D1251346

The Emergence
of the
Deaf Community
in Nicaragua

The Emergence of the Deaf Community in Nicaragua

"With Sign Language You Can Learn So Much"

Laura Polich

Gallaudet University Press
Washington, D.C.

Gallaudet University Press
Washington, D.C. 20002
http://gupress.gallaudet.edu

Library of Congress Cataloging-in-Publication Data

Polich, Laura.
   The emergence of the deaf community in Nicaragua / Laura Polich.
      p. cm.
   Includes bibliographical references and index.
   ISBN 1-56368-324-5 (alk. paper)
      1. Deaf—Nicaragua—History—20th century.   2. Deaf—Nicaragua—Social conditions.
3. Nicaraguan Sign Language.   I. Title.

HV2608.P65 2005
305.9′082′097285—dc22   2005040079

∞ The paper used in this publication meets the minimum requirements of American
National Standard for Information Sciences—Permanence of Paper for Printed Library
Materials, ANSI Z39.48-1984.

Contents

Foreword

In 1912 the supposed remains of "Piltdown Man," an archaic fossil ancestor of modern humans, were unearthed in England. Two skulls, a jawbone, and some teeth were uncritically accepted as evidence for the evolution of modern human beings in Western Europe. The prevailing dogmas of the age undoubtedly influenced the science. It was two years before the start of World War I. Was not Europe the most advanced region of the world? Were not Europeans the most advanced and civilized people on earth? Surely this meant that modern human beings had first evolved in Europe. Forty years elapsed before the obvious fraud was noted. In 1953 scientists discovered that the Piltdown remains were a mélange of doctored medieval human skulls, a 500-year-old orangutan jaw, and teeth from an elephant, a hippopotamus, and a fossil chimpanzee. The file marks, chemical processing, and paint that had been used to antique the "evidence" were clearly unmistakable. Dogma had blinded the vision of the archaeologists who had studied the Piltdown remains in 1912. Piltdown confounded the scientific record for decades.

Sign languages such as American Sign Language (ASL) have both the complexity and full communicative potential of any human vocal language. Sign languages differ from the gestures (known as home signs) used by deaf individuals who have been raised isolated from either instruction in sign language or from contact with persons who communicate in sign language. Though deaf people can communicate with these home signs, they lack the power to freely express the range of thoughts that syntactic processes make possible. Syntax essentially allows language users to form a potentially infinite number of sentences expressing novel thoughts using a finite number of words. It is clear from many examples that people who lack language are limited in their social and employment potential.

The myth that has developed concerning the spontaneous generation of Nicaraguan Sign Language derives from two dogmas held by a group of linguists trained at the Massachusetts Institute of Technology (MIT). The first is that human beings possess a genetic blueprint for a "Universal Grammar." The Universal Grammar is instantiated in some organ of the brain and specifies the syntax for every language that was, is, or will be. No one would argue with the claim that human beings possess the biological mechanisms necessary to acquire a language. The process takes somewhat longer than many linguists believe, at least ten years, but any "normal" child raised in a "normal" environment will learn to speak without any apparent effort. However, the theory of Universal Grammar proposed by Noam Chomsky claims that all of the details are, in computer terms, "preloaded" and merely have to be activated by minimal exposure to a language.

The second dogma at work in Nicaragua is the claim that a novel sign language, Nigaraguan Sign Language (NSL), spontaneously developed after a mass of deaf children were placed in a school for the deaf by the Sandinista government. This group of deaf children possessed only simple, varied home signs when they arrived at the school. According to Judy Kegl, Ann Senghas, and their colleagues, no deaf education or instruction in sign language had been available prior to the 1979 Sandinista revolution. They believe that the students created NSL and that this ostensibly is proof of the existence of Universal Grammar. The NSL story has been widely publicized and accepted as truth.

Laura Polich has carefully and meticulously examined written records and interviewed more than 200 persons to reveal the facts behind the emergence of Nicaraguan Sign Language. What she has found contradicts the dogmas currently accepted as truth. Deaf education actually began in Nicaragua in 1948 in several special education schools. These schools used the oral method to develop the students' competency in spoken Spanish, even when that was impossible for some profoundly deaf individuals. However, one of the teachers who worked with deaf students between 1948 and 1976 told Polich that the students used their hands to communicate among themselves and sometimes even with their teachers. Another teacher reported "it was impossible to stop them." In short, groups of deaf students had attended special schools in Nicaragua for many years, and they used gestures to communicate with each other.

Laura Polich documents a number of facts that must lead to a reappraisal of the account of the spontaneous appearance of a complex sign language. According to the Nicaraguan deaf community, the sign language used in Nicaragua today gradually developed. It began with the gestures used in the special schools, and, as Polich notes, "the chain of transmission" was unbroken from 1946 to the present. Several outside influences also contributed to the development of NSL. Among the earliest was Thomas Gibson, an American Peace Corps volunteer in Nicaragua, who taught an ASL class prior to the 1979 Sandinista revolution. His brief but effective instruction was recalled by many witnesses, and when he had to return to the United States, he left behind several ASL manuals. Another catalyzing influence was the return of Adrián Perez, a deaf student who spent eight years in Spain in a boarding school where deaf students used sign language outside the classrooms. During the 1980s deaf education instructors from Costa Rica, Sweden, and Finland came to Nicaragua and brought their sign languages with them. Lastly, a signing deaf community began to emerge in the 1980s. These facts are meticulously chronicled by Polich.

The dogma of the "white man's burden" that justified the excesses of nineteenth-century colonialism undoubtedly played a part in the Piltdown hoax. The uncritical attitude of British anthropologists (the file marks and paint placed on the Piltdown remains that were apparent in 1953 surely were evident in 1912) reflected the belief that modern humans must have evolved in Europe. Noam Chomsky's politics, which are much in evidence among many linguists trained at MIT, may also have played a part in the uncritical attitude of the MIT group that attributed progress to the Sandinistas and their Cuban and Soviet support systems. However, the Sandinista revolution of 1979 did not lead to openness and a freeing of previous strictures that might have impeded deaf children signing to each other. In fact, contrary to the MIT linguists' account, progress toward achieving competency in sign language was set back when the Sandinistas appointed a Russian school director who forbade any use of gestures or sign language in the instruction of deaf students. Polich found that "the pre-revolutionary schools in Managua were much more eclectic and open to sign language than the post-revolutionary schools for deaf children, which were severely, adamantly, and dogmatically oral" (see chap. 7). It was only after the director returned to the Soviet Union that NSL began to develop.

The Emergence of the Deaf Community in Nicaragua shows that sign language is a powerful, liberating force that has dramatically improved job and social opportunities for many deaf Nicaraguans. Nicaraguan Sign Language is the result of a long process entailing the efforts of many people, often against great resistance from educators, politicians, and the attitudes held by the general populace. Polich realistically notes that the struggle is not over—the opportunities open to deaf people in Nicaragua still are not at the point where they or we can say that all is well. There are no deaf doctors, lawyers, or other professionals, and deaf individuals as a group are economically depressed compared to their compatriots. The picture painted by Laura Polich reveals an incomplete canvas that needs a great deal of work. The status of deaf people in Nicaragua has improved, but it is far from perfect; their efforts merit our support.

PHILIP LIEBERMAN
Fred M. Seed Professor of
Cognitive and Linguistic Sciences
and Professor of Anthropology
Brown University

Note on Names

THE NAMING system in Nicaragua results traditionally in each person being identified by four names. Most people have two birth names, although they usually only use the first one in everyday usage. Oldest sons are typically named after their fathers. Women commonly are given an individual first name and a second name associated with Catholic religious traditions. Then each individual is identified by their paternal family name followed by their maternal family name. The pool of traditional family names used in Nicaragua is relatively small, and this tradition of using both paternal and maternal family names helps with identification.

The president of the National Nicaraguan Association of the Deaf (in 2003) was Juan Javier López Gómez. He is commonly referred to as "Javier," although "Juan Javier" is how he is listed on his national identification document. The order of the family names is important: Paternal comes first and maternal second. Javier's father's family name was "López," and his mother's family name was "Gómez." Since both López and Gómez are very common family names, giving both helps to distinguish him from the many others who might also be named "Javier López." Thus, when asked to "give one's full name," Nicaraguans will respond with four names.

In this narrative, as characters are introduced, I have tried to give their full names if I am aware that this "full name" is important for their identification in Nicaragua (e.g., Olga Tenorio Hernández or Rúthy Durán Collado), but succeeding references are only to the names by which they are commonly known in Nicaragua (e.g., Olga Tenorio or Rúthy Durán), unless, as in the case of Javier López Gómez, both family names are regularly used.

When women marry, they do not change their family names, but may choose to identify themselves with their husbands by adding *de (husband's family name)*. Thus, Rosemary Bohmer de Selva had a father whose family name was Bohmer and a husband whose family name was Selva.

Introduction

The mid-July heat made it nearly impossible to breathe in the National Nicaraguan Association of the Deaf's (ANSNIC) small office without air conditioning. Because both audio and video were being recorded, it had been necessary to close the outside windows to shut out the traffic noise from the street, but the blare of television and laughter from the adjoining room meant the inside door leading to the rest of the building also had to be shut. In this oven-like atmosphere, Natalia Galo, a deaf woman a few years over thirty, had been responding for about an hour to questions about her experiences growing up and her present life. But now we were all exhausted, and I moved to bring the interview to a close.

"Just one last question before I turn off the camera," I told Yolanda Mendieta, the Nicaraguan Sign Language (NSL) interpreter with whom I was working. Looking at Natalia, I asked in Spanish: "What is it like to be deaf?" Yolanda's hands went immediately to work, translating my words, and after gravely following Yolanda's motions, Natalia turned to me and signed her reply.

"I am content. I feel contented to be deaf."

Curious, I continued: "If you could change anything, what would you change?"

"I'm deaf, that's all," Natalia answered. "I would be fine always being this way, being deaf. I feel like myself. I don't know what to say, but I would be deaf, even if I could be born again, I would be born deaf the second time. It is what I am meant to be. It is the same as for you, being hearing."

I persisted. "But what if you would be reborn the only deaf person in Nicaragua—everyone else would be hearing—would you still choose to be born deaf?"

"Me the only deaf one? No way. I remember being little, and how lonesome I felt, and it wasn't until I went to school that I felt happy. I met other deaf children. What a wonderful surprise! It's true that they didn't use the sign language we have now; at that time, it was just gestures. But I was so happy to find myself with other deaf people. If I were the only deaf person, I just know I would have no hearing friends. I wouldn't be able to understand them!"

Feeling that there was something more here, I asked, "And what if you could be reborn and there would be many, many deaf people—thousands and thousands—but there was no sign language? What if there were deaf people all over the place, but all of them only spoke with their mouths, orally, and none ever used their hands? Would you still choose to be born deaf?"

"No, no, not that way. If there was sign language, yes, I would still choose to be deaf. It is impossible to understand only through speaking. With writing, you can get a little, but it is only so-so. But with sign language you can learn so much."

In 1968, when Natalia was born in Nicaragua, there was no deaf community nor any commonly accepted form of sign language used by groups of deaf persons in that country. Until she went to school, Natalia believed she was the only deaf person in the world, and the only one shut out from understanding the mouth movements that served her parents, relatives, and neighbors so well. The realization that first school day, that others like her existed, was so profound for her, that even twenty-five years later, as she told of starting school, the joy of her discovery was palpable.

Still, until she was a teenager, Natalia's prognosis for participation in society depended on her ability to master oral communication—a skill with which she, like many other persons born with profound congenital hearing loss, has never had any success. In her teenage years, however, Natalia began to participate actively in what would become Nicaragua's present deaf association, a group that used a language modality that was completely accessible to her—sign language.

Participation in the deaf community opened a new world for her—one of unhindered communication and full participation as a social actor. Today, Natalia at times helps to support her family by sewing in the assembly plants in the free trade zone.[1] She lives with her husband, who is also deaf, and her two hearing daughters. Because she signed to her oldest daughter at the same time that the child learned spoken Spanish, Natalia is now able to attend Mass, and, with her daughter interpreting, understand what is happening. The ritual, she says, used to be a complete mystery to her. Natalia's immediate family regularly participates in activities at ANSNIC, and maintains social contacts with other deaf families. Because her family has a refrigerator with a freezer compartment, she sells ice and popsicles to the neighbors to make a little extra money. The one bleak spot that Natalia mentions is that her own mother has refused to learn any sign language, so face-to-face communication with her parents is fragmentary and labored. We can see, then, that Natalia is an active social player in Nicaraguan society, just like any other thirty-year-old woman in that country. The only difference is that she prefers to participate using a non-oral language.

In 1968, there was no deaf community in Nicaragua; but in 1997, when I did my dissertation fieldwork, there was. The role of deaf persons in the greater Nicaraguan society started to change about sixty years ago, and it shifted dramatically in the past twenty-five years when a deaf community formed. This evolution took place within such recent memory that ethnographic and historical information about the period before the community existed can still be collected. The main actors involved in the community's formation are still available to be interviewed. The Nicaraguan experience, then, offers a fascinating focus for examination of how deaf communities form, as well as a wonderful opportunity to think about why they form.

HUMAN ACTORS constantly produce and reproduce the structure we know as society. They do it by using language. Lack of access to a society's language is a serious obstacle to social participation, and thus, to ever being an active member of society. Deafness has been an obstacle to this social agency, because language has historically been so closely tied to orality (the assumption that language, at its core, is produced by vocal means, and that communication via non-oral means is nonlinguistic). But, when other modalities can be tapped for language use, the range of possible social actors is widened.

For long periods in human history, because deaf persons do not naturally acquire oral language, the wider society has considered it impossible for deaf people to play active social roles. Deaf people were expected to exist in a protected environment (in which they might be well-treated or mistreated) but never participate independently and actively in society. Without oral communication, they were cut off, isolated, and marginalized. With the advent of special education procedures designed to teach oral language skills to deaf persons (we have written documentation of such methods from the seventeenth century), access to social agency within the oral society became a possibility, and deaf people could then set as a goal being able to speak intelligibly. Unfortunately, oral competency has been an elusive quest for many.

But in social groupings in which the preeminence of orality was not accepted, and in which language was shifted to an alternate modality—in deaf communities using sign language—full access as social actors has been available for those previously disenfranchised. Deaf communities provide a vehicle for deaf persons to participate as social agents in society. While deaf communities have been studied and described (Erting 1994; Higgins 1980; Higgins and Nash 1982; Padden and Humphries 1988; Prillwitz and Vollhaber 1990; Schein and Delk 1974; Van Cleve and Crouch 1984), the history and formation of these groups has been harder to document, although this area has received more attention in the past fifteen years (Fisher and Lane 1993; Gerner de Garcia 1990; Monaghan 2004).

This is probably a result of the fact that, until the 1960s, signed languages were not considered to be independent languages, but rather systems of mimicry and gestures or a manual reproduction of an oral language. While not common today in the United States, I have met a few deaf people who were educated before linguists took much interest in signed languages, and who go out of their way to sign in English word order because they consider American Sign Language (ASL) to be "bad English." William Stokoe's monograph, *Sign Language Structure: An Outline of the Visual Communication Systems of the American Deaf,* published in 1960, discussed how signed languages could be rule-driven, were not a reflection of the majority oral language, and, in fact, (because they use a spacial/visual modality rather than an oral/auditory modality) have some grammatical constructions with no equivalent in oral languages (Maher 1996). Since signed languages were considered to be either nonlinguistic (gestures only) or a poor imitation of the majority language, naturally, there was little interest in, or study of, the groups who formed around signed languages.

Deaf communities were regarded as a social deviancy, because hearing society assumed that deaf people congregated in communities, not through choice, but because they lacked other options (Goffman 1963). Having no access to "normal" social structures, deaf communities were considered "last resorts"; hearing researchers assumed that deaf people would form such groups out of a shared sense of stigma, and that anyone who could fit even minimally into a mainstream group would naturally prefer to do so. This attitude resulted in a paternalistic, depreciating view of deaf communities, and I found no study of this type (e.g., Best 1943; Upshall 1929), which looked carefully at how or why the group formed at the beginning.

In fact, most of the information we have about the existence of the earliest known deaf communities is in the form of co-incidental allusions, when the author's main point lay elsewhere. Pierre Desloges was refuting the assertion that the Abbé de l'Epée was the founder of the sign language used in Paris in the late eighteenth century when he mentioned that there was a well-established deaf community and language long before the Abbé appeared. Because the Abbé's role, not the community, was his focal point, he gave no details about what the deaf community was like, or when or why it might have formed.

Likewise, thirty-six years after the American Asylum of the Deaf was founded in 1817, the New England Gallaudet Society was organized in 1853. Since the earliest reports from the group (published in the *American Annals of the Deaf*) describe it as a "regional" group with each state represented on the board of managers, the existence of multiple, smaller, preexisting deaf communities is implied. But the founders of the society never included in their reports to the *Annals* any history of either state or local groups, so we really do not know how any local groups had emerged, or what their characteristics were (*American Annals of the Deaf* 1857).

The society of Martha's Vineyard, from the 1600s to the 1800s, when it was isolated from the mainland, appears to have accommodated to the fact that it was composed of both hearing and deaf, by the group expectation that everyone would learn the sign language, not just deaf persons. Nora Groce, interestingly, describes an area in which a deaf community did *not* form, even though there was a high rate of congenital deafness (Groce 1985).

As you read about the Nicaraguan deaf community in the following chapters, it is important to keep the Martha Vineyard's society in mind. Because sign language was not limited for use by only deaf persons, lack of oral competency was not an impediment to social participation. For the period in which the island was isolated, at least, it appears that the deaf members of the society had opportunities equal to (or nearly equal to) their hearing peers to become full social actors, and thus, never had any need to form a separate group.

THE NICARAGUAN deaf community offers us an excellent opportunity to examine the events of the past sixty (but especially the past twenty-five) years to discover what elements and catalysts seem to be important to produce a deaf community. The formation of deaf communities is linked closely to the societal roles that deaf persons are allowed to play. Where deafness is construed as incompatible with any type of social agency—where deaf persons are prohibited or strongly encouraged not to leave their birth homes, and thus, remain isolated from one another—no deaf community will form. Where social agency is considered to be possible only through oral proficiency, a certain number of deaf persons will strive to attain such agency, and a few will succeed. The others will consider their inability to acquire oral fluency to be a personal failing within a legitimate status quo and will participate marginally, if at all, in society outside of their families.

But at the point where a sufficient number of deaf persons find that not only is social agency through oral means *not* the only avenue, but that an alternate language form could do just as well, a deaf community will form and its members will become social agents within that group. They will use the group as a bridge to wider active social participation. At the periphery of the deaf community, a subset of bilingual individuals will form and become intermediaries for individual deaf members with the society of the oral majority. Thus, participation in the deaf community will offer these individuals ample opportunities to be social actors within the subculture, and through the subset of bilingual individuals, participation as a social agent in the wider society will also be possible.

My interest in Nicaragua dates from 1987 when I spent the year as a volunteer with the group, Witness for Peace. Afterwards, I was an audiologist in Yakima, Washington, for five years before entering the doctoral program in language and culture at the University of Texas at Austin, which, at that time, was hosted, in part, by the Department of Communication Sciences and Disorders. Because of my interest in the function of the ear and my experience with Central America, I was especially curious about the lives of persons with atypical hearing (i.e., hearing loss or deafness) in economically less-developed countries. I wanted my dissertation to envelope both themes. As the second poorest country in the Americas, Nicaragua certainly qualified as less-developed, and my previous residence in the country gave me leads about which groups worked with persons having atypical hearing. As I was preparing for my first research trip in 1994, my adviser, Madeline Maxwell, told me that Nicaragua was on the map in the world of linguistics because Judy Kegl had publicized the existence in Nicaragua of a distinct sign language that, according to Kegl, had been devised by deaf children first brought together by the Sandinista Revolution. I contacted Kegl who graciously recommended additional sources I should seek out in Nicaragua.

When I returned in January 1997 for a year of field study, I expected to be examining how children with atypical hearing are prepared and transitioned into the regular education system (which is the Ministry of Education's official goal for those in the classrooms for hard of hearing or deaf children in the special education schools). Naturally, I wanted to learn the sign language I had seen children using at school. I was told that the best way to do that, in addition to observing the children at school, would be to take language lessons at the deaf association and observe the language use there as much as possible. I followed that advice, dividing my time between the special education school, the deaf association, and observation at the hearing and speech clinic operated by the Parents of Disabled Children group (known as Los Pipitos).[2]

In addition to private and group lessons in NSL, my observations at the deaf association included regular attendance at Wednesday literacy classes for young adults and Saturday afternoon social hours when older deaf adults were likely to appear. My curiosity about ANSNIC's history ultimately piqued a wider study of the historical view of deafness in Nicaragua. I had arrived assuming, in accordance with what I had been told that, prior to the 1979 Sandinista Revolution, no attention had been paid to children or adults with deafness. And I also believed that the sign language had arisen quickly and spontaneously after the Revolution when elementary-age children were first brought together for schooling (Kegl 1994). Over the course of 1997, I learned that history was not that simple. I began to interview anyone who had ever been involved with education of deaf children and to ask the older deaf adults about what they remembered.

For one thing, there *had* been education available for deaf children since the 1940s in Nicaragua. And the story of how the sign language grew was also more complicated. Even the date of the deaf association's founding (April 22, 1986) was not as unambiguous as I had thought. The conclusion I drew from further research was that the story, as I had first accepted it, seriously underestimated the adolescent contribution to the formation of a deaf community and its language. I focused my time in Nicaragua to reconstruct the history of education for deaf children there, especially the events surrounding the foundation in 1981 of a vocational center accepting deaf adolescents and young adults. I also sought to document the history of any Nicaraguan organizations of deaf adults. (Ultimately, I only found one.) I hypothesized that if more of the history of what happened in Nicaragua were known, it would shed light on our wider understanding of how any deaf community and its sign language had/could/would emerge. In part because deaf people in Nicaragua have historically not been considered worthy of much note, and thus, are not much remembered, but also because doing any kind of historical research in Nicaragua is exasperating, finding the history of the deaf community in Nicaragua turned out to be more labor-intensive and time-consuming process than I had ever expected. But now that the parts I have found are gathered in one place, I hope it will be both a contribution to other researchers working on NSL and its precursors (e.g., Senghas and Coppola 2001; Senghas, Senghas, and Pyers 2004, etc.) as well as provide deaf Nicaraguans with a written version of their history.

When I asked Nicaraguans (both hearing and deaf) to remember deaf people in their neighborhoods from thirty to fifty years ago, many had difficulty. Typical Nicaraguans could not remember any, or at most, one or two. They were never identified by name, for no one could remember their names. They were simply identified in the neighborhood as "the deaf-mutes," and no one could tell me any details about them other than perhaps the kind of work that they performed in relationship to a family business. None could remember any of them as married, having children, or even working at a job except under the supervision of family members. They did not have their own households.

The deaf persons remembered by typical Nicaraguans were isolated, language-less, and lived in lifelong dependence. In fact, my inquiries suggesting that a deaf person fifty years ago might have been a responsible parent or homeowner seemed ridiculous to most with whom I spoke. The one exception was a man, remembered by the last name of Perezalonzo, who came from a wealthy family, who sent him to Spain for education, and who, then, evidently helped him set up a business. When he was remembered, it was *because* he was such an incongruity—a person who was deaf and yet who earned a living independently.[3]

I had a little more luck when talking with the eight people I could find who had worked in education for deaf children during the 1946–1976 period. Considering that we are talking about a thirty-year time span, it is interesting that they, collectively, could come up with only about twenty names (often only the first names), and no one could tell me how to contact any of them. About half (usually those whose last names were remembered) were said to have emigrated at the time of the Sandinista Revolution. The others were lost to time, and my inquiries about how I might proceed to locate their past students were met with a simple "I have no idea."

Emigration of important informants has been a serious difficulty for this research. Instability in the pre-revolutionary period (from 1977 to 1979) encouraged many Nicaraguans to leave the country and settle elsewhere. The drastic governmental changes resulting from the success of the Sandinista Revolution (in July 1979) meant a massive outflux of Nicaraguans in the early 1980s. The Contra War, which resulted in a universal military draft in Nicaragua, encouraged outflow during the rest of the decade. Today, the emigration trend continues, but for the past fifteen years, the major cause has been the poor state of the domestic economy. While there are pockets of emigrated Nicaraguans living in Canada, Europe, or South America, the vast majority have settled in the United States, especially in Florida and California. It seems that every Nicaraguan family has multiple members living abroad, and the resources they send back are an important source of income for many (Marenco 1997). Thus, various persons who were important actors in the history of education for deaf children or the formation of the Nicaraguan deaf community now live abroad, and, it is impossible to locate most of them with precision.

Several of the younger members of ANSNIC thought my question, about who the deaf members fifty years and older were, was ludicrous. Everybody knew that the oldest deaf persons who participated in ANSNIC events were a little over forty, so how could any older deaf person exist? When I asked them why they thought deafness had only begun to appear in Nicaragua around 1960, they admitted that there probably had been some deaf people born before that time, but they didn't know any personally. The question, in fact, started them thinking and questioning: "If we are this many now, then there should have been a reasonable number fifty years ago. Why don't we know who they are?"

The deaf association has a list of those who, over the years, have registered as members since the group was founded in 1986. By copying that list, transferring the information to a database, and ordering the list by birth date, Yolanda Mendieta and I had a record of the oldest registered deaf association members.[4] It was excruciatingly rare that anyone born before 1960 attended deaf association events, and it was not common to see those born before 1970 there either. Yolanda and I set out to find their homes and interview as many of those born before 1965 as possible.[5] These were the persons likely to have been present in the 1983–1989 period when the deaf association was being organized, and the ones likely to remember what life was like for deaf persons before the association existed.

One hundred and six registered members of the ANSNIC (30% of the total registered members) were born before 1966. Through sheer persistence, some amount of luck, and Yolanda's connections, we were able to find and interview thirty-six of them (33% of the 106). The eldest subgroup consisted of the twenty-four registered members born before 1959 (6% of the total registered membership and 21% of our interview target group). We found eight of them (33%) and received information on the possible whereabouts of four others, but twelve of those twenty-four (50%) were impossible to trace. No one, deaf or hearing, knew where they might be. We also found approximately one-third of the registered members with birth years between 1959 and 1965, but we did get hints on the possible whereabouts of another 33% (but were unable to physically locate them, typically because they had left Nicaragua). For the whereabouts of this younger subgroup (birth years 1959–1965), only 33% were completely unknown.

I only interviewed two deaf persons not on the association's rolls at all, but Yolanda and I heard references to more (but never with enough details to actually find them). We witnessed a definite linguistic divide between those who had either never had schooling or had left the educational system by 1972, and those who had continued or started their education after that year.

This book is based fundamentally upon interviews with these older members of the deaf association, hearing individuals who were involved in providing education to deaf children in the 1946–2003 period, hearing people who had deaf relatives, and the many members ranging from age fifteen to forty who participate in activities at the ANSNIC clubhouse in Managua, the capital. A list of those interviewed is included as an appendix, and I thank them all. In working on this topic from 1994 to 2004, I have been fortunate to be able to talk with hundreds of people, and many have become personal friends. I emphasize that the story gleaned from these many individuals is the basis for this work, because although I combed all the libraries and archives I could find, it has been most difficult to find contemporary written records to corroborate interviewees' memories.

Nicaragua is a country that has destroyed or lost the archival portion of its collective memory more than once during this century. Devastating earthquakes in 1931 and again in 1972 destroyed all the country's major libraries, so all repositories of governmental and institutional records were lost forever. Internal warfare played havoc with record-keeping early in the century, and had an even worse effect in the turmoil of the 1970s, which resulted in the Sandinista Revolution in 1979. Political bickering and machinations have meant that at each transition of government power (e.g., 1979, 1990, 1996), more records were destroyed or "lost" because each new government chose to begin with a clean slate. I searched as assiduously as I could, but many documents that would be most helpful to substantiate the history this book recounts simply no longer exist or are unofficially stored where I could not reach them.[6] I was unable, for example, to find any of the pre-revolutionary planning documents or reports from the Junta Nacional de Asistencia y Prevención Social (JNAPS) about the administration of the Centro Nacional de Educación Especial (the special education school in Managua now renamed the Centro de Educación Especial Melania Morales), and likewise, the post-revolutionary official special education pupil counts prior to 1988 have been "lost."

In 1994 and 1995, with the help of the Scott Haug Foundation, the Austin (Texas) Sertoma club, and the Pan-American Roundtables, I made preliminary summer field trips to Nicaragua to identify the groups that worked with persons who have hearing loss. The Ministry of Education, the Association of Parents of Disabled Children (Los Pipitos), and ANSNIC graciously answered my multitudes of questions. In 1997, with the help of scholarships from the Fulbright Foundation and the Pan-American Roundtables, I spent a year in Nicaragua regularly attending deaf associa- tion activities and classes and visiting the Melania Morales School in Managua. I was also, during that year, able to visit all (at that time) twenty special education schools with one or more classrooms for deaf pupils, which were located outside of the capital. With my scholarship money, I funded a survey of more than 225 deaf persons about their backgrounds and present living conditions.[7] I have twice surveyed (1997 and 2000) all of the teach- ers in classrooms for deaf children about their educational backgrounds and knowledge of deaf persons. In one- or two-month visits to Nicaragua in 1999, 2000, 2001, 2002, and 2003, I was able to interview more people, search the National Archives, and, with the help of Yolanda Mendieta, make a concerted effort to locate the oldest members of the deaf association.[8]

This book discusses the conclusions that I came to on the basis of my nine-year investigation. I found that the use of a "standardized" sign lan- guage in Nicaragua did not emerge as an independent entity until there was a community of users meeting on a regular basis and *beyond childhood*. The adoption and molding of NSL did not happen suddenly, but was a process that took many years and was fed by multiple influences. Adolescents have a profound urge to seek a community in order to assert and attain their social agency in a society, but to do so, they have to be in contact with each other on a regular basis. For deaf adolescents in Nicaragua now, community is found in ANSNIC.[9] Once social circles and sign language have been estab- lished, the central organization becomes less important, being a crucial fo- cus during young adulthood, but of less importance later on. The larger Nicaraguan society only began to recognize that non-oral deaf persons could be social actors after an organized deaf association formed. And finally, al- though I will illustrate the tremendous changes that the past sixty years have produced, the fact remains that the work of asserting full social agency for deaf persons in Nicaragua is not complete. It has only begun.

"Eternal Children" 1

EXACTLY WHEN the damage to a child's hearing occurs is often unknown. Some disease processes, such as rubella, affect the development of the ear in the fetus, and the child is born deaf. Other children are born with normal hearing, and disease or an ototoxin destroys the ear's ability to hear later.[1] When hearing loss takes place before the child has developed any oral skills, it is usually very difficult to ascertain the cause of the loss. Elena Gonzáles, the older sister of Camila, a thirty-three-year-old Nicaraguan woman who had never been educated or learned any language system, remembered that her parents wasted little time decrying a situation which they believed was God-given:

> We don't know if Camila was born deaf or hearing normally, but when she was three days old, she had gastritis and was very sick, and the doctors gave her lots and lots of injections of gentamicin. My parents were simple people of the countryside, and they just accepted her and didn't question. We knew [when she was older] that she couldn't hear, but there was no way to do anything about it.

Elena Gonzáles remembers that the family developed a system of home signs to use with Camila, which worked in many ways but did not allow the communicative access that a true language would:

> We used home signs. It was possible to understand the basics. Camila stayed at home in Nueva Guinea and helped my mother. She was my mother's right hand. When my mother would misplace something, all she had to do was indicate to Camila what it was, and immediately Camila would know where it was. But there were problems too. We wouldn't know that she was sick for a long time. Finally we would notice that she was just sitting there holding her stomach or something, and then it would be obvious that she wasn't well. It was easier with Camila when we were younger. It was easier to understand her, but now it is more difficult. I don't remember having such a hard time understanding her then as I do now. But, we never knew her as a person. We never knew what she was thinking or feeling.

13

Even in homes where a more elaborate system of home signs combined with some oral words is worked out between the child and parents, the limitations on communication remain significant. While the deaf child may learn to understand what the parents mean on occasion, there is typically little, if any, dialogue or self-expression encouraged from the child. Luís Gonzáles volunteers with the deaf association in Matagalpa, Nicaragua.[2] He visited the homes of some of the teenage members, observed the communication interaction in the homes, and interviewed the parents about their communication preferences.

> I talked to Evert's mother about how she communicates with him, and she says she mostly talks with him but also uses some signs. But what I noticed is that it is a language of orders where they tell him, for example, go get that, go clean that, go take a bath, go to the store and get some coffee. Sure it's communication, but Evert doesn't get much out of it. And I also went to Luís's house and talked to his mother, and she told me their family has no problems with communication, that they have always just treated Luis as though he were normal by talking to him, and he is able to understand everything. But that just isn't true because I asked Luis about this [in sign language] and whether he understood what his mother said to him. He told me he didn't understand anything at home. He says he doesn't understand anyone or even know what is going on at all.

A direct result of the communication barrier is that the child is denied not only access to routine parental explanations and teaching about how the world works, and how the child should act within that world, but also to a vast amount of incidental learning that is rarely transmitted consciously, but which most children overhear as they play around and are co-present at the conversations of adults or older siblings. Deaf children and adolescents are then considered to be naive and unsophisticated. Without the ability to express more complicated thoughts, or understand discourse directed to them, the uneducated deaf are assumed to be cognitively limited and in need of protection. Elena Gonzáles remembers that her mother treated Camila differently than her other daughters, and so did the rest of the family:

> I really have very few memories of what it was like growing up with Camila. We just played and tried to protect her. My mother overprotected her. Camila never went out to parties or things like that. My parents never let her go out alone, not in the town or anywhere. She was always at home, or if she went

out somewhere in the town, someone took her. My mother particularly kept Camila away from boys, and worried about that. If she was at a family gathering and some boys started to eye her, my mother sent her inside immediately and wouldn't let her get near any boys.

Traditionally, in Nicaragua, children born with handicapping conditions are thought to represent a punishment from God for previous sins of the parents or another relative. Similar attitudes toward disabled children have been documented for Mexico and the Dominican Republic (Ramsey and Noriega 2000; Gerner de García 1990). Gregorio Mercado, the father of Edner Mercado, now a young adult, agreed that this interpretation of deaf children had been common, and that some people continue to think this way:

> They see the child as a punishment from God (*un castigo de Díos*) or a judgment from God, and they don't want it known publicly that they have this child. So they never take him out or let other people outside the family see the child. Many people say that a child has a disability because the father sinned too much, had too many women, or because the father beat the mother too much. They say, "Look, because of how much you have sinned, God has punished your child with this disease." They see the child as being ill.

Parents in Nicaragua with the financial means have been known to set aside a suite of rooms for the child and hire a full-time nurse to care for the child's needs, and provisions were made for support throughout the child's natural lifetime. Even as these children became teenagers and adults, they were still considered to be in need of protection. There were other cases not so benevolent. As these children became stronger and less amenable, they might also wish to roam, in which case physical restraint might be used. Aura María Cajina remembers visiting a childhood friend whom she knew had a daughter with Down syndrome. (Not only deaf, but children with any disability, have been regarded and treated in this same manner.) After the first day in which the girl was never presented, Aura asked about her and was told that the girl was kept in a back room chained to a bed because she had become "unmanageable" since becoming a teenager. Aura said that it was only because she was a very close friend that she felt she could ask, and they probably only told her about the girl because of the previous bonds of friendship. "If I hadn't had that kind of relationship with the mother, I would have been too embarrassed to have asked, even if I had noticed the daughter's absence."

Other informants stated that they learned of the existence of relatives who had children with disabilities only when they were informed, after the fact, of the person's death. Silvia Ayón remembers that she learned that her husband's cousin had a disabled son when other relatives shared the news with them that the "boy" (*el niño*) had died. "That night my husband and I were sitting there talking," Silvia said, "and we started putting things together that we had heard before, and we realized that the 'boy' was probably in his forties when he died."

But before many parents of children with disabilities became resigned, they often felt great pressure to find a cure for the sickness that their sin had brought down upon their innocent child. Gregorio Mercado placed himself in this category.

> I went anywhere or to anyone that I was told could cure my son's deafness. I felt I had to. Other people are like me too. They feel they have to search because it was their sin, in the first place, that caused the problem. But all the time I was searching, I also treated my son differently. He was "sick." I couldn't expect the same of him that I expected of my other children. I disciplined my other children, but I gave my son preferential treatment. I never demanded very much of him.

But deafness is rarely an illness that can be cured by medication or surgery. When the inevitability of the child's condition becomes apparent, it has been typical to marginalize the child and concentrate one's energies on the children seen as more able to benefit.

As a researcher, I would be satisfied if I could say that this view of the deaf as non-agents, and the implication of their "uselessness" were a remnant of the past, but I am sorry to say that it appears to be a view which retains adherents to this day. While interviewing a woman who had served for various years in the special education system (I am consciously not identifying her more closely), I asked her if she had ever personally witnessed the marginalization of any deaf children. "Yes, of course" she replied.

> Over the years I have seen many. But it is funny you should mention that to me today. I saw exactly a case like that two days ago, and I cannot get the image out of my mind. I have a relative who has lived in another suburb for many years, and I have always visited her. Just two days ago, my relative led me to a gap in the wall in her backyard and showed me a woman who is abandoned in the neighboring backyard. She is kept there by her relatives. I think her

mother is dead. I could see her. She was filthy and was sleeping on a pile of cardboard in a corner. They have her there in that dark patio where little sun gets in, caged up, like an animal.

I asked the special education worker whether she knew the abandoned woman, and she said that the woman had not always been enclosed. When she was very small, she had been allowed out on the streets, and the special education worker had seen her then and heard her voice, which she recognized as a "deaf voice" from her work with children in special education. But that had been when the child's mother was alive. Later, the special education worker told me she had heard that the mother had died, and "I knew that the family was ashamed of the girl and didn't want her running outside." When the family began keeping the girl in their fenced backyard, the special education worker's relative got into the habit of passing her food and old clothing over the backyard fence, but suddenly there were some renovations and the passageway between the two houses disappeared.

> It's been years. I assumed she had died. But then my relative showed me where the renovation in the fence was getting loose, and so now one could peek through again. She is still there, and the picture in my mind haunts me.

It is not only everyday Nicaraguans who view the deaf as what I will call "Eternal Children," incapable of social agency, and in need of protection throughout life. The Nicaraguan Constitution guarantees to all citizens the basic rights to a "social security," and the deaf would be included in this broad, if ambiguous, guarantee.[3]

In addition, the constitution charges the state to "procure" to establish rehabilitation programs for disabled persons in order to improve their employment prospects. It is significant that the constitution employs the word *procure* and not *mandate* or some other similar term, like *order*. Thus, the state may make an effort to provide such programs, but is not obligated to do so.

The legal code of Nicaragua is based on the Napoleonic Code of the early 1800s. Among the sections of the legal code denoting the rights and duties of the citizens, there is a distinction made between the citizens who are capable of representing themselves in a court of law and those who are considered legally incompetent and therefore in need of legal guardians to attend to their affairs. Among those listed as incompetent, the blind and deaf-mutes are enumerated specifically, along with the demented. The law does not make any distinction between *sordomudo* (deaf-mute) or *sordo* (deaf). There is no compilation of laws concerning the disabled, nor are the terms used in the various legal codes standardized.

Article 299 of the Civil Code states that deaf-mutes and blind persons who "do not have the necessary intelligence to administer their own goods will be placed under a guardianship." This guardianship is typically requested of the court by the relatives of the person presumed to be incompetent, and the court requests an examination from a physician attesting to whether or not the person in question is capable of administering his or her own person or goods. While it is probable that the court would prefer to have a deaf person examined by someone familiar with deafness, such as an otolaryngologist, or audiologist, the law only specifies that the examiner be a physician. If the deaf person is found not to be capable of administering his or her person or goods, the court would appoint a guardian, who typically is a close relative of the person declared incompetent.

When I closely questioned Dr. Napoleon Ríos, a practicing lawyer in the Nicaraguan capital of Managua, about this matter, he told me that while the legal code does not make a distinction between a deaf person who speaks intelligibly and one who does not, that, in point of fact, people with these differing capabilities would be treated differently in a court of law.

> Look at J. G. [a deaf Nicaraguan woman known to both of us]. She uses a hearing aid and talks and writes. She would be considered a normal person. She is able to show that she has the necessary intelligence to take care of her own person and goods, and the law would not allow her to be discriminated against or to be pushed aside in favor of a guardian.

But Dr. Ríos pointed out that the law in Nicaragua was written before there was a sign language commonly used by the deaf in that country. He believed that Nicaraguan Sign Language (NSL) had only existed since the 1980s, so legal precedents have not had the time to accumulate. According to Ríos, NSL is not recognized in the Nicaraguan legal code as a true language, and there are no guidelines for the use of interpreters in the courts of law. Ríos is unfamiliar with any other lawyer who has even a minimal knowledge of the deaf, and he believes that most would not consider the sign language of the deaf to be a true language, nor would they fight for a deaf client's right to have an interpreter in court.

Interestingly, in September 2004, Ann Senghas published an article in the prestigious journal, *Science,* about how NSL has evolved over the past fifteen years, and she stated explicitly that it was a fully functioning language, on par with the other thousands of human languages. The Nicaraguan press called this journal article "a theoretical revolution." (See article published in the evening newspaper, *El Nuevo Diario,* on September 16, 2004.) The National Nicaraguan Deaf Association (ANSNIC), naturally, was enthusiastic that an international source expressed what they have believed for years, and the association provided reporters with multiple interviews. However, other educators of the deaf were not so pleased. The parents' group, Los Pipitos, made no comment, nor did the Ministry of Education.

In 1997, there was a case in which a deaf Nicaraguan woman accused a deaf man of assault (Mairena Martínez 1997). Although both parties were over the age of twenty-one, the legal case for each was directed by their hearing parents. The parents of the deaf man wanted him to testify for himself, and they requested that the deaf association provide a voice interpreter that he might do so. But the parents of the deaf woman refused an interpreter from the deaf association for her, insisting on acting, themselves, as her "interpreters."

Her parents were not fluent in NSL, so her testimony, which her parents transmitted to the court, consisted of the translation of whatever sign language her parents could understand supplemented with gestures. Questions to her from the court were answered by her parents. ANSNIC's interpreter (who was there for the defendant), naturally, would not disclose details of what had happened in court, but did note that the woman's parents only addressed her when she was needed to answer a specific question. The commentary of the lawyers, the judge, and the other set of parents was not relayed to her. Neither the judge nor the lawyers made any objection, or even seemed aware that the plaintiff might not be fully informed about what was happening. As deaf-mutes, both of these persons were technically "incompetent" to testify for themselves and needed guardians (in this case, their parents) to act as their legal representatives. The legal representatives were free to accept or reject the interpreters from the deaf association.

Although not legally bound to do so, the courts of Nicaragua have, over the past ten years, become aware of the use of sign language interpreters, and the deaf association regularly receives calls asking for interpretation assistance at police stations, jails, and in court. But, to date, there is no case law or legal precedents that would *require* provision of interpreters either at competency hearings or in criminal cases where individuals are either plaintiff or defendant. Dr. Ríos's commentary remains valid in 2004.

In 1997, there were also no required qualifications for interpreters. ANSNIC's president's sisters, both hearing, had begun informally to learn sign language in 1990, and over the years had taken over most of the interpreting duties. They were infamous for not translating what they did not consider important for the deaf person to know, for interjecting their own opinions, and even taking over the conversations they were supposed to translate. I personally experienced such behavior on multiple occasions between January and May 1997 when I asked one of them to translate for me. Between 1995 and 2002, the Royal Swedish Deaf Association funded two training courses, one more informal and one formal, in which ten persons have participated. The second, the formal course, continued over a period of two years, and the ten participants received a certificate in the end. The graduates of this course translate for official and nonofficial meetings and for deaf persons involved with legal proceedings, and they interpret the mass said by the Archbishop of Managua, which is broadcast on national television every Sunday. In most of the country, there is no access to local sign language interpreters.

Thus, in Nicaraguan law, the deaf person is presumed incompetent and must obtain a statement to the contrary to be able to exercise the powers accorded to all adults in society. If a guardian is named, the guardian's consent is required for any legal transaction, whether that be buying a house or other property, entering into marriage or any other contract, or exercising custody of children. (Children are considered an extension of the person. If someone is not competent to administer their own person, neither can they administer the person of their children.)

In criminal cases, according to Dr. Ríos, a deaf person would be tried just as any other citizen, but the fact of deafness would probably be considered an extenuating circumstance, moving the judge to leniency. Dr. Ríos explained:

> There is a presumption that a deaf-mute would have little social knowledge and would be illiterate, and so the judge would probably view that person as

impressionable and incapable of acting with malice, and that person would probably be dismissed to a relative's custody. I have never seen a deaf-mute convicted of a crime. It would be a historic occurrence here. But also, consider the problems if a deaf person were condemned. Our prison system is atrocious, and there is absolutely no provision available for dealing with someone who could not hear.

While I was in Nicaragua in 1997, I was told that the situation regarding legal status for deaf persons was changing. Two years previously, on August 23, 1995, "the Law for the Disabled," (Law No. 202) had been passed by the National Assembly.[4] This law covered all disabling conditions, not just deafness. In Nicaragua, however, passage of a law was only the first step. No law need be applied until its "reglamentation," (i.e., implementation)—the specific conditions under which the law will be applied—has been published in *La Gaceta*. (For example, if the law prohibits an act and calls for a punishment for that act, the definition of the act and guidelines for sentencing are spelled out in the reglamentation, not in the law itself.) The reglamentation for Law 202 was finally published on August 25, 1997. (The dates of the passage of the law and that of the reglamentation are not accidental. August 25 is celebrated by all the organizations that deal with persons with disabilities as "The Day of the Disabled.") The deaf persons I spoke with were especially enthusiastic about Article 12:

> Businesses are obliged to employ persons with disabilities and may not deny them their rights or salaries, but [persons with disabilities] will enjoy the same conditions under which other workers are contracted. (Translation mine)

That part of the law was not specific for deaf persons, but applied to all disabilities. The only part of Law 202 which specifically addressed persons with deafness is that of Article 13 in Chapter V:

> i) The messages of the government which are transmitted by television or other audiovisual media must be accompanied by a specialist for phonetic-auditorally disabled [persons]. (Translation mine)

From what I could see through 2003, Law 202 has been window dressing and a sop to international welfare and material aid groups who are promoting projects to improve the quality of life of persons with disabilities in Nicaragua. (There are so many international groups funding "projects" that benefit persons with disabilities that they have multiple councils, including the Federación de Coordinación de Organizaciones Nicaraguenses de la Rehabilitación y la Integración (FENACORI), an umbrella group for non-governmental charitable organizations, which exists to encourage communication and reduce overlap among the organizations.) Few concrete effects of the law were apparent even six years after the reglamentation.

The unemployment rate for members of ANSNIC continues to be significantly higher than that of the bulk of the population, and no one could tell me of any businesses that had hired deaf workers in order to be in compliance with this (admittedly, very vague) law. The ambiguity of the language of Law 202, Article 13, Chapter V has meant that little sign language interpretation has actually been done on behalf of Nicaraguan deaf people. The press conferences routinely given by the country's president, the taking of office of the new president, or commentary of government officials to the press, all of which are aired on national television, are evidently not considered "government messages" because they are not interpreted into NSL. In August 2002, the elaborate presentation called the "uncovering of the buried treasure," a performance watched by most Nicaraguans with a television set, would surely have qualified as an official message from the government, but it was not translated either.[5] While admittedly on the books, this law does not appear to have had much, if any, effect on deaf persons.

On a more positive note, however, I want to point out that in 2003, an uneducated deaf man was an eyewitness to a murder scene (Romero 2003), and police did promptly contact ANSNIC to ask for assistance in questioning him. This was done by a team of older members of the deaf association and a Spanish/Nicaraguan Sign Language interpreter. (The deaf eyewitness was not a member of the deaf association or fluent in NSL, so it was necessary to interpret his home signs along with the standardized sign language he knew.) Ultimately, his testimony was not found to be relevant, and he disappeared from the news. But this incident did show that the justice system is using NSL interpreters, even if the language has not yet been officially recognized.

One model of deafness, then, is that deaf persons, mainly because they do not talk, are inherently incapable of being independent social actors. While their humanity is recognized, and therefore, their right to food and shelter is commonly admitted, they are not expected to become fully-functioning adults in society. They are seen as needing the help of a guardian to protect them from legal exploitation. This model of deafness prevailed in Nicaragua before 1946 and is one that is, unfortunately, still seen occasionally today. It is the model written into the country's legal statutes. As "eternal children" deaf persons are not expected ever to act independently during their lifetimes.

2

Special Education

WHEN A DEAF person is considered an "Eternal Child," there is no expectation that the individual will ever become an adult, in the sense of changing from a dependent member of a family to an independent actor in society at large. Because the deaf child's access to the majority language is blocked, so too is the child's access to education and training in the skills necessary to support oneself as an adult. But if some means of communicating with the child can be found, this opens the possibility of education. If the deaf person could be trained in skills or literacy, in time, he or she should be able to assume an adult role in society. Thus, insofar as remediation is an option, an adult position in society becomes a possibility.

Prior to 1946, there were no educational options for children with mental retardation, deafness, blindness, or motor problems in Nicaragua. Wealthy families might hire private tutors in their homes, or send their children to boarding schools in other countries, but no formal education was available within the country. On February 4, 1946, Presidential Decree No. 11, signed by Anastasio Somoza (senior), authorized the creation of Special Education School No. 1 in the capital, Managua, for children "who have problems with vocalization, hearing and other [disabilities]" (*La Gaceta* 1946). Thus, from some point before 1946, an alternative to the model of deaf persons as "Eternal Children" began to form. Deaf persons began to be seen as potentially "Remediable Subjects."

The establishment of educational institutions for the deaf is a sign of a transformation and paradigm shift. The decision to form schools is evidence of a change from a view of deaf people as incapable of agency to deaf people as possible social actors. The most important work for the later formation of such an institution is not done at the moment of school establishment, but beforehand when the possibility is debated of whether deaf children (or children with other disabilities) could profit from education and an affirmative conclusion is drawn. The decision to provide

Figure 1. Important Dates in Education for Deaf Children in Nicaragua

1946	Special Education School No. 1 is founded in Managua with Dr. Emilio Lacayo as director.
1952	Dr. Apolonio Berríos is named director of Special Education School No. 1.
1962	Special Education School No. 1 is moved to a new site in Managua—on land owned by the Mántica family. The school is by now commonly referred to as the "Berríos School." There is one class for deaf children taught by Soledad Escobar de Flores.
1974	Dr. Apolonio Berríos dies. Olga Tenorio Hernández becomes director of Special Education School No. 1. The deaf pupils are split into two classes (older vs. younger) with twelve students in each class.
1974	Special education schools are opened in León and Chinandega.
1977	The National Center for Special Education (CNEE) opens in Managua at a site in Barrio San Judas. Twenty-four deaf children previously enrolled at the Berríos School constitute half of the new school's deaf enrollment, along with twenty-five deaf children new to schooling. (The Berríos School ceases to exist.)
1978	The Boarding School for Disabled Children (Escuela Hogar para Niños Minusuálidos) opened in Ciudad Darío.
1979	The school year starts in March, but is interrupted from May to August by a national revolution, culminating in a change of government on July 19, 1979. The post-revolutionary Ministry of Education (MED) makes special education a department within the Ministry. Existing special education schools are subsumed into the national educational system.
1980	Negotiations between MED and the National Welfare Institute (INSSBI) conclude that MED will be responsible for providing education to disabled children ages five to fourteen, and INSSBI will educate those fifteen to twenty-five years of age.
	A location for the vocational school is identified in the Villa Libertad suburb. Classes at CNEE are intermittent due to the need to train new special education teachers. Regular classes resume around October at CNEE with ten classes of deaf children with twelve students per class. Plans are made to widen the network of special education schools across the country to twenty-two.
1981	The vocational school, Centro Ocupacional para los Discapacitados (COD), opens at the new site in Villa Libertad.
1982	The emphasis of the boarding school at Ciudad Darío is changed from accommodating children needing physical therapy to focusing on those with hearing loss.
1992	The COD is "privatized."
1999	The privatized COD is closed.

schools is the point where non-agency is no longer regarded as inevitable, and the hearing majority changes its view of deaf children. Schools for the deaf have traditionally been formed by hearing persons, and control of those institutions typically remains in hearing hands. When schools for the deaf are in the planning stage, it is not deaf people who are changing their own concepts of their own social agency, but hearing people who are modifying under what conditions they will accept deaf people as social actors.

The conviction that deaf people could be remediated through education had been promulgated for centuries in other countries that had had considerable influence on Nicaragua. In Spain, Fray Pedro Ponce de León educated deaf nobles in the 1500s, and that country instituted schools accepting deaf pupils of all classes by the nineteenth century (Fischer and Lane 1993). The United States had adopted education for deaf pupils in the early 1800s (Lane 1984). Benito Juárez, the "father of Mexico" in so many ways, included a school for deaf children in 1856 among his multiple reforms (Lane 1984b). All of these countries started with educational institutions that used sign language as the major means of instruction, but they later turned to oral education in the late 1800s.

The first school for deaf children in Central America was founded by Maria Cristina Valentine in 1938 in Tegucigalpa, Honduras, but apart from surmising that it had an oral philosophy, nearly no details are known about the school. In the introduction to a book written by Valentine, *Education of the Deaf-Mute in the Home*, published in 1949 (the Gallaudet University Library has a copy), Valentine mentions that she based her book on experience gathered in the school she had set up, but she provides no details about its functioning or how large it was. Her book focuses on what to do with deaf children; it was never meant as a history. We know that the Nicaraguan government authorized a scholarship for two deaf sisters to an unnamed school in Tegucigalpa in the 1940s. They probably went to this school, but the scholarship's cancellation notice in *La Gaceta* in 1946 (it was cancelled because they had finished the course of study at the school) did not list the school's name, so we cannot be sure. The sisters did not appear to take any interest in special education, and four months after they finished their schooling, they were named to positions in regular high schools.[1]

More well known is the work of Dr. Fernando Centeno Güell, a physician of Spanish origin, who set up the first special education school in Costa Rica, the Escuela de Enseñanza Especial, in Guadalupe, a town close to the capital in San José. Dr. Centeno Güell started working with a small group of children in 1939. In 1940, a classroom specifically for deaf children was added (Jara 1971). The curriculum was strictly oral, and the school received guidance from the Lexington School for the Deaf in New York, as well as advice from other schools for the deaf in Spain and

Argentina. It is probable that the success of that school was watched closely by interested parties in Nicaragua, because Dr. Centeno Güell was later invited to have a hand in the organization of the first special education school in Nicaragua.

Apolonio Berríos Mayorga, who was born in León, Nicaragua, in 1908, attended medical school in Mexico City in the 1930s, ultimately choosing psychiatry as his specialty.[2] According to his sisters, María Berríos and Angela Berríos, Apolonio wrote to his father while he was in Mexico that he had become very interested in mental retardation, and that he wanted to have a positive impact on the lives of persons with developmental delay when he returned to Nicaragua. When he arrived home in 1938, his sisters remember that Apolonio brought six trunks filled with books and materials on the subject. He worked in Leon for two years and then moved

Dr. Apolonio Berríos Mayorga in 1938 in Mexico City as he was finishing his medical studies and preparing to return to Nicaragua. Photo courtesy of Maria and Angela Berríos.

to Managua to open a medical practice in 1940. Dr. Berríos's sisters also remember Apolonio, on visits home to León, remarking upon the large number of children with Down syndrome that he was encountering in his practice in Managua and his wish to improve their situations.

It should be noted that the late 1930s is also the time when Dr. Pedro Berruécos in Mexico City became concerned about the problems surrounding deafness and began to seek expert advice from Dr. Max Goldstein of the Central Institute for the Deaf in St. Louis, Missouri, on how to educate deaf children. In 1951, Dr. Berruécos would found the Instituto Mexicano de la Audición y del Lenguaje (IMAL) in the Mexican capital, which included a school for deaf children as well as a training institution for audiologists and speech-language therapists. The IMAL would later provide Nicaragua with professionals trained in these areas.[3] Dr. Berríos was already back in Nicaragua by the time that the IMAL was founded, but it is possible that he met Dr. Berruécos during his studies in Mexico City. Dr. Berríos's knowledge of deafness probably stemmed from discussions with Mexican colleagues like Dr. Berruécos around the larger topic of whether disabled children should or could be educated, and how.

When Apolonio Berríos moved to Managua, he became acquainted with a circle of wealthy and prominent Managuans who lived in the Barrio San Sebastián: medical professionals and others who had children with disabilities and wanted an educational option for them. The Barrio San Sebastián is a neighborhood that borders Lake Managua close to what was then the center of the city, and which contained many nice homes. It was destroyed in the 1972 earthquake, and its affluent population built new homes in the suburbs. One of the few reminders of old Managua, standing only a few blocks from the old cathedral and town plaza, is the strikingly beautiful three-story green house still known as the Mántica house. During its life, it has been used for many different purposes, even being at one time a museum. Though deteriorated, it still provides an enormous contrast to the plank shacks with dirt floors that surround it today. The Mánticas were supporters of the special education school from the beginning. From the early 1950s up to 1962, the first special education school was located directly across the street from the house.[4] The school was moved in 1962 to another property owned by the Mántica family, and the old building was torn down to make a parking lot for the Palace of Telecommunications (i.e., post office).

Felípe Mántica (senior) and his wife, Margarita Abaunza de Mántica, became close friends of Dr. Apolonio Berríos. The Mánticas's youngest daughter, Margotita, was cognitively delayed, possibly (according to her brother, Carlos) because of a very high fever she contracted as a toddler. Her parents hired a special nurse to care for her, and would later pay for special tutors to work with Margotita at their home. But, as civic-minded individuals, they concurred with Dr. Berríos and others that Nicaragua needed a school that would educate children with disabilities.[5]

It is thus slightly ironic that education for the deaf in Nicaragua probably stemmed not from an interest in deafness, per se, but from the fact that it was so closely associated with, and probably identified as a subset, of developmental delay. It is clear that the majority of the group of founders were more interested in mental retardation than they were in deafness. And it is a fact that from the beginning of provision of education to deaf students in Nicaragua to the present, they have always been educated in schools also charged with education for students with developmental delay, rather than in separate schools specializing in education for deaf children, as has been true in other countries. There are no existing records of the enrollment in Special Education School No. 1 from 1946 to 1976, but everyone I interviewed was adamant that deaf students were always outnumbered by students with developmental delay.[6] Data collected after the Department of Special Education was created at the Ministry of Education (in 1979) shows that deaf students have typically comprised 20% of the special education system's enrollment, with 70–80% filled by students with developmental delay.

Special Education School No. 1 received government assistance for rent, teacher salaries, and custodial staff, although the Rotary Club of Managua donated the furniture. The school opened with twenty pupils, ten of whom were deaf (the others had developmental delay), under the direction of Dr. Emilio Lacayo, a psychiatrist, a duty for which he received 500 córdobas monthly (*La Gaceta* 1946).[7] Dr. Fernando Centeno Güell and Dora Santiestéban came to Nicaragua from Costa Rica to help set up the school and hire the teachers. The first curriculum was strongly influenced by Montessori principles, and instruction for the deaf class was oral in focus.[8]

The school's bylaws, published in the official newspaper of record (*La Gaceta* 1947), required that the director of the school always be a physician, preferably a psychiatrist, indicating that, at that time, the school (and probably its founders) was influenced by a medical model in which a disability was seen as a state of illness that could be changed through appropriate intervention. Oviedo (1996) described this same perspective at work when a Venezuelan school for deaf children was initiated in Caracas in 1958: "Deafness was seen as a medical disease that could be overcome by therapy." If children could be trained "in oral Spanish," they could be considered "cured."

In 1952, Dr. Emilio Lacayo was named Minister of Education, and the directorship of the school was transferred to another psychiatrist, Dr. Apolonio Berríos Mayorga, who had identified closely with the school from its inception. Among Managuans over the age of forty, the name Apolonio Berríos is very famous, but it is not first identified with the school and children with disabilities, unless one had a child enrolled there or taught there.[9] When I have mentioned the name of Dr. Berríos to people, he is immediately recognized as the doctor who attended the sick without charging. Many have described to me the long lines of people waiting outside his dispensary, and I have also been told multiple times that he did not require any set fee. There evidently was a donation box outside the dispensary, which he suggested that people contribute to as they were able, and he is said to have used that money to buy medicines which he gave out free.

Dr. Berríos is also remembered for his conviction that antibiotics (especially gentamicin) were good for just about any ailment, and vitamins were useful in all cases, especially when given by injection. When I interviewed Carlos Mántica in 2003, he laughingly remembered the time in the early 1960s when he had been sent by his father to discuss with Dr. Berríos the plans for the new school that the Mánticas were building. Carlos said that he had no sooner entered and sat down in front of the doctor's desk when Dr. Berríos gave him a vitamin injection before he could explain that he had come to talk about architectural matters, not to consult him about his health.

Dr. Berríos remained the director of the school until his death on March 19, 1974. According to Olga Tenorio (who began her employment at the school as a new college graduate in 1948), when Dr. Berríos assumed the directorship, the school's official name was changed to Escuela

Nacional de Orientación y Educación Especial. Dr. Berríos también implementó a full day program (running from 8 a.m. to 5 p.m.). He identified himself so closely with the school that he sent his own car to transport children to and from the school, and he provided a free school lunch program by combining donations from patrons and various local businesses with money from his own pocket.[10] Olga remembers that to honor the doctor's dedication to his work, the school was re-named "Apolonio Berríos Special Education School" after he died in 1974.[11]

Not one of Nicaragua's first teachers for the deaf had formal training in deafness; all learned empirically on the job. Dr. Centeno Güell provided some training to all the teachers for a month when the school opened, and Dora Santiestéban, a recognized teacher of blind children, was named to a position at the school when it opened with a salary of 200 córdobas (*La Gaceta* 1946). There is no evidence that she was particularly familiar with deafness, but Olga Tenorio believes that Miss Santiestéban helped train those who taught the deaf also.

I would like to clarify for my readers that, as archives in Nicaragua are fragmentary, finding written sources to verify the history of the first special education schools has been time-consuming and difficult. The structures built to house the first schools have been torn down. Some documents have been lost as they were passed from hand to hand, and others were considered of no historical significance and evidently deliberately destroyed in "spring cleanings."[12] There are a few typescripts in the documentation center at the Ministry of Education, all of which are undated and anonymous, but through internal evidence, they can be shown to be remembrances written out by Olga Tenorio in 1986 for a retrospective workshop on special education. The National Archive of Nicaragua is opened only periodically when there is funding. Fortunately, I happened to be in Nicaragua in 2001, one of the years it was open and I was able to search for information pertaining to the school.[13]

In the National Archive, the boxes labeled "Ministry of Public Education (MEP)" only run up to 1979. Beginning with those labeled "1946," I examined all the MEP boxes. None of the correspondence that would have been expected to exist between the special education school and the Ministry of Education appears to have survived. In Box No. 112, which covered the years 1950–1964, I found a copy of the 1949–1950 budget for the Ministry of Public Education. This was the first information I had found about budget other than the original decrees to set up the school that were published in *La Gaceta*. It appeared to be nearly complete and gives us an interesting view of how special education fit into the national picture of education.

Budget of the Secretary of Public Education for the Fiscal Year 1949–1950
Chapter 38: Special Education School Managua

Director	$C 500
Secretary	$C 250
3 teachers for mentally-retarded, deaf and blind (each $C 200)	$C 600
1 teacher of music and rhythm	$C 100
Doorman and servant	$C 100
Expenses for maintenance and unforeseen expenses	$C 200

There were probably ten to fifteen deaf students as the 1950s began.[14] Thus, for the fiscal year 1949–1950, the MEP spent 21,000 córdobas on special education, which included the salaries listed above and a small amount for maintenance (essentially equivalent to the secretary's salary, and thus, probably not sufficient to cover all the school's costs). This equaled 1,750 córdobas per month. To gain some perspective, the Minister of Public Education earned 1,700 a month in salary (or approximately the same amount that supported the entire special education school), and the total expenditures for the MEP that year were 8,288,170 córdobas. Thus, special education represented 0.25% of the total education budget.

This fact should be interpreted in a larger context by noting that from 1981 to 1984 (probably the years in the last three decades during which Nicaragua's educational funding was at its highest), only 0.8% of the budget of the Ministry of Education went to special education (MED 1984). During that period, the proportion of the budget for special education was actually higher than the proportion of special education students among the total primary school enrollment at that time, which was 0.3%. Still, special education has never been among the top priorities in education in Nicaragua, and has never reached all the children who could use it.

The special education school suffered from high teacher turnover during its first six years, but that later stabilized. Olga Vivas, Ignacia Calero, and Odilí Delgado were named to teacher positions in 1946 (*La Gaceta*

1946) to teach deaf students, mentally retarded students, and blind students, respectively. The next year, however, Olga Vivas and Odilí Delgado received scholarships to study in the United States. Olga stayed in the United States, but Odilí did return to the special education school in Nicaragua. In 1949, Concepción Morales taught the deaf class, and she was followed by Thelma Córdoba de Porta, who stayed only a year or two. In 1952, Dr. Berríos appealed to another resident of the Barrio San Sebastián, a woman married to one of his relatives, to come and take over the deaf class. Soledad Escobar de Flores came and stayed twenty-two years. She stepped down after the 1974 school year, and her class was divided into two sections. Two new graduates of the Panamanian Institute of Special Habilitation (IPHE) taught the classes in 1975. María Teresa Castillo taught the younger children, and Rúthy Durán, the older ones.[15]

In 1961, the Mántica family brought Spanish educator, Florentina Gonzáles y Ciprés, from the México City school, Parque Lira de México, to tutor their daughter, Margotita, on a two-year contract that was later renewed, so that the educator stayed until 1965. The Ministry of Education, with the encouragement of the Mántica family, took the opportunity to hire Ms. Gonzáles y Ciprés to give a class on special education for regular teachers during her spare hours. According to Olga Tenorio, about thirty teachers participated, but after Ms. Gonzáles left, the class was not repeated or expanded upon. No normal school (the teacher-training institutions in Nicaragua) added instruction for special students to its curriculum. In the early 1980s, under the Sandinista government, the public library located in the Huembes Market was named for Ms. Gonzáles, and she was brought from México for a ceremony honoring her when the library was inaugurated. (The library was closed, for lack of funds, in the late 1990s.)

Isaura García, a longtime special education teacher, taught at Dr. Berríos's special education school from 1960 to 1962. (She left to study in France and returned in 1968 to work at a different school for special students founded in the meantime.) Isaura remembers that there were two large classes in 1960: one for the deaf and one for the mentally retarded. Soledad Escobar de Flores taught reading and writing to the deaf children in the morning, while Olga Tenorio taught them drawing in the afternoon. Isaura, herself, taught the mentally retarded group in the morning, and

Mercedes Rivas de Berríos (Dr. Berríos's wife) replaced her in the afternoon. Isaura was unable to remember the number of deaf students apart from saying it was a large group "because I never paid attention to the deaf students. My concern was my class, and since I couldn't communicate with the deaf students anyway, I didn't think about them any." Roberto Cano (born 1955) attended the school in 1961, but he did not stay the full year. He remembered only one deaf class, a large group seated in the classroom by age. He was unable to estimate the number in his class "because I was one of the littlest there, and I just tried to stay out of the way of the big kids, but it seemed like a lot to me."

In 1962, the special education school moved to a new building in the Barrio Monseñor Lezcano (a neighborhood of Managua), near the National Stadium. The Mántica family and the 20–30 Club provided the building and equipment.[16] The land upon which the building was located remained the property of the Mántica family, who allowed its use for Dr. Berríos's lifetime. The building was a long rectangular structure, which was sturdy enough to withstand the 1972 earthquake with no damage.[17] Facing the street entrance was the doctor's office where he received patients. The house for Dr. Berríos's family was behind the office, and behind that, separated by a very large patio that included a space to store the car, was the school building (which thus was not adjacent to the street). Upon Dr. Berríos's death in 1974, the land was repossessed. The house and school building were replaced by a large car parts store (Repuestos Mántica), which is still there today. The MEP rented a space for the special education school for two years (1974–1976). By 1977, the new Centro Nacional de Educación Especial, or National Center for Special Education (CNEE) had been built in the Barrio San Judas. The pupils from the old school were absorbed into the new one, and the Apolonio Berríos Special Education School ceased to exist.

According to Olga Tenorio, in the new 1962 building, three classrooms were allocated for the deaf and three for the mentally retarded. In spite of this, it appears that there continued to be only one class for deaf students, and Soledad Escobar de Flores was the teacher. The class appeared to oscillate between eighteen and twenty-five deaf pupils. The second of the three classrooms was reserved for the hardwired, stationary "auditory trainer." If the equipment was similar to systems used in the United States in that era, it utilized vacuum tubes, was bulky, and was not portable.[18]

Aerial photograph of the Centro Nacional de Educación Especial in Managua, 1977, the year that it opened. Photograph courtesy of the administrators of the Escuela Melania Morales in 2003.

The teacher spoke into a microphone, which amplified the sound and passed it to students through individually adjustable sets of earphones. Thus, if a child had some residual hearing, the amplification system would allow them to hear the teacher's voice. The equipment was a donation, but Olga cannot remember whether it came from México, Argentina, or pre-revolutionary Cuba. While a third classroom was included for the deaf section in the new building, its use remains a mystery.

The few deaf adults I could find who were students at the school in the 1962–1974 period, as well as some of their hearing relatives, recalled only one teacher, and hence, one class for the deaf. Angela Obando, whose son, Douglas, entered the school in 1969, was certain that Soledad Escobar was the only teacher for the deaf, although Olga Tenorio provided speech and voice training after she returned in 1965 from her study in Mexico. Noel Rocha, an extraordinary deaf man born in 1953, attended the Berríos school from 1965 to 1972. When asked to reflect on who was at the school in the 1960s, he could not remember any teacher of the deaf except Soledad, but he was able to fluently list twenty-five student names, and said there were more whose names he couldn't remember. He definitely remembered Olga Tenorio, but did not believe she had her own deaf class.

Noel grouped the names he gave according to older ones and younger ones, and said he remembered that the older students were separated from the younger ones. But when asked who taught the other class, he was stumped. He remembered that when he was older, he was allowed to help with the younger children, but he could not remember if he went to another classroom, or if everyone was in one class. The division into older and younger was also recalled by Salvador López (born 1947), Miguel Angel Moreno (born 1953), and María Lourdes Palacios Mairena (born 1954, but attended the Managua school only two years—1960 and 1961—before going to study in Mexico), yet none of them could remember any other teacher for the deaf than Soledad Escobar de Flores.

In the National Archives, I found only one other budgetary document from the Pre-revolutionary MEP relating to special education (the budgets from all other years appear to have been lost), and it sheds light on the school's staffing at that time. It is dated July 26, 1963, and is not complete (so I cannot calculate what percentage of the total budget the special education school received that year). But it does contain (on pages 20–21) the pay rates for the ministry's employees at Special Education School No. 1.

Special Education School

I.D.# Post	(Basic Salary + Academic Credits + Years of Service = Total)
1047 *Director*: Apolonio Berríos Mayorga (MEP)[19]	1,200+100+360=1,660
1048 *Secretary-Treasurer*: Mercedes Rivas de Berríos	300+0+0=300
1049 *Teacher Class A*: Olga Tenorio Hernández (MEP)	600+100+120=820
1049 *Teacher Class A*: Soledad Escobar Barrera (MEP)	500+50+225=775
1049 *Teacher Class A*: Mercedes Rivas de Berríos	450+0+0=450
1049 *Teacher Class A*: Adelfia Rivas de Cabezas	450+0+0=450
1049 *Teacher Class A*: Carmen Castrillo de Chaw	450+0+0=450
1049 *Teacher Class A*: María Estela Rivas	450+0+0=450
1049 *Teacher Class A*: Apolonio Berríos Mayorga (MEP)	300+0+90=390
1050 *Music Teacher*: Josefina Paguagua de Pérez Alonso	200+0+40=240
1051 *Doorman*: Marcos López López	260=260
1052 *Servant*: Rosa Montiel de Alvarado	260=260
1052 *Servant*: Flora Ruíz Ortíz	260=260
1049 *Teacher Class C*: Isabel Mungía Mungía	450=450

Salaries were paid to seven teachers, but there must have been fewer actually directing classes because on closer inspection, one sees that Apolonio Berríos Mayorga received one salary as director, but he also received another as a teacher. Dr. Berríos's sisters are adamant that he never taught a class at the school, "he was only the director," and no deaf person who had any contact with the school has ever referred to a male teacher, except Josefa Guttiérrez (who began attending the school in 1971) who remembered that "one day our teacher, Soledad, was sick and her husband came and took her place. He was very stern and strict." It is likely that Dr. Berríos only filled in on that one day, but he was not a regular teacher. Mercedes Rivas de Berríos (Dr. Berríos's wife) received a salary as secretary/treasurer, and she also received a second salary as a teacher, but it is clear from all the interviewees that she taught the girls "handwork," such as embroidery and crochet in the afternoons, and was never considered a teacher of academics. Olga Tenorio and Carmen Castrillo can be linked to the mentally retarded classes; and as a Class C teacher, Isabel Mungía was more like a teacher's aide. Josefina Paguagua taught music to all the students. Adelphia Rivas was remembered as Mercedes Berríos's only sister.[20] Although listed as a Class A teacher, María Estela Rivas is remembered by no one and is probably a phantom name. Soledad Escobar de Flores was the teacher of the sole class for deaf children.

The need for more teachers trained to work with speech and language development was evident, and in 1963–1965, three Nicaraguans went to Mexico to study speech and language therapy at the IMAL. One of those who received her degree as a teacher of the deaf, as well as a voice and language therapist, was Olga Tenorio Hernández. Upon her return to Nicaragua, she continued at the Berríos school, ultimately assuming the directorship of the school in 1974 upon the death of Dr. Berríos.

Silvia Ruíz de Ayón and Antonio Ayón, the other two who went to Mexico at the same time as Olga Tenorio, were motivated to seek training when their third son, Antonio (known in Nicaragua as Toño) was born deaf in 1959. They could find no one, at the time, who worked with preschool deaf children. Silvia Ayón remembers that Dr. Pedro Berruécos, director of IMAL, came to Nicaragua in 1961 to give a lecture, and that she sought him out afterward for advice on what to do. He referred her to the John Tracy Clinic in Los Angeles, California, which provides training in speech and language development to parents via correspondence, and she began working with Toño, but Dr. Berruécos later found a scholarship that would allow Toño to attend the IMAL school while Silvia enrolled in the teacher training course. Her husband decided not to split the family and opted to accompany her to Mexico with their other children and take the training himself. Upon their return, the Ayóns went to Dr. Berríos, offering their services as teachers at the Escuela de Educación Especial. [21] But Dr. Berríos was not willing to give them paid teacher positions (although he said he would have been happy to have had them as volunteers), but he was also scandalized when they said they wanted each class limited to seven to ten children in order to provide individualized attention (certainly not, in his mind, a cost-effective manner of educating deaf children).

The Ayóns, faced with earning a living for their six children, set up a private school in their home in which they worked with children who had learning disabilities and who were deaf. From 1964 on, they taught twenty-eight children annually, fourteen in a morning session (i.e. two groups of seven) and fourteen in an afternoon session. Their curriculum was fiercely oral and emphasized speech training.[22] For a while, their students included Adrián Pérez, who would later be educated in Spain and be a founding member of the National Nicaraguan Deaf Association (ANSNIC). Jenifer Grigsby (later the first president of the deaf association) worked with Silvia Ayón for years in the little private school; then when she was "mainstreamed" into the Colegio Teresiano (a prestigious private girls' school in Managua), Jenifer continued to come to the Ayóns in the afternoons for tutoring. Silvia believes that half of the children she and her husband taught over the years were deaf. She estimates that she, personally, has worked with twenty deaf children; and of these, she judges that six learned to talk.

In 1967, Dr. Eloy Isabá, an otolaryngologist, and his wife, Dr. Alma Acuña de Isabá, an audiologist and speech therapist, returned from Mexico, where Dr. Isabá had also received her training in audiology at IMAL (and thus was also very oral in orientation). She set up a small program for children with speech and language problems (including hearing loss), which enrolled six to fourteen children annually. Dr. Isabá did not actually work directly with the children, but supervised a staff of speech therapists, some of whom later became teachers of the deaf in the public school system.

Upon her return from France to Nicaragua in 1968, Isaura García became director of the Special Education School No. 2, founded in 1965 through the efforts of Dr. Mauricio Ocón and Dr. Gonzalo Meneses Ocón. After the 1979 revolution, this school was renamed Escuela Manolo Morales. It was included as a public special education school from 1980 until 1983. Support was withdrawn because the school was not following the official special education curriculum.[23] Some deaf children appear to have been "integrated" at that school (e.g., educators, such as Noel Lam Herrera, coordinator of deaf education when I interviewed him in 1994, included the Manolo Morales School when asked to list the pre-revolutionary schools for the deaf), but, when I interviewed Isaura García in August 2002, she stated adamantly that education of the deaf had never been the goal of the school, and she did not want the school characterized as ever having been a school for deaf children (she said its focus was upon children with developmental delay).

The December 1972 earthquake in Managua had an impact upon educational options for deaf children by the total disruption of daily living that it caused in Managua. According to Marcos López, Dr. Berríos's chauffeur, who was inside the house during the earthquake (Dr. and Mrs. Berríos were spending Christmas with their son in Mexico City), the house and school weathered the quake intact, but many teachers and students had their homes destroyed. Julio García remembers that he had to quit school after the earthquake because his family's house was destroyed, and they moved to the countryside to be near relatives. No schools near their new home accepted deaf pupils. The families of Miguel Angel Moreno and Noel Rocha were similarly in need, so both young men left school to look for work.

The Ayóns's home was also destroyed. They relocated to Altamira, a nearly undeveloped suburb at the time, and reopened their school in their new home. The Special Education School No. 2 was relocated to a private building in the Reparto Serrano, a suburb of Managua. Dr. Isabá was able to reopen her program at the same location, and ran it until the Sandinista Revolution. In a personal interview, she stated that she closed her little school in 1979 in order to focus on her audiological practice.

In 1973, Guillermina Morgan, a social worker who had been working in the MEP, was named to be the liaison with the various special education schools. She handled all administrative matters (such as payment of teacher salaries), and, because she had finished a course of training in deaf education at the IPHE in Panamá, she also began to visit regular education schools to give talks about children with special needs, and what resources were available for them.[24]

Until 1974, education for the deaf was only available in four schools in Managua, Nicaragua's capital. Deaf children from other areas of the country either moved to the capital or went without education. Early in the 1970s, however, groups of professionals and parents began the work necessary to establish schools for children with disabilities in cities outside of the capital. Like the previous schools, these new schools accepted children who were blind, deaf, or mentally retarded. Classes were grouped according to disability.

Under the inspiration of Jilma Balladares de Herdocia, and with the support of the 20–30 Club, a special education school was founded in 1974 in León, in the historic district of Subtiava.[25] It faces the imposing colonial church, a site it still occupies although the school has grown in size. The first year, there were twenty deaf pupils divided into two classes. At the same time, Dr. Zela Porras lent her support to the founding of a special education school in Chinandega, which opened the following year with one of the classes including ten deaf students.

In 1976, the University of León opened a master's-level degree program in Educación Especial Polivalente (multidisciplinary special education) with three instructors brought specially from Spain. The program was interrupted in 1979 by the turmoil around the Sandinista Revolution, and the Spanish faculty members departed. Natalia Popova, a Russian teacher of deaf children, who had immigrated to Nicaragua after her marriage to a Nicaraguan (Marenco Tercero 2003), took over administration of the program for its final semester, allowing twenty-three students to receive degrees in 1980. These students filled important vacancies in the special education system, which was expanded after the revolution in 1979.

Beginning in 1978, a church missionary from the United States, "Tommy" Wallace, and his Miskito wife worked with children with disabilities, including some who were deaf, in their home in Puerto Cabezas; but they left the country at the time of the revolution and did not return. There were two other persons (names now unknown) who worked with them, because, according to Guillermina Morgan, the Ministry of Education had been paying four salaries for the school in Puerto Cabezas.

In 1978, the Italian-born pastor of the Roman Catholic church in Ciudad Darío, Monseñor Carlos Santi, raised the funds to build the Escuela Hogar para Niños Minusvalidos (Residential School for Handicapped Children), intending that the school would deal with children with motoric problems, such as those caused by polio and cerebral palsy. Later, in 1981, when the necessary physical therapists could not be found, the focus of the school was changed to educating children with mental retardation (local pupils only) and children with hearing losses (who come from all over the country and are boarded at the school).

In the mid-1970s, Hope Somoza, the wife of then-dictator Anastasio Somoza, was head of the Junta Nacional de Asistencia y Prevención Social (National Board for Social Assistance and Problem Prevention or JNAPS, which Nicaraguans pronounce as "hoh-tah NAHPS"), a Nicaraguan institution that promoted various social projects. She became interested in the area of special education, and when the United States Agency for International Development (USAID) requested proposals for funding, the Institute for Social Welfare and the JNAPS submitted a proposal to build a new and expanded special education school in Managua.[26]

Ground was broken for the school in 1976 on a large plot of land in the Barrio San Judas in what, at the time, was an isolated part of the capital. Now a teeming section of southwest Managua, Barrio San Judas was countryside until 1973, when it began to be settled by people who previously lived in the center of the city, but who had lost their houses in the Managua earthquake in December 1972.[27] Sewer connections and electricity came slowly to this sector, which has always been known as a working-class neighborhood. The school today is still isolated, although public transportation, something that was not available until the 1980s, does pass by it. On all sides of the school, very low income housing has appeared.

Rosemary Bohmer de Selva, the then-head of the psychology department at the Jesuit Central American University (Universidad Centroamericana, UCA) was also named the director of the new school, the CNEE. She says that she worked at the school during the day, and directed the UCA's psychology department in the evenings. The Apolonio Berríos School was closed, and the students were absorbed into the new school. In June 1977, the CNEE opened with at least 120 pupils, probably including forty-nine students in four classrooms for the deaf. [28] Twenty-five of the forty-nine were transfers from the first special education school, and twenty-four were new to schooling. The students transferred from the old school were not kept together in classes. About half of each class, both older and younger, were transfers, and half were new pupils. The older two classes were composed of students who had passed the age of fourteen (they ranged from fourteen to nineteen years of age), the age at which elementary school in Nicaragua traditionally ended. Fourteen was the age at which Dr. Berríos had previously begun to seek apprenticeships or jobs as helpers in manual trades for the boys, and the age at which girls typically stopped school and helped out at home.

The decision made in 1975 (after Dr. Berríos had died and Soledad Escobar de Flores had retired) to separate the deaf class into two classes: an older group (who were beyond fourteen years) and a younger group, as well as the decisions made when the new school was set up to retain pupils in special education routinely during adolescence (giving them some academic training, but also providing workshops for the boys to learn manual trades and for the girls to learn sewing) set precedents that would lead later to the establishment of vocational schools after the revolution.

Rúthy Durán, who had studied deaf education in Panamá and Uruguay, and who had taught at the special education school in León and at the Apolonio Berríos School, was named head teacher for the deaf section at CNEE. Olga Tenorio, the former principal of the Berríos school, became one of the speech therapists for the new school.

Like the other special education schools previously established in Nicaragua, the CNEE accepted children with mental retardation, blindness, deafness, and motor disabilities. In addition to the children who were transferred from the Berríos school, the students were recruited from lists prepared in anticipation by the JNAPS. According to Rosemary de Selva, the first director of the school, there were no financial or social prerequisites for acceptance.[29] The school's funding was provided by funds from the lottery, and there was never any need to charge tuition or other fees. Some parents who could afford to do so, were encouraged to contribute to the school in order to encourage their sense of participation; but no child was required to pay anything, and there was no set tuition. Children came to the school from all areas of Managua, and from all social strata. A set of school buses, each with a driver and an attendant, made the rounds twice a day to pick up and drop off the children.

The school had an evaluation team of social workers and child psychologists who placed the children in classes according to their levels, and there was access to a team of physicians (pediatricians, a neurologist, a physiatrist, and an audiologist) to which any children needing medical care could be referred. The CNEE had eight pavilions of classrooms, and each pavilion had an attendant who focused on the children's personal needs or acted as a teacher's aide as necessary.[30] The teaching staff included the classroom teachers, a speech therapist, and two teachers of physical education. Among the equipment available to the deaf section was one room set aside to house a group auditory trainer (similar to the one in the Berríos school. It may even have been the same machine). In total, the school employed eighty staff members and served around 120 students in 1977.

The two teachers of physical education employed at CNEE in 1977 found a group of very enthusiastic adolescents in the fifteen to nineteen year range, most of whom were deaf. The children were interested in participating in individual sports events, an option not open to them at their previous school. The group took part in practices during and after school. They also competed successfully against other "regular" Managua schools in various track and field events. The team was sent to a meet in Costa Rica in 1978, as well as to meets in Venezuela and Honduras in early 1980. (All trips were evidently at school expense. According to Rosemary Bohmer de Selva, the funds from the lottery were sufficient for this kind of school-sponsored activity.) Another group of students had learned to perform folk dances under the direction of Haydée Palacios, a well-known teacher of dance in Nicaragua, and they accompanied the athletic group to Venezuela. Rúthy Durán, the teacher of the older students at CNEE, served as one of the chaperones.

Rúthy recalled that the long-distance trips involved groups of twenty to thirty students who were gone for a week to ten days. While in each of the foreign countries, the group met with representatives from the various local deaf associations. In all of these countries, Rúthy remembers, the representatives of the deaf associations used sign language, and the adolescents, who at the time did not use a standardized sign language, nor

CNEE athletic team as they leave for the trip to a competition in Costa Rica in May 1978. Front row, left to right: Rúthy Durán (teacher), Isolda Zavala, Cristina Guevara, Ana Maria Chau. Back row: Javier López, Sócrates Avilés (teacher), Arcadio Díaz, Douglas Vega, Norman Burgos (teacher) Mauricio Zepeda, José Dolores Méndez, Roberto Useda. Photo courtesy of Rúthy Durán.

CNEE athletic team at competition in Honduras in January 1980. Front row: Douglas Vega, Arcadio Díaz, Javier López, José Dolores Méndez, Mauricio Zepeda. Back row: Liseth Balmaceda, Lesbia Portillo (teacher), Norman Burgos (teacher), Isolda Zavala, Mayra Mena, Roger Aguilar, Ana Maria Chau, Cristina Guevara, Tamara Garcia (teacher), Rúthy Durán (teacher), Haydée Palacios (dance teacher), Maria Lourdes Palacios. Photo courtesy of Rúthy Durán.

CNEE athletic team competition in Venezuela in January 1980. Front row: Mauricio Zepeda (Mauricio's sister), José Dolores Méndez, Arcadio Díaz, Ana Maria Chau, Javier López, Mayra Mena. Back row: Isolda Zavala, Rúthy Durán (teacher). Photo courtesy of Rúthy Durán.

have a very clear idea of what one would look like, were enthusiastic about what they saw.

Starting in 1975, rumors of the first challenge to the oral methodology began to enter Nicaragua through adoption of Total Communication methods in Costa Rica.[31] In 1974, Gallaudet College, in Washington, D.C. (the world's only college founded to educate deaf students) had made the first contacts with educators in Costa Rica. In 1974, Dr. Gilbert Delgado, who was active in international outreach at Gallaudet College, made his first trip to Costa Rica and contacted Gloria Campos, a teacher of the deaf who had worked at St. Joseph's School for the Deaf in New York from 1972 to 1974.

This meeting resulted in the later founding of the Programa Regional de Recursos para la Sordera (Regional Resource Program on Deafness) (PROGRESO), a center on deafness based in Costa Rica at the University of Costa Rica. In 1975, linguists from Gallaudet College (e.g., James Woodward and others) began to study the sign language they found in Costa Rica and declared it a language distinct from American Sign Language (ASL), and they urged that LESCO (Lenguaje de Señas de Costa Rica or Costa Rican Sign Language) be used with Spanish in classes for the deaf in the Total Communication method. Through Gallaudet, information about the Total Communication methodology spread to the Costa Rican teachers of the deaf; and from Costa Rica, the word spread to Nicaragua.[32]

Historically, Costa Rica was very oral in its deaf education focus. Both schools for deaf children in Costa Rica, Dr. Centeno Güell's school founded in 1939, and Alejandro Larena's school founded in 1965, were strongly influenced by Spanish methods and were fierce in the avocation of oral education. In 1972, Gloria Campos, a teacher married to an American, had moved to New York where she worked at St. Joseph's School for the Deaf and learned Signed English and about the Total Communication method. She returned to Costa Rica in 1974 and brought with her the use of the one-handed fingerspelling alphabet and sign language in combination with speech.

There was already some sympathy for sign language in Costa Rica at this time, and it came from deaf people. Former pupils of the oral school of Professor Alejandro Larena had formed the National Association of the Deaf of Costa Rica (ANASCOR) on June 8, 1974; and from the beginning, they used sign language.[33] (A large group at this school had previously spent multiple years at a school for deaf children in Spain.) Gloria Campos encouraged Mima Bravo, a member of ANASCOR and an extraordinary young deaf woman, to apply to Gallaudet College for a scholarship, and Mima went to the United States.

Total Communication, which originally meant the use of whatever communication system or modality would work, whether voice or sign or writing, came to be identified with what is now more often referred to as Simultaneous Communication, a method in which speaking and signing are performed at the same time. Usually, the grammar of the sign language is ignored and signs are matched to the spoken message, which retains its grammatical form. Thus, this method is also known as Sign-Supported Speech or Manually Coded Speech. Supporters have also added invented manual signs to stand for the grammatical features of the spoken language in an effort to make the grammatical features of the spoken language visible to deaf children. The hope in the mid-1970s was that this combination of speech and signs would provide a better way for deaf children to learn the majority spoken language through a visual medium that was more salient to them than speech. Knowledge of this methodology passed from Costa Rica to Nicaragua; and in 1978, some Nicaraguan teachers attended workshops on Total Communication.[34]

In August 1976, Delgado arranged funding from the Organization for American States for Gloria Campos, the teacher, and Rafael Valverde, a young deaf man, to meet up with Mima Bravo (already studying at Gallaudet) on the Gallaudet campus, where photographs were made for a first draft of a dictionary of Costa Rican Sign Language. The signs were debated at the Costa Rican Deaf Association from June to September 1977, and agreement among the members about the correct form was reached on 520 signs. A dictionary of those signs, dated April 1979, was published by the Ministry of Education under the title *Hacía una Nueva Forma de Comunicación con el Sordo* (Towards a New Form of Communicating with the Deaf), although a 1978 letter from Dr. Delgado to Soledad Chavarría of PROGRESO indicates that the dictionary was available by early 1978. (Gallaudet University has a copy of this dictionary in their collection.)

In 1978, multiple workshops were given in Costa Rica on Total Communication, and Charlotte Baker-Shenk presented a workshop on the linguistic features of signed languages. When Mima Bravo returned to Costa Rica that year, she pressed hard for incorporation of Total Communication into the Costa Rican educational system.[35] Gerilee Gustason, a strong advocate of Signed English (one of the constructed sign language systems used in the Total Communication methodology), gave a weeklong workshop in Costa Rica. Educators from all Central American countries were invited to participate in the workshops; and in 1978, some Nicaraguan teachers, including Luz María Sequeira [the second in command of the special education school at that time], attended a workshop in Costa Rica. One Total Communication workshop appears to have been held in Nicaragua, probably before June 1980.[36] The teachers who had gone to the workshop could not remember specific dates. Unlike PROGRESO at the University of Costa Rica, which has notices from these early workshops in its archive, all correspondence and files generated by the CNEE before the 1979 revolution (and, in fact, anything prior to 1990) have been lost, and no official record remains, so the names of the trainers in Nicaragua remain unknown.

While Total Communication was never adopted officially as a methodology in Nicaraguan schools for deaf children, it did introduce the novel concept that sign language might have a linguistic content, rather than being nothing more than pantomime or rudimentary gestures. When interviewed in 2002, Adrián Pérez Castellón reflected on changes with sign language and its use in Nicaragua, which he had noted for the 1974–1984 period. Adrián, Nicaraguan by birth, was deafened by meningitis at age eighteen months (in 1965). His family sought in every way to give him the best education they could: He was a pupil with Antonio and Silvia Ayón, he was "integrated" into regular classrooms (which he hated because he never understood what was happening in class) and his second cousin, Rúthy Durán, came to his home to tutor him.[37] In 1974, his father obtained a scholarship for him through the Spanish ambassador to the Brother Pedro Ponce de León Special School for Deaf Children in Astorga, Spain.[38] In the Spanish school, Adrián says that, while classes were oral, sign language was commonly used in the dormitories and on the playgrounds, and he naturally picked it up, too. Adrián was able to visit Nicaragua twice while he studied in Spain, once in 1976 and again in 1980. He thus has memories of a period before he knew sign language (prior to 1974), an awareness of what it was like to use sign as a language (his time at school), two definitely separated encounters with his future signing partners in which he did not feel that he was using sign as a language (his visits home) and memories of "after," when signing *had* become a system—both in states of low, and later, higher involvement with the deaf association. According to Adrián's accounts, something happened between 1976 and 1980 to engender a different attitude toward signing.

When he left Nicaragua in 1974, the only other deaf persons Adrián knew were his classmates at the school run by the Ayóns. When he returned for his first visit home in 1976 (which lasted three months), his cousin, Rúthy Durán, introduced him to her pupils at the Berríos school.[39] (They included Javier López Gómez, Douglas Vega, and Mauricio Zepeda.) Adrián remembers that during the first visit, "[I] tried to communicate with them in sign language [the system Adrián had learned in Spain], but it had no effect, and they also did not seem interested in learning any of what I had learned in Spain. We worked out a system of oral words, gestures, written words, and "mimicry" [acting out] that was alright for communication."

Adrián returned to Spain, and the political situation was too precarious for him to return for either the 1978 or 1979 school vacations.

The revolution was finished by 1980, and when he returned to Nicaragua for the vacation, Rúthy again brought him to her school to meet her same pupils, now older teenagers, who were still at the CNEE waiting to transfer to the COD (Centro Ocupacional para los Discapacitados or Vocational Center for the Disabled, a school which opened in 1981). Rúthy has a picture of Adrián with her students in the workshop at CNEE taken during his visit. When asked about his visit that year, Adrián remembered that he was pleasantly surprised to find more signs in use in Nicaragua, but, communication was still different than what he was used to in Spain because individual signs were chained together and getting one's meaning across was still more awkward than it was in Spain. Javier had acquired a sign language dictionary by then, and Douglas had taken a great interest in sign language too. Both had learned many of the signs, but Adrián said that

Adrián Pérez with older students at the CNEE during his 1980 visit before the workshops were transferred to the vocational school in Villa Libertad. Front row: Aquiles Guerrero, Roger Aguilar, Gerardo Lezama. Back row: Adrián Peréz, Eduardo Benevides, Javier López, Roberto Useda, Mauricio Zepeda, José (last name unknown), Leonel (last name unknown). Photo courtesy of Soledad Rostrán.

communication at this time was still a combination of everything: signs, gestures, oral words, written words, acting out—whatever worked. He said that in 1980, he still did not see a sign language, such as he knew existed among the students at the school for the deaf in Spain.

In 1982, after finishing a certificate in dental technology (making dentures), Adrián returned to Nicaragua for good. He remembers that after he returned, Javier López, Isolda Zavala, and Mayra Mena came to find him at his house to visit. Adrián said that, this time, there was a decided increase in the use of signs, but that they were still "primitive" and not as "rich" as the sign language he knew from Spain. At this time, Adrián had a job as a dental prosthetist. While he still socialized with them, he was only able to meet with them occasionally.

Adrián volunteered that he only noticed a significant increase in sign language use and increasing fluency after the group of deaf young people started meeting at Rúthy's or Gloria's houses after 1984. Adrián was emphatic that the change in language usage had not been rapid, but there had definitely been a trend to more fluidity in signing, and "they could express more complicated things than before." At the meetings, this sign language (which Adrián distinguishes from the sign language he learned in Spain) became the common mode of communication. With his knowledge of another sign language, Adrián picked up the local variations quickly. When a position came available in 1990 for a teacher of sign language, he was happy to quit his warehouse job to take it, and he remains in that position today.

Adrián, by his fluency, would have been an encouraging influence on the growing Nicaraguan Sign Language (NSL); but, as he pointed out, when it was only himself signing (in 1976)—one person trying to use a more standardized sign language among others who evidently did not— his Nicaraguan contemporaries were not particularly interested. (They were happy to meet him, and visited multiple times during those three months, so if they were already using a full signing system among themselves, they most likely would have taught it to him or he would have recognized it due to his familiarity with another signed language.) But, by 1980, when he returned the second time, he found his friends more receptive to sign language, although grammar, at that time, seemed to have developed little at that point.

Adrián is always listed as one of the APRIAS founding members (his registration card number is 38), but he did not, at first, participate as actively as others (Javier, for instance, has registration card number 2). Adrián was the first elected president of the Asociación Pro-Ayuda y Integración a los Sordos (Association to Help and Integrate the Deaf, or APRIAS), the first deaf group to organize formally in Nicaragua, in 1986; but after only a few months, he resigned because he felt the duties were too onerous to complete along with his job in the dental workshop. (Jenifer Grigsby was then elected president.) Adrián is, however, a witness to the growth of the language, and he described that growth as slow, taking place over a long time.

Thomas Gibson's witness to the state of sign language use in 1979 was briefer than Adrián's, and was never repeated. A Peace Corps volunteer, he was assigned to teach sign language to the teachers at the CNEE for two years. He arrived in April 1979 and had only just begun to teach before the impending Sandinista Revolution encouraged his superiors to withdraw him from Nicaragua and send him to Costa Rica to finish out his assignment. Mr. Gibson and his sign language made an impression on everyone. I was told about him whenever anyone reminisced about the CNEE in 1979, although no one I interviewed in Nicaragua could remember the last name of "Tomás."[40] Rúthy Durán remembers that Thomas gave Douglas Vega, one of the older deaf pupils, a sign language dictionary from the United States, and that he and Javier López Gómez studied it intensely and were abuzz with enthusiasm about learning signs from whatever source they could find (mostly Thomas). Rúthy remembers that "they followed Tomás around like puppy dogs." Although she had heard about sign language, and probably assimilated some by that time, Rúthy also remembers later watching Javier and Douglas converse with signs. "Their hands went so fast, and they didn't talk. I was amazed to see that they were understanding each other very well. And I remember saying to myself, 'Oh, *that* is what they mean when they say the deaf communicate through sign language alone.'"

Gibson says he did not find any sign language in Nicaragua in 1979. Even though he was at the CNEE only three weeks before being evacuated, Gibson told me (in a telephone interview) that even that short time emphasized to him what a challenge he faced in his proposed assignment because "the sign language I witnessed in Nicaragua consisted of home signs. There was very little contact and communication between members of the deaf population. . . . The faculty at the [CNEE] was a dedicated group, but lacked even the basic knowledge of sign language."[41] Gibson, for example, recounted his memories of going to a potluck-type gathering of deaf people at the home of one of the students in May 1979. There was a total lack of older deaf persons; and while the young adults all wanted to interact with Gibson, communication was quite draining for him because they only had home signs and gestures at their disposal.

Gibson had the sign language knowledge to have recognized any regularized signing if he had seen it, even if the vocabulary items might have been unfamiliar to him. He had previously worked for five years as a teacher in a residential school for the deaf in North Carolina and during that time had socialized with the adult deaf community. Because he was billed as someone who knew sign language, it is certain that any regularized signing that might have existed (and was known to either the teachers or students at CNEE) would have been exhibited to him. And, if there had been any deaf community or older signing adults known to any of the students or teachers, he would certainly have been invited to meet them, or they would have gone out of their way to meet him. (He had been present in the country for language training for four weeks before he began his "work" at the CNEE in May 1979, so the teachers and students were aware of his pending arrival, and would have had time to alert any older deaf persons they knew.)

Gibson also said that he never returned to Nicaragua after 1979. He thought my letter, asking about his experiences there, was "kind of spooky" because he was no longer a teacher of the deaf, no longer had any special contacts with deaf persons, and hadn't used his knowledge of sign language for some time. The letter reminded him of events that he had not thought about for years. Gibson's remembrances (like Adrián's), then, are actually valuable "snapshots" of the linguistic knowledge and usage of the deaf in Nicaragua at that moment. In 1979, he says he saw absolutely no older deaf adults, nor any standardized or regularized signing.[42] There was one striking exception: a young man with "curly, kinky, yellowish hair" whom Mr. Gibson recalls was able to string ASL-like signs together well enough to carry on a coherent conversation. This had to have been Javier López Gómez. Sign language had become one of Javier's avocations.[43]

"Remediable Subjects" 3

PRIOR TO the Sandinista Revolution in 1979, there were seven special education schools in Nicaragua, five of which accepted pupils with hearing problems.[1] According to a 1980 Ministry of Education report (MED 1980), before the revolution, there were 512 children enrolled in these schools, of whom about 100 were deaf; and there were thirty-three teachers. Probably nine of them taught students with hearing impairments. All of the teachers for the deaf used oral methods of instruction and had the common goal of "restoring the deaf to society" by teaching the children oral Spanish. For all of the country's educational institutions, the most important goal for teachers of the deaf was to "make the children talk."

This goal did not change with the new government that entered in 1979, although the coverage of special education was broadened. The Sandinista revolutionary philosophy included a dedication to universal education. All of the schools within the republic were incorporated into one national system under the supervision of the Ministry of Education (MED). While the pre-revolutionary Ministry of Public Education (MEP) had, in the 1970s, assigned one administrator to act as liaison to the special education schools, the new minister of education, Dr. Carlos Tunnerman, decided to raise special education to the level of a department.[2]

Under the reformed national educational system, private schools were allowed to continue to teach special subjects, such as religion, but they were required to follow the national curriculum for the academic courses. All of the special education schools were also incorporated into the national system. In addition, the decision was made to set up at least one special education school in each of the fifteen *departamentos* (administrative districts, similar to the states in the United States), with the result that the number of special education schools increased from seven in 1979 to twenty-four in 1981.

Within the newly reorganized ministry, the separate Department of Special Education was established in late 1979, and Jilma Balladares de Herdocia of León was named its first director. Doña Jilma was a society matron in León. When her youngest daughter, Martha Lucía, was born with Down syndrome, she became interested in special education. She took Martha Lucía to Dr. Centeno Güell's school in Costa Rica, for an evaluation, and observed classes at the school. Later, during a visit to Spain, she toured special education schools there, and returned to León convinced that a special education school was needed in her hometown. She convinced her friends in the León chapter of the 20–30 Club to take on the project of finding a building and equipping it; and in 1975, a small special education school opened across the street from a local León church in the area known as Barrio Subtiava. Doña Jilma had also convinced the National Autonomous University of Nicaragua in León to initiate, in 1977, a three-year program to train teachers in special education.

When Dr. Carlos Tunnerman, previously the rector of the university in León (Universidad Nacional Autónoma de Nicaragua), was appointed minister of education in 1979, he naturally thought of Doña Jilma and her efforts on the part of providing education for children with disabilities, and he asked her to be the national director of special education. She accepted and began a round of international fundraising, which resulted in the construction of many small special education schools in areas outside of the large cities, usually in the towns that serve as the administrative center (*cabezero*) for each department. In these small schools, one or two of the classrooms were devoted to *audición* (deaf education), with enrollments fluctuating between five and twenty deaf students per school. Managua, Ciudad Darío, León, and Chinandega continued to be homes to the larger special education schools in the country, enrolling between 30 (Chinandega) and 120 (Managua) deaf students among a much larger population of children with mental retardation.

Doña Jilma appointed Natalia Popova to be the first coordinator in the area of deaf education on the national team of teacher trainers.[3] Natalia had immigrated to Nicaragua in 1972 with her León-born husband, and in 1974 was working with Doña Jilma to prepare teachers of the deaf for the Chinandega and León special education schools. Natalia had been trained to teach the deaf speech development, and to use fingerspelling as a teaching adjunct.

Because the number of special education schools was planned to expand rapidly, there was an urgent need for more teachers, and that included a need for more teachers of the deaf. Popova moved to Managua in early 1980 to take up her post. Intensive training classes for prospective special education teachers started the regular academic year in March 1980.[4] In Managua, the classes were held at the National Center for Special Education (CNEE), as it was easier to bring the teachers of the deaf who were staffing the "country-side" schools to the capital city for the duration of the course, rather than train them at the schools to which they would return.[5]

It must be remembered that both the 1979 and the 1980 academic years were very disrupted in terms of instruction. In Managua in 1979, there was instruction for the fifty deaf pupils at CNEE from March to June 1 when the civil war made it dangerous to transport students into the Barrio San Judas. The school reopened on August 1, 1979, but, because of transportation and administrative difficulties, instruction was intermittent up to the regular close of the school year in November.

The 1980 school year opened on schedule, but regular classes were discontinued so that the teachers could attend training classes, including those of Natalia Popova and other members of the technical team, which drew prospective special education teachers from the whole country, not just Managua. Select pupils were invited on specific days to be part of demonstration groups for the training class, but regular instruction did not take place during the training classes. Although the National Literacy Crusade (Cruzada Nacional de Alfabetización), which mobilized thousands of students, teachers, and workers to spend March through August 1980 in the countryside teaching previously illiterate peasants to read, had less of an influence on the special education classes at CNEE than it did in other schools, it did cause some interruptions to classes at other times that year (Arrien and Matús Lazo 1989).[6] The year 1980 is remembered as a time of upheaval and readjustment in Nicaragua.[7] The school year ended, as usual, in November.

According to Nora Gordon (who taught a class for deaf kindergartners at the CNEE in 1980), when the regular classes resumed in 1980, the

Students in the hairdressing class at the Centro Ocupacional para los Discapacitados in Villa Libertad, Managua, August 4, 1986. Front row: Gloria Sánchez, Luz (last name unknown). Back row: Mabel Midence, Juanita Theodolinda López, Giaconda Cardoso. Photo courtesy of Cyndi Norman.

students who had comprised the oldest two classes in 1979 (taught by Rúthy Duran and Soledad Rostrán, each of whom had been assigned new classes at the school's reopening) were scheduled to transfer to the new vocational school, the Centro Ocupacional para los Discapacitados (Vocational Center for the Disabled or COD). But they could not do so in 1980 because the building was not ready, so the young persons (ranging from sixteen to twenty-one) continued to go to the CNEE for instruction in the workshops (which were still located at the CNEE, until they could be transferred to the COD when the building was ready), but they came in the afternoons when the younger students had already gone home.

Thus, the amount of interaction among deaf children at the CNEE (during recess, for example) in 1979 and 1980 was limited. Instructional days were intermittent, and the class sizes were growing throughout the year. The supplemented enrollment (about 120) of deaf students was probably not gathered together in one place regularly until March 1981 when that school year started. By that time, all students over the age of fifteen had been moved to the COD.

At the CNEE, the number of classrooms for the deaf doubled from five in 1979 to ten in late 1980 when the school reopened (after the Literacy Crusade and after Popova's training course). The number of pupils at the center who were deaf increased from 50 to 120. Over the next four years, the classrooms for deaf students at the CNEE increased gradually to eighteen with approximately 200 children, ages five to fourteen. The CNEE's enrollment of deaf students remained stable until the late 1990s when it increased to approximately 250, a figure that is typical for the school at the present.

I would like to focus for a moment on this increase in the number of deaf children on the CNEE campus.[8] It has been suggested that the Managua campus brought together 500 or more deaf pupils soon after the revolution. This figure confuses the *total* number of students *at* the school with the *subpopulation* who were deaf. In 1979, there were no more than 200 children in total enrolled at the CNEE; and in 1980, the year of upheaval, total enrollment probably started well under 400, but increased as the new students trickled in. Not until 1981 did the school's *total* enrollment reach approximately 500. But remember that only about one-quarter of them were deaf.[9] To date, in 2004, no school in Nicaragua has ever gathered 500 deaf students on one site. In 1983, the total number of deaf students enrolled in special education *in the whole country* was 359, and the total number of deaf students in the special education system nationally did not reach 500 until 1994. At the end of the year after the revolution (1980), there were ten classrooms for deaf children at the CNEE with approximately twelve children in each class. Rather than increasing to 500 in 1980, the enrollment went from approximately fifty in 1979 to approximately 120 in 1980.

The special education school in Managua has always contained, by far, the largest number of deaf pupils (after the year 2000, approximately 240–260, with 251 in 2003), followed by León (usually averaging about forty students per year, but with only thirty-eight in 2001 and twenty-two in 2003), Chinandega (also typically averaging forty deaf students, but with thirty-five in 2001 and only twenty-nine in 2003), and the boarding school at Ciudad Dario (typically with an average of fifty deaf pupils; there were forty-eight in 2001, but only thirty-four in 2003). The rest of the special education schools in Nicaragua have had only one to three classrooms for the deaf, and typical enrollments are 9 to 15 deaf students per school. In 2003, the total number of deaf students in all of the special education schools was 573, down from a high of 641 in the year 2000, and the enrollment of deaf students at the Centro de Educación Especial Melania Morales (the new name for the CNEE after 1986) was 251.[10]

Outside of Managua, twenty-three special education schools were functioning in 1981; but throughout the 1980s, there was some fluctuation in those numbers (as the Contra War made it necessary to close schools, either intermittently or permanently, in targeted areas). Over the years, the system has averaged twenty special education schools that have *audición* (deaf) classrooms, with the overwhelming number located in the Pacific portion of Nicaragua, where the majority of the population, who are Spanish-speaking, live. From one to three of the schools have been located in the central area, and from one to three on the Atlantic Coast, mainly in the two largest towns, Puerto Cabezas (Bilwí) and Bluefields. (The Atlantic Coast includes a multilingual population.)

The immediate result of Natalia Popova assuming supervision of all teachers of the hearing impaired was a standardization of methodology and curriculum. Popova had been trained in Moscow to use a method emphasizing speechreading skills, with fingerspelling as a backup. This is not a strictly oral methodology since it does provide the student with a visual alternative to the spoken word on the lips; but it is also not the Rochester Method (which she has said, on occasion, she adopted), in which *all* linguistic input and production is accompanied by fingerspelling.

According to former students at the Apolonio Berríos Special Education School and Soledad Escobar de Flores, the teacher at the school in the 1950s and 1960s, a two-handed alphabet had been used for finger-

Group photograph of adults who had attended the Escuela Especial Número I ("Berríos school") as children during a meeting at a carnival at the Association of the Deaf's branch in San Marcos in 1996. Front row: Miguel Angel Moreno, Josefa Gutiérrez, Roberto Useda. Back row: Luis Morales, José Dolores Méndez. Photo courtesy of Josefa Gutiérrez and Ann Senghas.

spelling before the CNEE opened.[11] Beginning in 1978, under the influence of the Total Communication method, *some* teachers and students adopted the one-handed alphabet (e.g., the one now used in the United States and Canada) with the minor modification that the handshape for "t" (which has a vulgar connotation in Latin America) was substituted with the shape in which the index finger is extended and all the other fingers are curled into a fist. With the arrival of Popova, this alphabet became essential because it was integral to the Verbal Communication Method, her preferred form of instruction.

Natalia Popova forbade the use of any sign language, whatsoever, by teachers. The ban was so strict that some teachers recalled feeling uncomfortable using typical gestures for fear that they would be accused of signing. A dressing-down by Popova was infamous among every teacher I spoke with who had worked under her supervision: The recrimination would be swift, loud, and public. Thus, any signed communication the teachers used with the children (and some did learn some of the children's home signs) was done secretly or in guarded circumstances. No one wanted to be reported for signing and have to face Natalia Popova when she found out about it.

The basic teaching sequence that Popova mandated for the teachers of the deaf included the introduction of an object or picture paired with the vocal production on the lips, with the introduction as soon as possible of the written equivalent also paired to the vocal production, with the children then producing the written equivalent through fingerspelling. Understanding or producing the vocal target was the preferred result, but using fingerspelling either for understanding or production was acceptable. As might be imagined, this system gave preference to concrete nouns (which could be easily represented) and easily enactable verbs. Using this method, it would be very difficult to introduce abstractions, either as nouns or verbs.

Among all of the teachers trained by Popova whom I interviewed, the most common adjective used for her and the methodology was "strict." The teaching sequence was laid out clearly, and the teachers were required to follow the prescribed method. Deviation resulted in censure. Only a few of the teachers had had any previous experience with teaching children with hearing losses, and they seemed to have adopted the new methodology wholeheartedly at first. The other, newer, teachers had no experience on which to base an opinion, and they tried carefully to follow the instructions they were given.

Although there is no evidence that students were physically punished at the CNEE for using signs, I have heard various stories, both from former teachers and former students, of teachers teasing students who used sign language for "acting like monkeys."[12] Other strategies to discourage signing, such as having students sit on their hands or hold objects while talking, were also described.

Most teachers who reminisced about those years stated that they never considered using the few signs they might have picked up from the Total Communication influence because the atmosphere at the schools was so "anti-sign" that they believed any form of signing would jeopardize their jobs. One teacher remembered listening to critical remarks made by Natalia Popova about a fellow teacher who was given to using many natural gestures to get her meaning across, and that teacher said, "I vowed to myself to be very careful in my use of gestures, because I didn't want anyone talking that way about me."

The curriculum written by Popova focused on planned receptive, and then expressive, language learning and was very detailed, although it did not, at first, cover a six-year curriculum.[13] With the younger children, teachers were encouraged to use a playful approach, and each school was encouraged to keep a full set of common objects and materials on hand that could be used for language stimulation. Classes remained small (approximately ten to twelve students per teacher) and whenever possible, were grouped by age level. Teachers in the schools outside Managua were often brought to the capital to observe "demonstration classes" at the CNEE.

One problem that had complicated educational planning before the revolution, and which continued afterwards, was the fact that very few of the children received in-depth audiometric evaluations. In the classrooms, children who were hard of hearing (i.e., who had usable residual hearing) were in the same classes as children who were deaf (i.e., those without any usable hearing). Few (if any) of the children had hearing aids.

This has always been a problem in Nicaragua. The first children to be fit with hearing aids received their devices through the auspices of Clare Cooper, an audiologist working on the ship S.S. Hope, which docked in 1966 in the harbor at Corinto.[14] Probably a total of fifty hearing aids were dispensed that year to children in Nicaragua, but there is no way to know how long they continued to function. When the ship left the country, there were no repair facilities for the hearing aids left behind.

Hearing aids for children continued to be rare throughout the 1970s. In the early 1980s, volunteer audiometrists from Guatemala provided some hearing testing in conjunction with the two audiologists in the country,

Dr. Alma de Isabá and Dr. Araceli Navas. In 1984, Terry Mitchell, an audiologist working with Tecnica fit a number of hearing aids for children in Managua. In 1984, Terranuova, an Italian material aid organization, provided the salary for an audiometrist, Laura Bucarelli, to spend two years in Nicaragua, and also provided the funds to purchase basic audiometric equipment, which was set up in the offices of the MED. Toward the end of her stay, Bucarelli began to train a former teacher of the deaf, Ileana Ruíz, to perform hearing testing. Ruíz subsequently finished an audiometric technician's course in Mexico, and from 1988 to 1999 was the person providing audiometric testing and some hearing aid fitting for children enrolled in the schools of the MED.[15] Since 1991, the Audiological Assessment Center (CAA), run by the Association of Parents of Disabled Children (Los Pipitos), has begun a sustained effort to encourage bilateral hearing aid use by children, and the audiometric technician there has fit donated hearing aids and aids purchased by parents.

Hearing aids in Nicaragua, however, have a very short working life because of climatic factors, such as high humidity and dust, which cause them to malfunction often. Repairs are expensive because no facilities exist in Nicaragua and the instruments must be sent to labs in Honduras or the United States. Earmolds are difficult to obtain, and batteries are expensive. Overall, hearing aids in 1997, for example, were probably only used by 10% of the children who could be expected to gain some access to auditory input.[16] Before 1966, hearing aid use by children in Nicaragua was probably nil.

Even though the hearing testing (by no means were all children in the educational system tested) produced audiograms in the 1980s, giving information about how much residual hearing children might have, the results do not appear to have ever been used to influence instruction (even up to 2003). Hard of hearing and deaf children continued to be grouped together in classrooms according to age, and the same expectations for speech development were imposed on children who had nearly no residual hearing as on children with significant residual hearing.[17]

It must be emphasized that the basic philosophy of education of the deaf did *not* change after the Sandinista Revolution in 1979, but simply was applied in a stricter and more consistent manner. The revolution may have brought a more welcoming attitude to universal education; but where

Preschool class of 1980 at a parade for Day of the Disabled in front of the Ministry of Education buildings in Managua: Front row: Alex Vargas, David Ulloa, Norman Cedeno, Henry January Benavides, Ivette (last name unknown), three unidentified girls, Henry Ellis, with Rúthy Durán (teacher) with her back to the camera. Ivette is holding a sign that reads "Think of me as a person." Photo courtesy of Rúthy Durán.

deaf education was concerned, the pre-revolutionary and post-revolutionary goals were the same: to make deaf children capable of interacting on a daily basis with a world that was unremittingly hearing. A deaf child who could understand and produce speech would no longer be mute, and thus could be incorporated as a social actor. *Sacarse la voz al sordo* (literally, "to drag the voice out of a deaf person," but here meaning "to make the deaf talk") was a serious and laudable goal of both school and family.

While the teachers and administration were careful to prohibit the use of any sign language in the classroom at CNEE, the children, during recess and away from school, seemed oblivious to the prohibition. As Esperanza Salvador, a teacher of the deaf in the early 1980s, remembered:

> We made sure that in the classroom, we taught the classes orally; but the kids outside were using signs among themselves. During recess, at the snack bar,

everywhere. Some of us used our hands, too, to communicate with the kids, but only in private or where no one could see. In the classroom, it was us emphasizing the oral and the fingerspelling, but outside, it was another matter.

Just how much of the manual communication that went on outside of the classroom was sign *language,* as opposed to gestures and pantomime, is impossible to tell. No one recorded it, and no one capable of categorizing it was there watching. Still, the reports from the few teachers who began to imitate the children and learn their communication systems, and from the children themselves, when they remember back as adults, is that at this point, it was, at most, a very rudimentary language system.

Morena Torres, who was ten when she enrolled in 1980 at CNEE, and had just come from El Salvador as a refugee, said that she began to sign in Nicaragua by watching "the older students who came to visit Rúthy Durán. . . . They would engage us [the younger students at the CNEE] also in conversations, and they used signs, and we just drank it up and started using them with each other. . . . Rúthy was able to communicate with the older deaf people. She signed to them and talked. We littler ones like to watch."[18]

Rúthy now denies that she knows any sign language, and I have never seen her show any comprehension while witnessing a conversation in Nicaraguan Sign Language (NSL) in the 1997–2003 period.[19] In 1997, in fact, she asked Javier to come to her house and teach her NSL, and he did give her a few lessons, but she said she found it very hard to learn. She says that the "real signing" started after she stopped participating in the National Nicaraguan Deaf Association's (ANSNIC's) activities (which was probably around 1988).[20] But we also know that Adrián Pérez, Mayra Mena (and the teachers who had gone to Total Communication workshops, bringing back a dictionary) as well as Thomas Gibson (and his dictionary) had, by this time, introduced some signs (and the concept of sign language) to Nicaragua. So the "signing" that Morena observed probably contained some standardized sign language, but it was likely to have been heavily weighted to home sign and gesture, which Rúthy admits she is very comfortable doing (and her former students corroborate her on this).[21] It would be unwise to conclude that the "signing" Morena watched was the same as the sign language now in use among the deaf community in Nicaragua. But Morena's memories do give us proof that the rudiments of the use of sign language were being laid down in the early 1980s, and that younger children, like Morena, were content to soak up whatever communicative interactions were accessible to them.

The children pooled the home signs they had invented to communicate with their families, incorporated the common Nicaraguan manual gestures, and invented new signs for events happening at school that did not have a counterpart at home.[22] Most of the now-adults who were children at the time, as well as the teachers I talked with, say that this communication system was not a "real" language. It wasn't anything like the sign language that they use now. The system was dependent upon shared background knowledge and was very iconic in form. Still, as Coppola (2002) has pointed out, deaf persons using a shared home sign system over many years exhibit regularities in their communication that their hearing partners do not when communicating with the deaf person. The home sign system(s) that developed at the school may not yet have been a language, but probably had some consistencies in form that increased over the years.

Beginning in 1983, a few of the teachers began to experience discontent with the strict oral methodology required of them, especially those who had deaf children of their own. They noted how difficult speech was for their children, how little progress they seemed to be making, and how a speech-only approach isolated their children socially. A training workshop held in Costa Rica at one of the schools for the deaf in 1983 was an eye-opening experience for Yadira Miranda, a teacher who had a deaf daughter:

> I was shocked to see how much success they were having with the kids. They had oral classrooms, of course, but they also had non-oral classrooms too. It was the first time I began to see what a resource sign language could be for the deaf, and it really changed my ideas. I began to see that forbidding the use of sign language was limiting the deaf. I had been very definite before about the need of the deaf to assimilate to hearing society, but slowly it dawned on me that it might be easier for us to assimilate to the deaf.

Three teachers had undergone the training together. One of them continued her dedication to the official methodology, but the third teacher, Rúthy Durán, like Miranda, began to reconsider her teaching methods. Back home, they recounted their experiences to another teacher, a Salvadoran woman named Gloria Minero who also had a deaf daughter. The three teachers, subsequently, began quietly to modify their teaching methods. One result was that they consulted with one of the secretaries of the school, a deaf adult named María Lourdes Palacios, the extraordinary bilingual woman mentioned earlier, about what she wanted to see in her own schooling. This is probably the first time that any deaf person in Nicaragua was asked to give an opinion on deaf education. Through Rúthy's contacts with former deaf pupils (those born during 1959–1963, who had by then been sent to the COD for vocational training), some of the young deaf adults were also invited to "demonstration" classes and asked to comment about what they saw.

These adjustments in methodology did not meet with official approval. Between 1984 and 1986, all three of the teachers resigned from teaching at CNEE. One took a position teaching nursery school, another ultimately supervised the workshops at the COD in Villa Libertad, and the third went to work for Instituto Nacional de Adaptación Tecnologica (INATEC), the technical education arm of the MED (at that time; it was later separated from the ministry and set up with an independent administration).

Up to 1980, the only institutions accepting deaf pupils were the pre-revolutionary schools mentioned previously. They provided an elementary curriculum with the goal of turning out youths able to read and write, and hopefully, speak, enough to gain employment in manual trades. At Special Education School No. 1, classes in manual arts, or (*manualidades*), including crochet and embroidery, had been included for the girls; and probably some beginning carpentry was included for the boys. All the students took drawing lessons, at which the deaf students were said to excel.

But upon finishing their schooling at fourteen or fifteen years of age, the students had few "real-world" skills. Dr. Apolonio Berríos took it upon himself to find placements for the boys in workshops where they could be employed as carpenter's helpers, construction helpers, mechanics' helpers, and so forth. The deaf youths, then, were typically placed in positions in which they had to function as the only deaf person among various hearing persons. The deaf students would learn the trade well enough to function independently at it, although most of them continued to have severe difficulties communicating with hearing people. But simply to be able to earn a salary, even if it was only the minimum wage, was considered a great step forward for these "remediated subjects" over the pre-1946 view that considered them incapable of ever leaving home.

In 1997, when I interviewed Soledad Escobar de Flores, she mentioned how proud she was of her students from the Berríos school who had obtained regular employment: One was a "helper" at a newspaper publishing plant, one had a job sweeping the streets, and another laid stone blocks to make roads. In 1975, the expectation that students would leave the Berríos school around age fourteen had changed, because the class that Rúthy Durán taught there included children from thirteen to sixteen years of age; and they completed the 1976 school year at that school also.

In 1977, when the CNEE was built, it included well-furnished workshops in carpentry and horticulture for the boys, and sewing and hairdressing for the girls. From 1977 to 1980, the prior expectation that deaf students would only be at the school until they were fourteen or fifteen years of age had changed (although policy on age requirements did not change officially, as is evident from the 1979 decision to send the pupils over fifteen to a vocational school). Of the four classes that included deaf students in 1977, two taught by Rúthy Durán and Soledad Rostrán included students twelve to seventeen years of age. (The other two, taught by María Teresa Castillo and Sabrina Gadea, were composed of pupils from four to ten years of age.)[23] The goal, as articulated by both Rosemary Bohmer de Selva and Luz María Sequiera, the school's first director and vice-director, was that, upon graduation, students would have some marketable skills.

For a few, this evidently worked. Two members of the older deaf classes in 1977 stayed at the school until 1980. Instead of going on to the new vocational school in 1981, they left and found work as carpenter's helpers. Douglas Vega subsequently learned a great deal about repairing engines and ultimately emigrated from Nicaragua. José Dolores Méndez, the other, has worked at a succession of different jobs over the years, including selling his own handmade belts and working at one of the factories in the free trade zone. (The rest of that class went on to the new vocational school.)

In 1980, after the revolution, a major policy change was made when the expansion of the educational system was envisioned. Administrators realized that the CNEE would not have the capacity to retain older students if it were to admit additional younger pupils. The National Board for Social Assistance and Problem Prevention (JNAPS), which had administered the CNEE, ceased to exist in July 1979. After long negotiations through 1979 and 1980, the decision was made that the CNEE would be incorporated into the public school system under the direction of the MED and would be responsible for the elementary academic education of children seven to fourteen years of age, (ultimately that became grades one to six, although in the beginning, fewer grades were offered as the curricula were revised). Pupils over the age of fifteen would be sent to one of three vocational schools that would be set up, and that vocational education would be offered routinely to disabled students fifteen through twenty-five years of age. During 1980, as the site in Villa Libertad was being prepared, the older deaf pupils continued to attend the CNEE for classes in the workshops, but they came in the afternoon after the younger pupils had gone home.

This expansion of the years in which students were expected to be in the educational system is the only major policy change in deaf education from 1946 to 1992. The methodology remained oral throughout this period, and the desired class size continued to be about twelve students per room. But children were now expected to enter school earlier (at five or six years of age, rather than eight or nine), and they were expected to be educated longer (the typical school-leaving age was expected to be twenty-one rather than fourteen, although students could remain until age twenty-five.) This is a significant change because students were now expected to be in the educational system throughout adolescence, rather than leaving the school system at just that point.

Three vocational schools were set up in 1980 to meet the needs of disabled youth: the Gaspar García Liviana Center, which targeted vocational training for youths with motoric problems; the Carlos Fonseca Amador Center, which was a training center for blind youths; and the COD, which was set up to provide vocational training for mentally retarded and deaf youths.[24] Again, as in 1946, the two groups were not placed in separate schools, but were evidently seen as subsets of a larger category. The 1979 revolution did not change educational policy in this respect.

The COD staff included administrators, psychologists, social workers, a speech therapist, and teachers of workshops in manual arts, tailoring, sewing, carpentry, cabinetry, hairdressing, horticulture, commercial baking, and daily living activities. The workshops were typically gender-segregated, with the males learning carpentry and cabinetry and the females sewing and hairdressing. According to a former social worker at the school, Nancy Guadamuz, the classes in horticulture and daily living activities were mainly geared to the students with mental retardation, and few deaf students participated. Likewise, the carpentry, cabinetry, sewing, and baking classes demanded the ability to do arithmetic calculations, and it was mainly the deaf students who were in these classes. Still, the classes were not separated by disability, so some classes included both deaf students as well as hearing students classified as mentally retarded.[25]

About nineteen deaf students above the age of fifteen transferred from the CNEE in 1981 when the COD opened. They joined about thirty-five deaf youths who had no previous training. The CNEE students obviously had received education in oral Spanish and had experience communicating with hearing teachers. The previously unschooled students presented more difficulties, since most of them entered with only the most rudimentary, if any, language skills. To the consternation of the staff, the communication methods that had worked at the CNEE (mouthing of words, fingerspelling, or writing Spanish words) did not do any good with the new arrivals. The new students had some home signs, and in time, they adopted the communal gesture-pantomime-home sign system that the older students had brought with them from the CNEE. Thus, in the first few years of operation, the previously educated deaf students were outnumbered by those just entering the educational system, and all of the deaf students were outnumbered by students categorized by the MED as "mentally retarded" (Grooteman 1990).

Within the COD, the gesture-pantomime-home sign system became an essential form of communication. Nancy Guadamuz, who worked as a psychologist from 1981 to 1985 at the COD, remembers:

In Villa Libertad, almost everything that one did with the deaf was done with signs (*casi todo lo que se hacía con los sordos era seña*). Let me tell you that only kids over fourteen came to Villa Libertad, and the emphasis was on making these kids employable. So some had been to the special education school (CNEE), but the majority had not. We used a mixture. Even though I know a little bit of fingerspelling and lipreading and working on articulation, we didn't emphasize that at the Center. We used signs (*se utilizaba señas*), like those we learned from the speech therapist who had gone to Costa Rica for a sign language course (likely in Total Communication). When we organized group meetings with the kids, usually one of the teachers was talking, but there was always another teacher signing (*haciendo mímicas*) to translate for the other kids.

Communication at the COD was a multimodal affair. Teachers and students used whatever means was possible to communicate, including oral speech and speechreading, fingerspelling, gestures, signs, pantomime, writing, and pointing to pictures. The emphasis was on effective delivery, not purity of performance. The students entering from the CNEE had a common vocabulary of signs that they had previously used at that school. When a common sign was lacking, signs from Costa Rica were added.[26] If no sign was available from those sources, and fingerspelling the Spanish word or speechreading it wouldn't do, a form was created at Villa Libertad to fill the need. Even though Guadamuz and others I interviewed about the COD (including some deaf persons) referred to this communication as "signs" (señas), I do not mean to imply that there was a standardized sign language at the COD in 1981. In fact, I emphasized that the presence of previously uneducated students and teachers who were not familiar with deaf students made the use of a standardized language unlikely. But manual communication was the norm, not the exception, at the COD.

At the beginning, many students trickled in, entering as social workers found them and informed their parents of the existence of the vocational program, so there was no single "first day" for everyone. They came with no educational background at all. It was important they be able to communicate with classmates as soon as possible, in order that they be integrated into the group. The speech therapist, then, gave individual sessions to teach the newcomers a basic "survival" vocabulary of signs; however, as soon as possible, the newcomers were integrated into a language group to learn enough "signing" to be able to function in one of the workshops. According to Nancy Guadamuz, most of the teachers became functional in signing. She said that, besides the speech therapist, who often acted as an interpreter, the teachers of sewing and the manual arts, the social workers, and the psychologists were able to communicate in signs.[27] The instructors for carpentry and horticulture, however, never seemed to be comfortable with using their hands to communicate.

When the students had completed a level of training that indicated that they could be employed, the COD sought placements for them with small area businesses sympathetic to the goal of employing the disabled. In those years, the most successful placements were in hairdressing establishments; but only a few of the deaf women trained at the COD are still working in hairdressing. Some of those who are employed at the Free Trade Zone are graduates of the COD in sewing and tailoring. The personal ties formed at the COD are, however, very important.

Asked if there was a deaf community at the time that the COD came into existence, Nancy Guadamuz replied:

> I wouldn't call it a "community." There wasn't anything organized or identified as such, but something like that was in the making. The students who came from the CNEE had their ties to each other and they had their own signs that they used with each other, but it wasn't consolidated in any way. That came later. The signs and the way of using them then are nothing like they are now, which I understand is a real language. But at the time, it was a way that a very heterogeneous group was able to learn enough so that everyone could understand.

According to María Teresa Aguilar (a social worker at the COD from 1981 to 1984, and later director from 1987 to 1994), budget reductions at the end of 1984 caused a complete shake-up in personnel in all of the vocational centers.[28] Many positions throughout the government were cut, including some jobs at the COD, and the remaining certified personnel jockeyed for jobs in other institutions that they considered more stable or having better long-term prospects. María Teresa also said that the COD was cut from two social workers and two psychologists to one of each. She left her social worker position that year to take another job that she thought would have a better salary. (She was gone for two years, and then the directorship of the COD opened, so she applied for that.) Turnover in certified positions (e.g., social worker, psychologist, etc.) from 1984 to 1985 was high, but the vocational positions (which did not require special certification) were more stable. Many of the professionals most fluent in manual communication appear to have left at this time to take other jobs, and they were replaced by others who were not familiar with signing or persons who had never even considered that manual movements could be used linguistically.

Meanwhile, in mid-1985, Natalia Popova left her position as co-ordinator of deaf education to accompany her husband and family to Moscow, where her husband had been named to a position at the Nicaraguan embassy in the then-Soviet Union. She took advantage of the availability of university education and studied for her doctorate. When she returned to Nicaragua in 1989, she did not resume her post at the MED, but began to work with Los Pipitos, an organization which had been founded in 1987.

After Popova left, the methodology at the MED for teaching the deaf slowly (but not immediately) became more flexible. Teachers were encouraged to use their creativity to reach students as they could. The curriculum was rewritten, and a special curriculum, with attenuated goals for the special education schools, was adopted. After about ten years, that decision was reversed, and goals similar to those of regular elementary education were reestablished. In the 1990s, deaf students were expected to accomplish in twelve years what regular education students covered in six. Unfortunately, a very high number of deaf students exited the special education system functionally illiterate. Throughout, however, the philosophy remained oral, with the goal of training the students to understand and produce speech remaining dominant. Not until 1992 was sign language officially permitted for instructional purposes in any of the schools run by the MED.

Thus, over a period of years, society's view of the deaf had changed—from the pity and disinterest which marks the "eternal child" model to the perception of the deaf as "remediable subjects." The prevailing model had changed from one in which participation in society was considered simply not possible for a deaf person, to one in which social agency was a possibility *if* the deaf person could attain mastery over a skill seen as crucial to social participation in Nicaragua: oral speech. As a remediable subject, the more a deaf person became "like the hearing" (understanding and producing speech), the more likely it was that social candidacy might be granted.

I found no evidence that families of hearing impaired children had any problems with this educational philosophy. In fact, I had multiple parents tell me that the present education system (in 1997) was "soft" because children were allowed to sign. They referred to the "old days" when oral methodology had been stricter, and they said, children had talked more.

Let us pause and ask, at this moment, whether the forty-six years between 1946 and 1992 produced any "remediated subjects."[29] The answer is "yes," of course. There were deaf persons who did acquire sufficient lip-reading skills to understand speech directed to them, and there were deaf persons who could speak intelligibly enough to be understood by most people.[30] I asked people I interviewed to tell me the names of the deaf people that they remembered as having "overcome" (*superado*) their deafness or who had become oralized.[31]

One teacher, who has been active in education for the deaf in Nicaragua for fifty-three years, gave a list of fifteen or twenty names, the majority of whom were persons who were dead or had emigrated, so I could not interview most of them. Among those she mentioned were two secretaries and a young man who presently works as an illustrator. Those three people *can* communicate through speech when it is necessary. Another teacher who has been active in deaf education for thirty-five years gave me a list of ten people whom she considered to have been successfully "oralized," including her son. Both of the secretaries and the illustrator were also on her list, and the remainder had emigrated.

This apparently high number of emigrés is actually not surprising. Nicaragua, like some of its other Central American neighbors, experienced high levels of emigration beginning in the late 1970s when civil unrest became acute. In 1979, those who did not agree with the Sandinista Revolution left. The emigration continued during the 1980s because of internal political disagreements, evasion of the universal draft during the Contra War, and the "super inflation" in the late 1980s. Some people returned to Nicaragua after 1990 when the Sandinistas lost power, but the poor economic situation of the country has continued to encourage an outflow. In the case of the deaf, it is logical that more of the successfully "oralized" deaf would have come from wealthier families, which would be the families more able to provide them with private lessons in speech and articulation; however, these were also the families more likely to leave in the 1980s. It is interesting that most of the reportedly successfully oralized expatriates are also reported to have married deaf spouses when they settled outside of Nicaragua.

I found no basis for concluding that more children were "oralized" under the stricter oral methodology that was standardized in 1980. Inevitably, when I would ask either parents or teachers for examples of children who had been successfully "oralized," 90% of the names given me are now adults who are members of ANSNIC, and who declare to me that their preferred language is sign language, and that they feel incompetent in oral language. For example, I asked that question of another teacher who had been involved in deaf education for the past twenty-one years. She remained silent for a long time, thinking, and then replied:

> I don't know what to tell you. I never thought of it that way. You ask me who the successes were under the old way [before sign language was allowed], and all the names that come to mind are kids that are now active in the deaf association [i.e., prefer sign language as their major mode of communication].

I also asked teachers with fewer years of experience in deaf education who the deaf people able to talk were. They added five more names. Of these, three had served at different times as presidents of the ANSNIC (i.e., were very active in the signing community), one was studied as a model of signing by sign language researchers (1986–1994), and the fifth person told me in reply to a direct question that he does not speak. Evidently, the "remediable subjects" model resulted in very few remediated subjects in Nicaragua.

"Social Agents"

4

WHEN THE National Center for Special Education, Centro Nacional de Educación Especial (CNEE), was established in 1977, it continued to be the common practice that groups of students would be taught by the same teacher for multiple years. Rúthy Durán, the teacher of one of the two older deaf classes at CNEE, had already taught many of those same students in 1974 and 1975 at the Apolonio Berríos School, and she was again named their teacher in 1977, 1978, and the parts of 1979 in which classes were held. She took a special interest in her students and invited them to her house to celebrate their birthdays and other special occasions, and she still has pictures taken at those festivities.[1] She also attended social events that some of the parents arranged for their child's classmates.[2] When the CNEE's sports team and folk dance ensemble (most of whose members were deaf students) went on trips to Costa Rica (1978), Venezuela (1980), and Honduras (1980), Rúthy was one of the chaperones: "Otherwise, none of the girls would have been allowed to go." She took pictures of these parties and trips and was proud to show them to visitors twenty years later. (These pictures formed the basis of my reconstruction of the 1977 enrollment list.)

Rúthy came to know the students, and probably their parents, in 1975. Some out-of-school activities were held in 1975, but it must be remembered that both Rúthy and María Teresa Castillo were doing "double-duty" in 1975, working from 8 a.m. to about noon at the Berríos school, grabbing some lunch, then catching the bus to León in order to teach from 2 p.m. to 5 p.m., and then taking the bus back to Managua. In 1976, María Teresa and Rúthy taught only in Managua in the mornings. (By that time, León had found other teachers.) Rúthy started the school year at the Berríos school in March 1976, but left on May 1 because she received a six-month scholarship from the Organization of American States to go to the Instituto Magisterial Superior in Montevideo, Uruguay, for a course in deaf education. María Elena Joffre took over her class while she was gone. When Rúthy returned for the 1977 school year, she started teaching again at the old school in March; but in the first few months, the class was moved to the new CNEE, and she went with it. The teachers at CNEE taught the students from 8 a.m. to noon (when the children went home) but were required to be at the school from 2 p.m. to 5 p.m., preparing their classes. Rúthy probably had a lot more free time for socializing after 1977.

No one educated earlier under Soledad Escobar de Flores at the Berríos school remembered any out-of-school-socialization as children. Soledad, herself, told me that her pupils did not meet outside of class, and that none of them married. The socialization that she heard happened at the deaf association (I interviewed her in 1997) astonished her. "There was none of that when I taught," she said. Her students usually commented spontaneously that, when they were children, socialization was limited to school hours (they were picked up and dropped off at their homes by Dr. Berríos's chauffeur using the doctor's car), that social ties were severed when they left school to work, and that they later found other deaf adults only by accident, meeting up again on public buses or in public places. But, beginning at least by 1975, a teacher and some parents encouraged formation of a social network among the deaf students outside of school, celebrating holidays and birthdays, such as Mother's Day. (Besides Rúthy's house, former students remember Roberto Úseda's mother hosting celebrations and some parties at Mauricio Zepeda's and Javier López Gómez's homes.)

In 1980, however, after the training sessions (including those taught by Natalia Popova) at the CNEE ended, and the special education schools started classes again, the members of Rúthy's previous class were all over the age of fifteen, and were slated to be among the first occupants of the vocational school, the Vocational Center for the Disabled, Centro Ocupacional para los Discapacitados (COD), in Villa Libertad. Rúthy took over the youngest class at CNEE, but she maintained social ties with the older students, and they came by her classroom to visit and went to her house on weekends.[3]

The older students could not go immediately to the new training center and spent most of 1980 in a sort of "limbo." For one thing, the decisions about how to divide the students, which school would get the workshops, and where the new vocational school would be located evidently involved long negotiations between the Ministry of Education (MED) and the National Welfare Institute (INSSBI), which started in 1979, but took until mid-1980 to finalize. The site at Villa Libertad needed renovation and cleaning and did not open until January 1981. The oldest classes continued to come to CNEE in the afternoons (when there were no elementary classes) to work in the workshops, and the athletic events continued because there were competition trips to Honduras and Venezuela in early 1980. Some deaf adolescents who had not been at CNEE, but were already on the list to go to COD, such as Julio Garcia (fifteen years at the time), remember spending a couple of months at the end of 1980 helping to get the COD buildings ready before the classes began the next January. (The COD, because of its goal of readying the students for jobs, ran on a regular work schedule from 8 a.m. to 5 p.m., five days a week, year round, not on an academic calendar.)

Rúthy also was instrumental in encouraging members of the older group to join a folk dance troupe with hearing students under the direction of Haydée Palacios, a famous teacher of dance in Nicaragua (who had previously given instruction in folk dance to the deaf students at the CNEE). The troupe performed widely, and some of the deaf students were the outstanding dancers. Palacios or an assistant gave them visual cues so that they could remain in synchrony with the music, and depending on the surface on which they were dancing, they could feel some of the vibrations of the music and stay in time. Gathering for practice sessions and performances gave them regular opportunities to see each other even though some were working, whereas others attended the vocational school, and still others were neither working nor training, but simply staying at home.

By this time, group members ranged from eighteen to twenty-one years of age and were very competent at riding the buses of Managua to get to their desired destinations. It was not unusual, according to Rúthy, for three or four of her former students to stop by on Sunday afternoons to visit her. The communication mode was similar to that used in the COD—anything that worked. As Rúthy told me:

> There wasn't a sign language at the time, not like there is now. But we were able to understand one another. We would talk for part of the time and use a

lot of the gestures that everyone around here [in Nicaragua] uses, and we had a set of some signs that the students had made up. (They aren't used now.) Like, for the days of the week: We had special signs that we had used with each other for years, and they had learned new signs at Villa Libertad which they taught me. And when everything else failed, we would write words down, or else act it out. I don't remember there being any big barriers. We always managed to figure each other out.

Improving socialization opportunities for deaf students was on Gloria Minero's mind in 1983. That year, she had enrolled her daughter, Morena, (whose speech and lipreading skills Gloria had been working on since Morena was diagnosed as deaf when a baby) in a regular education class because of its greater academic challenge. With Gloria's daily tutoring, Morena made progress in school subjects, but was teased by the other children for her unusual speech and her difficulty following a conversation. She had no friends at her new school. When Gloria walked in on her daughter talking to herself in a mirror and asked what she was doing, she was shocked with the response: "Nobody else wants to talk to me, so I'm talking to myself." To console Morena, Gloria promised her that she would work on organizing some social events for deaf adolescents that would include her daughter when she had finished the teaching year and had more time (i.e., December 1983 or January 1984).

Additionally, in 1983, Yadira Miranda, Rúthy Durán, and another teacher had visited Costa Rica and come away impressed at how sign language could augment an oral program, and they told Gloria Minero (mother of Morena), also a teacher at the CNEE, about what they had seen. Yadira, Rúthy, and Gloria began to experiment with use of signing in their instruction, but this did nothing to enhance relationships with Natalia Popova, their supervisor, still a staunch advocate of strict oral instruction.[4] In 1984, the situation was so strained that Rúthy chose to request a new assignment mid-year at the MED's newly created preschool program.[5]

After the 1983 school year ended, Gloria consulted Rúthy about her promise to Morena. Rúthy knew the deaf students attending the COD and where they lived, and she agreed to invite them to meet on weekends at either Gloria's home in Barrio Liberia or at Rúthy's home in Barrio Monsenor Lezcano. Morena had been enrolled for the 1983 school year at the Clementina Cabezas Elementary School in the Barrio San Judas, which is

Gloria Minero with her granddaughter in Santa Tecla, El Salvador, August 1999. Photo by Laura Polich.

not far from the CNEE. At that time, Morena and Gloria were living in Barrio San Judas. They did not move to their house in Barrio Liberia until after the school year ended in 1983. Gloria never hosted any of the meetings of the deaf youth at her house in Barrio San Judas, and she says that the first meetings were specifically timed to be *after* she had moved.

Rúthy seems to have provided the bulk of the young people who were invited to the early meetings. Gloria and Rúthy were both working together at CNEE at the end of 1983, but not at the end of 1984 (Rúthy had left). Thus, it is likely that the earliest meeting was in December 1983 with only a few attendees; but the group grew as the meetings continued on a regular basis in 1984. The early meetings were organized by both Rúthy and Gloria, and they were attended mainly by Rúthy's 1977–1980 former CNEE students and Gloria's daughter. Yadira Miranda, and her daughter, Liseth, also joined. The first invitees told others about the meetings, and the number who arrived grew rapidly. Gloria's new house lent itself to the purpose because it had a large enclosed space (meant as a garage, but two sides of the room were made of decorative metalwork so it was open to the natural sunlight). Some of the early meetings also took place at Rúthy Duran's house, but its porch was quite small and could not accommodate the number that Gloria's house could.

One point I have been unable to understand clearly is why Gloria targeted the students that Rúthy knew for the meetings. They were all at least two years older than Morena, and some as much as eleven years older. If socialization for Morena was Gloria's goal (which is her answer when asked directly), wouldn't she have invited the students in Morena's age group who still attended the CNEE? She was, at that time, still a teacher at CNEE, so she had access to children closer to her daughter's age. Morena was definitely the youngest member of the founding group, and there is evidence that she had disagreements with some early members who evidently did not believe she belonged. But Morena has a very outgoing personality, so she overcame this barrier and was definitely as involved in the association as her mother was up to the point in 1990 when Gloria had a falling out with some of the officers of the association. Morena's participation faded at the same time. When I asked others (including Rúthy) about this discrepancy, I was told that the students Rúthy knew were the obvious ones to invite because they already knew each other and already socialized together. This seems to indicate that while these 1983+ meetings were an important unifying force, that earlier socialization (which had been going on among this group since their attendance at the Escuela Apolonio Berríos School) was also an important ingredient in community formation.

At some point in 1984 or 1985, Gloria suggested to Rúthy and Yadira that if deaf young adults wanted to have an impact on anything or improve their futures, they would need to organize themselves formally into a self-help group that could advocate for the improvement of the lives of deaf people. The political philosophy of the Sandinista government encouraged formation of grassroots organizations, not only as ways of encouraging communal volunteer activities (e.g., vaccination campaigns, literacy campaigns), but also as channels for special interest groups (e.g., AMNLAE (women's organization), UNAG (agricultural and cattle growers and workers), ANDEN (teachers' union), etc.). Gloria believed that an association of deaf persons could work for more education and increased jobs for its members.

Gloria, Rúthy, and Yadira started to work on a legal structure for the group by writing a constitution and bylaws, a process that took about two years to accomplish. The bylaws appear to have been written with little input from the deaf youths, although they were certainly in agreement with the plan (but probably not skilled enough in written Spanish to participate much in the process). It was not an easy task for the hearing teachers, either. Rúthy remembers that they worked on the documents for hours, often finishing so late at night that she slept at Gloria's house because it was too late to find transportation home.

Meetings were held on Saturdays and included opportunities just to socialize. Games or basketball were routine. Festivities around holidays and birthdays gave excuses for parties. But Gloria insisted that the young people think of their futures and improving their job skills, so basic literacy and arithmetic classes were also added. Although signing soon became a popular form of communication, throughout the group's organizational period, it continued to be seen only as an auxiliary form of communication, with oral proficiency as the ultimate goal.[6] Mid-year in 1986, Gloria was forced to resign her teaching job at CNEE because, while fleeing the civil war going on in neighboring El Salvador, she had entered Nicaragua illegally, and her legal status as a refugee was not in order. She spent the rest of that year regularizing her papers, but, thinking back on it later, she said, "not being able to work that year was what gave me the time to devote to organizing the association."

The young people found the meetings and the chance to socialize with other young deaf adults to be stimulating, and they invited other friends and acquaintances to the gatherings. The group started with eleven young people, but soon that number began to grow. Work on the legal paperwork had advanced to the stage that a vote was taken on what to call the new organization. An obvious name would have been something like

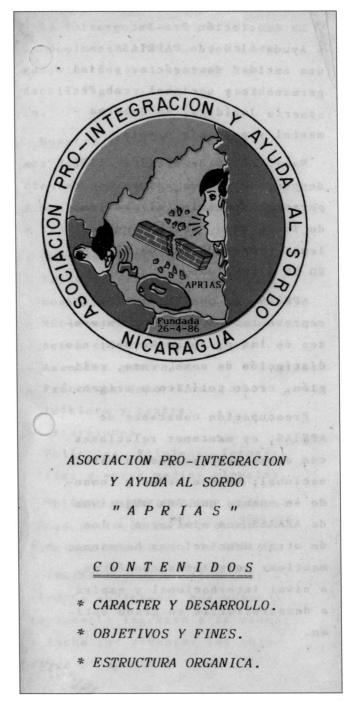

ASOCIACION PRO-INTEGRACION
Y AYUDA AL SORDO

" A P R I A S "

C O N T E N I D O S

* CARACTER Y DESARROLLO.

* OBJETIVOS Y FINES.

* ESTRUCTURA ORGANICA.

Pamphlet describing APRIAS with its logo. Given to Laura Polich by Javier López and Adrián Peréz during a visit to the National Nicaraguan Association of the Deaf's headquarters in May 1994.

Nicaraguan Association of the Deaf (which in Spanish would be Asociación Nicaraguense de Sordos, or ANS). But, there already was an organization known as ANS. It was the Association of Sandinista Children, and as Javier López Gómez explained, no one wanted the deaf group to be confused with the children's group. Other possibilities were suggested, but the one that won the vote on April 22, 1986, (now considered by the National Nicaraguan Association of the Deaf to be its official founding date) was suggested by Gloria Minero: Asociación Pro-Ayuda e Integración a los Sordos (Association to Help and Integrate the Deaf) or APRIAS (pronounced "ah-PREE-yes").

The statutes took the rest of 1986 and most of 1987 to finish. They were ratified by the members in a meeting on December 21, 1987, which took place at the Colegio Roberto Vargas Batres (the preschool where Rúthy Durán taught). Her name, however, is not included in the Certificación de Fundación, which was written by Daysi Zamora González acting as Secretária de Actas y Archivo.[7] Thirty-three members and Gloria signed the ratification document after the statutes had been read aloud by Yadira Miranda. (If anyone doubts that it was the cohort clustered around the 1962 rubella epidemic that were the founding members of the deaf association, this document should clarify that point immediately. Eighty-five percent of those listed on the founding certification were born between 1959 and 1965, while only 12% were born before 1959. By the time this step in the official process was accomplished, Douglas Vega had emigrated, and his name does not appear on the list.)

This certification and the Escritura de Constitución No. 2 of April 17, 1988, were two of the necessary legal documents presented by Mr. Ramiro Lacayo to the Consejo del Estado (national legislative body; since 1990 called the National Assembly) in the organization's petition for legal standing (*personería jurídica*). The exact date that the petition for legal standing was presented cannot be ascertained because it has been "lost" from the archives of the National Assembly, and the present officers of the deaf association say they do not know where copies of those documents might be.[8]

In any case, simply presenting the petition was not the end of the complicated process. It was not until June 15, 1989, (recorded in *La Gaceta* 1989b) that the then-president of the Republic of Nicaragua, Daniel Ortega, declared that the Asociación Pro-Ayuda e Integración al Sordo-APRIAS was a legally constituted entity and capable of legal standing in Nicaragua.[9] (This is an interesting commentary on Nicaraguan law and how it is enforced. As Dr. Ríos's commentary in earlier chapters has noted, none of the deaf members who did not talk were considered legally competent to even make the choice to sign the document. Dr. Ríos knew this when he submitted the paperwork; but as he told me, no one ever pointed that inconsistency out as the documents worked their way through the approval process. Because he firmly supported APRIAS, he felt no need to bring it to any official's attention.) On November 7, 1989, *La Gaceta* published the statutes of the organization, another legally prescribed step. In April 1990 the organization was officially registered at the Ministerio de Gobernación.[10]

The original statutes envisioned an executive council of five officers, each with a given area of responsibility: general secretary (president); organizational secretary; secretary of archives (secretary); secretary of finances (treasurer); and secretary for information, education, and culture. The officers were to be supported by a Comité de Apoyo, an advisory committee, composed of five hearing persons "sensitized to the problems of deafness." The first Comité de Apoyo included Rúthy Durán, Gloria Minero, Yadira Miranda, Mario López, and Esperanza Acevedo, all parents of deaf children except for Rúthy Durán. The officers were to be elected to terms of three years and were eligible for consecutive reelection once. Meetings were to be held at least every three months, and the day-to-day functioning was to be carried out by the executive council, which was to meet at least every fifteen days. The first executive council included Jenifer Grigsby Vado, Javier López Gómez, Adrián Pérez Castellón, María Lourdes Palacios Mairena, and Daysi Zamora Gonzáles.

It is significant that this first council was heavily weighted to persons competent in oral speech: Jenifer Grigsby had many years of speech training with Antonio and Silvia Ayón. Her speech is intelligible, but she also signs. María Lourdes Palacios was trained in Mexico at Instituto Mexicano de la Audición y del Lenguaje (IMAL) and is very comfortable with both speech and sign language. Daysi Zamora Gonzáles is a hard of hearing person, wears a hearing aid, and does not now self-identify as "deaf." Adrián Pérez Castellón was sent to an oral education program in Spain for eight years, and many persons who knew him in the early 1980s commented on how well he spoke. Javier López Gómez was also included in the lists of "successful" deaf persons I collected, and many hearing people noted that they considered it a shame that Javier (in 1997) no longer used his voice because they considered him to have good oral skills. Daysi stopped attending association events in 1990, as did Jenifer. María Lourdes occasionally attends, but it is not a major social outlet for her. Javier and Adrián now teach sign language at the deaf association and do not voice while signing.

The official slogan and logo of APRIAS are described in the statutes:

Article 38: The slogan of APRIAS will be "Together Let Us Break This Wall of Silence."

Article 39: The logo of APRIAS will be: Within a circle in which one can read the name of the Association, there is a sketch of Nicaragua.

Within the sketch one sees the profile of a face of a talking person whose voice breaks the wall behind which one can see part of the face of a deaf person.

The wall represents the barrier of silence and of communication which separates the deaf from the hearing world.

Below the wall one see the two large lakes of Nicaragua and one can read the date of the foundation of APRIAS. (*La Gaceta* 1989b, p. 1514)

Thus, we can see that, at this point, the model of deafness underlying the organization of APRIAS was integrationist: that the goal of deaf persons should be to fit into hearing society as closely as possible, a philosophy congruent with the official educational policy of the time. While the interest in joining a formal organization of the deaf may have been sparked more by young adults' interest in participating in a society of peers (in other words, in being social actors), at this point, the assumption remained that deaf members should strive to be joined, through speaking (breaking the silence), into mainstream hearing society. Although the use of signing was common during APRIAS meetings, oral speech was still more prestigious than sign language.[11] When I asked various early APRIAS members why those five individuals were elected to the first executive council, the answer was swift: "Because they could talk the best, so we considered them smarter than the rest of us."

The sign language had to have been developing, changing from a shared system of home signs and mime to one with an underlying grammar and common vocabulary, because while no sign language was evident in 1979, it was in 1986. Realistically, we will never be able to say at exactly what point this happened: We are looking at a "fuzzy" system (as in fuzzy logic), not a binary one. There was likely no particular day when the communication system in use at the meetings at Gloria's house was not language, while on the following weekend it was. Thus, the communication system during the meetings at Gloria's house was probably a system that started out simultaneously with a lot of home sign and gesture (which we generally consider nonlinguistic) and a weakly developed grammar (which is seen as linguistic), and over a period of time shifted to a system with a little bit of home sign and gesture and a stronger grammar. The work of Ann Senghas points out that this shift is not yet complete. Signers who learned the language at an older age tend to remain moored to the "little linguistic and lots nonlinguistic" end of the spectrum, whereas earlier language learners tend to take better advantage of the grammaticization that is going on, and show usage more toward the "lots linguistic and little nonlinguistic end." Senghas's work also proves that Nicaraguan Sign Language (NSL) did not spring forth fully formed grammatically (Senghas, Sotaro, and Özyürek 2004). The grammaticization of the language continues and can be expected to continue into the indefinite future. As a language, it is still very young.

APRIAS was founded within the remediable subjects model and functioned under it for many years. The group's name, logo, and slogan attest to this philosophy, which the deaf adults whom I have interviewed say was not challenged by any of its members until 1990. It is easy for outsiders to read meanings (e.g., Deaf Pride) into the official formation of a deaf association that do not appear to have been there at the time. As a group, most deaf persons in Nicaragua in the late 1980s still believed that the few of their number who had managed to learn speech deserved their admiration and respect, and inability to speak intelligibly was a personal failing. Before APRIAS coalesced, the only deaf "communities" which we can trace were small face-to-face social groups that gathered after school and on weekends at one or another's house. With the formation of APRIAS, however, the deaf community in Nicaragua became an "imagined community" in the sense that Benedict Anderson described in his book: "a deep, horizontal comradeship" (Anderson 1983, 7), which extended beyond the friendship ties linking particular individuals who socialized together. Any deaf person in Nicaragua could belong to the imagined community of APRIAS, which was conceived as a national organization with deafness its only criterion for membership. Still, in Nicaragua, it was a community first imagined as a way station to the oral majority, not as a stop on its own.

In 1987, Gloria Minero took a new job supervising the vocational workshops at the COD, a position which made her an employee of a different governmental agency: INSSBI (pronounced "EENS-bee"), the Instituto Nicaraguense de Seguridad Social y Bienestar, the social welfare arm of the government. Naturally, she met leaders in INSSBI and discussed the association on which she was spending most of her free time, APRIAS. In 1987, Socorro Carvajal, an official at the time in INSSBI whose job included coordinating material aid for social welfare purposes donated by international organizations, went on a trip to Sweden as INSSBI's representative to meet with the heads of various governmental and nongovernmental organizations, which were providing material aid to Nicaragua at the time. Among these organizations was the Swedish International Development Association (SHIA), the Swedish umbrella organization for groups working with the handicapped.[12] At that time, SHIA had a program for the war-wounded in Nicaragua; and when Socorro Carvajal met with an official of SHIA, she mentioned how well that program was going, but noted that there were other handicapped groups that were also in need, and she specifically brought up the deaf. The official with whom she spoke put her in touch with a representative of the Royal Swedish Association of the Deaf (SDR), who, on hearing how young the organization was and how few other alternatives there were for deaf persons in Nicaragua, took an interest in the possibility of aiding the fledging group.

A grant proposal from APRIAS to the SDR was approved, and $50,000 was donated in 1989 for the purpose of buying and equipping a permanent meeting place for deaf people in Managua. (According to SHIA's administrator at the time, buying permanent locations is not typical SHIA policy; but in Nicaragua's case, the cost of housing was not high, and it would add a sense of permanency.) Gloria Minero was adamant that the site purchased had to be close to multiple bus routes, the usual form of transportation for deaf adults. A suitable house was found in Colonia Los

Robles (from 1979 to 1990, the area was known as "Pancasán"), near the Jesuit-run Central American University.[13]

There was criticism about the site chosen (it was in an upper middle class suburb), but a patio that could be used for basketball, a living room large enough for big groups, and the proximity to transportation carried the vote; $35,000 of the grant was used to buy the house. The remaining money was used to buy folding chairs, tables, a freezer, a television, and some office equipment, so that the former home could be used as an office for the organization and a meeting center for the group's activities.

The meeting center was inaugurated on November 18, 1989, before an invited audience of parents, teachers, and public officials. It is symbolic of the group's underlying philosophy at this time that Jenifer Grigsby, the president, who was completely capable of signing what she wanted the audience to understand, instead delivered an oral address appropriate for the occasion, while Gloria Minero, standing next to her, and completely capable of voicing any speech Jenifer might have wanted to give in sign language, interpreted the speech into sign language for the members of the group. The group's goal of assimilating to hearing society was showcased in this instance. Speech was preferred. However, the deaf members watching the signed translation probably had the advantage that day, because Jenifer's speech was rendered unintelligible through a distorting microphone. But the next day, a newspaper article carried the text of the speeches and noted that the group's membership list included fifty names.[14]

Since 1983 (the beginning of the meetings), the use of sign language grew among APRIAS members, and most older deaf adults claim that it was at these meeting that they learned sign language and began to appreciate the communication possibilities it opened for them. Most of them were communicative strangers in their own homes and rarely understood what was happening around them; however, at the APRIAS meetings, everything was available to them. Although Gloria never could forsake speech, she began to appreciate more and more the usefulness that the signs had for the deaf. During this time, she became the main interpreter for the young people outside of the COD. When the first church wedding between two members of the group took place in 1989 (Senghas 1997), Gloria interpreted the ceremony and mass.

Gloria remembered that the association instituted weekend workshops in 1985 (and others were held in other years) to "rescue Nicaraguan sign language" ("*talleres de rescate de señas nicaraguenses*"): Gloria's own words. With later help contributed by Yana-María Graver, an American volunteer working in León, a hand-drawn, photocopied elementary dictionary of signs from these workshops was published and distributed in 1992. Before 1987 (i.e., before she went to work at the COD), Gloria remembers great diversity in the signs used: "There was a lot of use of rudimentary gestures (*gestos rusticos*) and ASL signs and mimicry (*mímicas*), which are not 'signs' but more 'iconic.' There wasn't much structure—that came later."

Many members of the deaf association, including Edda Salguera and Juan Carlos Alemán who attended the early meetings, agree with Gloria that the sign language was evolving. In a 1997 interview, Juan Carlos remembered that communication at the meetings was "through finger-spelling and gestures." (He was specifically commenting on the first meetings he attended in 1985, when he was fifteen years old.) He continued, "There really wasn't a sign language per se. It was the same way that we communicated at the [Managua Special Education] school, which was a mixture, mostly gestures, but some signs. Little by little, [we] started learning the sign language, but it was the "old" sign language, based on gestures, most of which has [now] been discarded. [Over time] the mixture changed to more signs and a little gesture. What we use now [in 1997] is completely different."

It is not just Juan Carlos and Edda who have this impression. Gioconda Cardosa remembers that she had used some signs at CNEE, but it was at the meetings at Gloria's house that she expanded her knowledge of sign language; although she stated that the signing was still "primitive" until after Javier was elected president in 1990, at which time signing was finally "taken seriously." Julio César García had only two years of education at the old Berríos school when the 1972 earthquake put a stop to his education. After an eight-year hiatus, he was one of the first students at the COD in 1981. He also remembered that the development of signing was a long process:

> In Villa Libertad [in 1981] we didn't know each other. There were no signs because we were all new to each other. Yes, it is true that those who came from

Juan Carlos Alemán (left) converses with Javier López (right) in front of the headquarters of the National Nicaraguan Association of the Deaf, May 1994. Photo by Laura Polich.

the CNEE had their own signs, but they were just individual signs, not placed together like we do now.

Juan [Leiva] and I were both new; neither of us had come from the CNEE, and so we learned the signs from the others. But it was mostly natural signs that they used, things that were like gestures or movements that everybody here uses. I would call them natural signs. It was very different from what we use now.

[I] learned to sign at the association with Javier. Yes, in Villa Libertad, they used signs, but they were abbreviated and not very understandable. When [I] first went to the association meetings at the home of Gloria Minero, the major form of communication was not through signs, which were only used as single words, when they were used, but mostly through shouting and through fingerspelling. Later, little by little, Javier taught us sign language.

Juan Leiva did not receive any education until he went to the COD, and he was there only for a few months before being expelled. He had, however, through this contact, made enough deaf friends that he was invited to the meetings at Gloria's house in 1984. He said that it was at the meetings that he began to learn sign language: "It was very hard at the meetings at first, because there was no common sign language, and it was hard to understand each other. But little by little, we learned." Mauricio Zepeda (b. 1959), who studied at the Berríos school, the CNEE, and the COD, also remembers that he learned sign language at the meetings at Gloria's. He remembers using "gestures and such when we were at school and later when a few of us would get together to hang out" (c. 1978–1980).

Exactly how Javier "taught" all the others the sign language, as Julio Garcia and Juan Leiva relate, is also not clear, but it is a claim commonly heard from deaf adults who attended the formational and early meetings of the deaf association. Ann Senghas (various personal communications, 1997–2004) can list multiple characteristics of Javier's signing that place him within the older group in the first cohort (centered on members born during the 1962 rubella epidemic) of signers; and Yolanda Mendieta, who often acts as his NSL/Spanish interpreter, can also describe multiple characteristics of Javier's language use that place him apart from the signers who predated the first cohort, as well as the younger members of the first cohort (born during the 1978–1980 rubella epidemic). Javier is, thus, a key figure in the first group to use a standardized sign language as their major mode of communication. How he managed to learn the language first while simultaneously teaching it to the others is difficult to explain.

Perhaps *taught* means that he was more enthusiastic about signing, used it more consistently, was patient about teaching what he knew to those less fluent, and took on the role of "language police," demanding that others conform to what was considered the "correct" version of signs. Both Ann Senghas and Richard Senghas, who attended one of the "rescue" workshops, noted a highly prescriptionist attitude toward language use, which was common in 1989–1994 at the deaf association (multiple personal communications with Ann and Richard Senghas 1994–2003). In 1997, I observed regular instances in which confusion over the "correct" version of a sign was referred to Javier for arbitration. His decisions were accepted with no dispute. Javier, in a sense, is identified as the "apostle" of NSL by older deaf adults. I had many informants tell me that Javier was the first to learn the language (how they don't know) and that he transmitted it to the rest of the deaf community, including themselves.

Throughout the early years, the activities of APRIAS centered both upon socialization and continuing education. During this time, Rúthy Durán, on her own; Gloria, through contacts through the COD; and Yadira Miranda, through her work at INATEC, were searching for employment possibilities for the young deaf adults.

Rúthy found openings for some of the young adults in learning to make leather goods, and later, others were trained to hand-paint pottery. None of these placements worked out in the long run, although at each one, the young people did learn some skills. According to Rúthy, communication was always a major problem. In addition, the jobs did not pay well, and ultimately, the deaf youth believed it was not worth their time to continue to work at such low-wage jobs. In other jobs that they held, Rúthy saw that they were, in fact, exploited, and noted that this tendency among employers to want to use disabled workers as nearly free labor had been, and continues to be, a problem.

Adrián Pérez Castellón described to me that he had been required to work for more than a year as an "apprentice" dental technician without receiving a salary before he was finally "hired" and paid a wage. He left that job after a few years because his salary never increased, although he saw the salaries of his hearing coworkers increase or saw them pass on to more responsible jobs. His brother-in-law obtained a warehouse job for him; but again, while he watched coworkers be promoted or have their salaries raised, his never was. When he was offered a position as a teacher of sign language at the deaf association in 1990, he was happy to leave the warehouse and immediately took the teaching job.

Similarly, Douglas Vega, one of the earliest members of the deaf community, emigrated from Nicaragua because, as he explained to Rúthy Durán, he could repair the machines better than the other mechanics, but he was never promoted nor had his salary increased. "He said he had no future in Nicaragua," commented Rúthy.

Through the COD, some female students were placed in beauty shops as hair dressers and manicurists, while some of the males were placed in jobs as carpentry assistants or workers in construction. Generally, these placements happened in the 1985–1987 period, before the hyperinflation of 1987–1989 began a very poor economic period in which shop owners found themselves needing to trim absolutely all expendable workers from their payrolls. As minimally trained workers who had difficulty communicating, the deaf workers were usually the first to be laid off. The economic situation of the country was still precarious when I did my fieldwork in 1997. Except for the workers trained in sewing, who were employed at the free trade zone factories, none of the workers who had been placed in the 1980s, and then subsequently laid off, had returned to jobs in the sectors in which they had received their COD training.

In the 1988–1989 period, a second wave of young deaf adults began to join the activities of the deaf association. This younger group had never been to the Berríos school, but had started their schooling at the newly constructed CNEE or soon after the revolution. They had heard about the deaf association and entered as regular members, not founders. They had also been exposed to signing as a language at a younger age than most of the founders and, according to Kegl and A. Senghas (1994; 1995, respectively), their signing was qualitatively different from the founding groups.

One of the members of this younger group, for example, was Ivonne Vega, the younger sister (by ten years) of Douglas Vega, one of the founding members. Knowing that the two of them had deafness in common, her older brother had made a special attempt to communicate with her from the time that she was four (when her deafness was discovered), and would often take her along when he went to visit his deaf friends. Ivonne recalls recruiting Jacqueline Aburto, a hearing woman who was to become her sister-in-law, to take her to the early APRIAS activities when she was twelve (thus, in 1984 and 1985) if her brother was not available.[15] Although the group catered to older adolescents, an exception was evidently made in her case since she was a relative to one of the founding members. She was probably an important bridge between the older deaf group and the upcoming generation.

In 1987, the movie *Walker* was filmed in Managua and Granada. The story of the film was based very loosely upon the imperialistic history of U.S. southerner William Walker's capture of the Nicaraguan government in the 1850s. The film included a cameo appearance by deaf U.S. actor, Marlee Matlin, as Walker's deaf fiancée who dies at a young age. Matlin made a trip to Nicaragua and was received by President Daniel Ortega; but she also attended a reception on May 8, 1987, arranged by APRIAS, and chatted with members; had her picture taken with them; and during the press conferences during the trip, articulated her sense of solidarity with the deaf in Nicaragua because of their common deafness. This was a historic first for members of the deaf community, who ten years later recounted it as one of their most memorable experiences. Matlin in her interviews emphasized that sign language was a language, and that it had played an important role in her life. This was some of the first good press that the usually denigrated *mímicas* received in Nicaragua.

With a fixed location in which to meet, the membership of the association continued to grow. In 1990, the SDR sent Anders Andersson and Kerstin Kjellberg, (at that time officers of the SDR) as representatives to visit APRIAS and evidently inspect how the financial assistance being sent to Nicaragua was being used. This was apparently one of the first major contacts that APRIAS ever had with deaf individuals who not only advocated the use of sign language and accepted deaf individuals into the world of employment, but also who had a cultural conception of deafness (i.e., that deafness is not a defect, but a difference). Andersson's description of the deaf in Sweden and their educational system had a profound impact on, at least, a small group of the Nicaraguan founders. He told them that deafness was not a disgrace and that they should be proud of their sign language. Sebastián Ferrar, the administrator of SHIA during this time (starting from the 1987 contacts with Socorro Carvajal until Sebastián was replaced in 1995 with a Swede, Göran Hanssen), remembered that Andersson was very bothered by the young deaf adults' unquestioning acceptance of the importance of orality, and that Andersson saw APRIAS as too "assimilationist." He urged the deaf members to rethink the value of oral skills, and to value more deeply the sign language that they were using with each other.

Before the new election of officers for APRIAS drew near, sometime in October 1990, a small group formed a "slate" that was understood to be more "deaf-centered" and less "integrationist" than that of officers, which had included both deaf and hard of hearing people, and most notably, a president who was very comfortable in producing oral Spanish in public. The new slate met with Sebastián Ferrar, the SHIA representative in Nicaragua, to ask for his support; but he told them that while he had no objections to their candidacy, the vote was to be taken by the members, and he did not wish to interfere. The fact that this group had formed must have been known to Gloria Minero and Yadira Miranda because one or the other of them translated the new slate's request for support. Ferrar is legally blind and was never able to learn NSL.[16] The campaigning itself was done mainly through personal contact, and there was little open opposition or inflammatory rhetoric. On the day of the election, November

4, 1990, the new slate won the contest easily, and one month later, was installed as the new officers of APRIAS.[17]

Various foreign researchers, including myself, have been told, in multiple versions, that this change of power in 1990 was abrupt and angry.[18] As the story goes, the change was more of a "defenestration" than a changing of the guard. The "insurgent" version of the story depicts Gloria Minero, the advocate of oral speech, handpicking Jenifer Grigsby as her preferred candidate and refusing to allow a change of leadership when Jenifer was not reelected. That version culminates with the pro-sign language contingent (including Javier López Gómez as the rightfully elected president) stealthfully entering the deaf association house and turning out the old regime, who, in retaliation, burned important papers. I can find *no* evidence that this version is correct, and there are many witnesses who refute that story. Sebastián Ferrar, the SHIA administrator at the time, states that the transition was orderly and correct, and Jenifer Grigsby agrees, noting that there was a lawyer present to be sure that all official changes (such as changing of signatures on bank accounts) were done appropriately. Daysi Zamora says that she turned in the Libro de Actas in up-to-date perfect shape, and everything was done correctly. Gloria Minero, in November 1990, was not actively participating in the association. Yadira Miranda remembers nothing unusual, nor does Adrián Pérez, one of the incoming officers, or María Lourdes Palacios, one of the outgoing officers. Most of these interviewees were offended that Gloria would be maligned in this way. There is no evidence that any official papers were burned. Gloria says she was completely detached from association affairs (due to a previous falling-out) by October 1990, and did not participate in any of the pre-election campaigning or in the voting.

Gloria was certainly convinced that good oral skills were important, but from many of the interviews I have done, it seems that, at the time, influential members (influenced surely by the attitudes of their parents and teachers) also were convinced that speaking was more important than signing. Javier, for example, drew the logo for the group, so he must have been convinced in 1986 of the importance of "breaking down the walls of silence." This is why it was a significant change to propose a second slate of officers, not all of whom were known for their oral skills, in 1990. The second slate movement was proposed and led by Javier (who was elected president). Adrián (also known for his good oral skills) was elected vice president. While there was outwardly little difference, this change in officers marked an important shift by the association—from an integrationist philosophy to one celebrating the deaf as community (and center of social agency for the deaf, with therefore no particular need to integrate as oral individuals into the general society).

From 1991, sign language became less an adjunct to oral speech, slowly becoming the dominant mode of communication within the association, and also by members when acting outside of the association, with no apology for their unwillingness to speak. During 1991, leading hard of hearing or orally functional founding members stopped participating in association activities. Jenifer Grigsby lost interest when she was defeated for the presidency. Quarrels broke out that made both Mercedes Murillo and Daysi Zamora (both identifying as hard of hearing) stop going to association events. María Lourdes Palacios cut back her participation to a minimum. Gloria Minero had been targeted in a gossip campaign and chose to sever her relationship with the association before the 1990 elections. In any case, Gloria left Nicaragua soon after, in 1991, to return to El Salvador, her native country, when the civil war there had calmed.

As an outcome of Kerstin and Anders's visit, the association began to receive funding in 1991 from the SDR to carry on three major projects: the collection of entries for a professionally published sign language dictionary, provision of sign language instruction for teachers of the deaf, and teaching of basic literacy classes to deaf members of the association.

As part of the dictionary project, the SDR provided computers, camcorders, and other equipment to draw the entries, as well as salaries for the four major collectors of the project. They also paid the salary for Juan Carlos Drueta, a deaf Argentine, to be an outside consultant in 1995 (R. Senghas 1997). Drueta had had an excellent oral education and communicated orally with Sebastián Ferrar, the administrator for SHIA, the funding source, which gave him an advantage over the Nicaraguan members who had to go through an interpreter to talk with Ferrar. (Remember that Sebastián was legally blind, so he never learned to sign.) There were disagreements over what was expected of Drueta, and arguments ensued. He came during parts of two different years, and his hearing wife taught sign language interpreting to a class of about ten hearing people who had shown an interest in becoming translators. At the height of the problems, there were insinuations that Drueta was not really deaf because he had intelligible speech. The dictionary project continued until the publication of the dictionary in March 1997.[19] Drueta is barely mentioned in the finished book.

The philosophical change was underscored in 1996 when the association began routinely to use the name Asociación Nacional de Sordos de Nicaragua (National Nicaraguan Association of the Deaf), or ANSNIC (pronounced "ahns-NEEK") instead of APRIAS.[20] The integrationist stance included in the group's bylaws was de-emphasized. Under the new philosophy, the association's apparent new goal is to be a central social focus for the deaf, and to provide as many educational and employment possibilities as possible.[21] By becoming members of the deaf association, deaf people are, de facto, integrated into a society, and they exercise their social agency, albeit as a subgroup in which their NSL is the major unifying factor. Because this mini-society retains ties through interpreters with the larger oral/Spanish-dependent society, members are, in a sense, integrated into the larger society by being situated in the smaller group. There is no need, and in fact, no wish, to disperse the members individually to integrate into the larger society to function in a hearing manner.

Thus, the third model of deafness, deaf persons as *social agents*, which is the prevalent model among members of the deaf association today in Nicaragua, is one adopted by certain deaf members themselves, not one imposed on them by the Nicaraguan hearing society. The model, however, is indebted to outside influences and outside precedents, and did not originate with Nicaraguan deaf members. Attitudes, especially from Sweden, Finland, and the United States introduced the philosophy; but starting in 1990, and especially after 1992, it was adopted by the leading members of ANSNIC, who started a campaign to include more sign language use in the schools, and to increase use of Spanish/NSL interpreters for deaf persons in daily life. Without the reification of sign language brought to Nicaragua from Costa Rica, the United States, Sweden, and Spain, or without the financial aid and the anti-integrationist perspective of the SDR, it is possible that this model would have been much longer in the making.

The model of deaf persons as *social actors*, as yet, has limited adherents among the Nicaraguan hearing majority, and is not well understood. Even many who favor the use of sign language by deaf people do not understand the implications of this difference in models, and still advocate the use of sign language as a stepping stone to learning more oral language. Thus, they expect that the individual deaf members will ultimately integrate, in a hearing manner, into society at large. The nonintegrationist view (which is what the deaf association's recommendations imply) is directly opposed today by influential personages in the educational sector. At MED, the philosophy remains determinedly assimilationist, and inclusion continues to be the official policy.

I had a conversation with the principal of a school with deaf pupils and mentioned that it appeared to me that the deaf students at her school were "starving" for linguistic interaction. (The students' main form of communication was through sign language.) I mentioned that it would be an excellent way to increase the language skills of her pupils if adults from the deaf association could be invited to simply come to the school and just engage in friendly conversation with the students (e.g., without the need to "teach" the pupils anything). "We tried that," the principal replied. "A few of the members of the deaf association did come a few times, but I didn't see that it accomplished anything. I didn't notice that the children talked (i.e., used oral speech) any more after those visits than before."

The director of special education in 1997, when I did my fieldwork, who told me that the aim of the MED was the "integration of the deaf," was Desirée Roman. (Desirée was also most encouraging of my research, agrees that NSL is a linguistic form of communication and very suited to the deaf, and is supportive of the deaf association.) She left that position in 2000. Interviews in 2001 and 2002 with her successor, Elizabeth Baltodanos, left no room for doubt that assimilation into oral society remains the official goal.

The conception of deafness has undergone significant change in Nicaragua over the past fifty years. It has gone from a view in which deaf persons were seen as incapable of becoming social agents in society, through a conceptualization of the deaf as possible agents as long as they were "remediated," to the perspective of the deaf as community, in which social agency is centered in the deaf community more than in the majority hearing society. Although there has definitely been an evolution in perspectives, I do not wish to imply that the changes were sequential, and that each new view meant that the previous perspectives disappeared. The progression has been more of a layering of possibilities. Today in Nicaragua, there exist three views on deafness. A small minority view the deaf community as the means of integration into society for the deaf, while a large majority holds tight to the need to remediate the deaf to enter society at large. But there is still another minority who does not view the deaf as ever being capable of entering society as actors. All of these views coexist simultaneously.

5

Being Deaf in Nicaragua in 1997

In the United States, which probably has the most reliable statistics, the literature on Universal Newborn Hearing Screening programs indicates that 3 children in 1,000 are born with significant hearing loss (Schow and Nerbonne 1996). In other countries, fewer reliable figures are available. In Nicaragua, for example, there are no reliable figures available at all. No census, including the last one carried out in 1995, has ever included questions about the presence of deafness or blindness, etc.[1] While the country's Ministry of Health does record epidemiological statistics, hearing loss is usually not a primary medical complaint, nor is it life-threatening; thus it is not included in the epidemiological databases. There is no national health or educational database in Nicaragua capable of collecting reliable statistics on the topic of hearing loss and deafness.

The exact number of deaf persons in Nicaragua is unknown, but through extrapolation from the rates of deafness prevalent in other countries, we would expect to find somewhere between 2,500 and 4,800 deaf adults in the whole country.[2] If deaf persons were distributed in the same pattern as is the general population, we would expect to find between 900 and 1,800 of them living in or close to Managua.[3] It must be noted that not all contemporary Nicaraguan deaf adults have had contact with the present deaf community: There are many still isolated within their birth homes, a few who choose not to have anything to do with other deaf people, and many who live in rural areas in which the concentration of deaf persons is so low that there is no access to any deaf group.

The core of Nicaragua's deaf community today is, undoubtedly, the group formed by the members of the National Nicaraguan Association of the Deaf (ANSNIC), which, in 1997, had a membership list with 359 names on it (but 3 are repetitions, so there are 356 different names on the list). The president of the association, Javier López Gómez, however, believed that 356 significantly underrepresented the membership, which he

placed at closer to 600.[4] He explained that obtaining an official association identification card involves multiple steps, including completion of
a registration form (the majority of deaf persons have very low literacy
skills) and the presentation of a certified birth record (the acquiring of
which involves a fee to the local office of vital statistics) with two pass-
port-size photographs (another charge). The association's president believes
that many persons who function as active members simply do not bother
to complete the paperwork, and thus, are not included in the official list.
From my personal observation, this is true, at least, of the younger members (i.e., those between the ages of fifteen and twenty-five who came to
literacy classes in 1997), few of whom had membership cards.

ANSNIC was formally organized in 1986 in Managua. For four years,
Managua had the only organized group. In the late 1980s, the deaf association began to attract interested deaf persons from the Carazo region
(e.g., the towns of San Marcos, Dolores, Diriamba, and Jinotepe), as well
as from the Masaya region, both of which lie about an hour by bus from
the capital. At first, they participated simply as members of the Managua
group; but in 1990, a regional chapter was formed in San Marcos, and in

ANSNIC entry in the parade for Day of the Disabled, August 1997 in Managua. Photo by Laura Polich.

1993, members from Masaya formed the second regional chapter outside of the capital.

In 1994, the hearing teacher for the deaf class in Matagalpa (three hours by bus from Managua) began to attend sign language classes in Managua on Saturdays, and she encouraged deaf adolescents to accompany her. These deaf young people began to participate in association activities in Managua and concurrently formed a small group at home with a broader membership. In 1995, Matagalpa officially became the third regional chapter.

By 1997, there were also deaf groups meeting in Tipitapa (about 10 km. outside the northeast city limits of Managua), León (a large city two hours northwest from Managua), Belén (close to Rivas, near the Costa Rican border), Bluefields (on the southeast Atlantic Coast), and Estelí (a large city three hours northwest of Managua); but none of these groups was large enough or coherent enough to form a regional chapter, although that is the expectation for the future. Group recruiting efforts started in Puerto Cabezas (now also known as Bilwí) on the Atlantic Coast in 1997 and in Waslala (northeast of Matagalpa; a very remote zone with very poor transportation) in 1996.

It is no surprise that the association would coalesce first in the capital and then spread outward across the country. Twenty-five percent of Nicaragua's population lives in the *departamento* of Managua, and thus, we would also expect to find the largest concentration of deaf persons there.[5] In addition to its own extensive city bus system, Managua is the hub for all the extra-urban bus routes. Thus, it is relatively easy to travel from the towns and villages of the western countryside into the capital.[6] Because most deaf people in Nicaragua have very low incomes, and are, theoretically, prohibited from obtaining driving licenses, the members of the deaf community rely completely upon public transportation for their mobility, and proximity to bus transportation is crucial in determining who does or does not participate actively in deaf association activities.[7]

The deaf association owns a house in a centrally located residential area of Managua, purchased for them by the Royal Swedish Association of the Deaf (SDR) in 1989, which is within three or four blocks of two main traffic arteries of the capital, and is thus, accessible to multiple bus lines. The stability of this meeting place since 1989, as well as its central location, has been important to the growth of the deaf association. The "Deaf

Ivonne Vega teaching at a school set up by the Nicaraguan Sign Language Project in Bluefields on the Atlantic Coast in May 1997. Photo by Laura Polich.

House" has become a Managua landmark, and persons seeking information about deafness or what to do with deaf relatives are routinely directed there.[8] (I can vouch for this because on various Saturday afternoons during my fieldwork, I was the only hearing person at the association, and thus, was summoned to be the designated speaker to members of the general public who had rung the doorbell to inquire about association activities or what kind of help they could obtain for their deaf relatives.)

There are deaf persons (it is impossible to estimate the number), both registered and nonregistered members, who choose not to attend the association events on any kind of regular basis, either because of personal rivalries or disagreements over how the association and its activities should be run. I conversed with various people in this category. They choose to socialize with other deaf persons by meeting at their homes, and thus, not on association territory. But even those deaf persons who are not registered members of the deaf association, or those who choose not to participate actively in the events at the Deaf House, are well aware of the association and where it is located. In fact, while I was there, it was not uncommon for individuals who identified themselves to me as persons who "never go to the association's activities" also to tell me that they were registered members of the association. And universally, any deaf person felt that entrance to the association house and participation in activities was a right of all deaf persons, whether they were officially enrolled in the association or not.

During my year of fieldwork, I did my best to collect enough information to allow me to describe the characteristics of Nicaraguan deaf community members as of 1997. There was no "scientific" way to do this. I could not survey a representative sample because there was no way to estimate a reliable "universe" of eligible subjects from which to choose a sample. Neither the Institute of Statistics and Census, nor the Ministry of Education (MED), nor even ANSNIC have ever done any careful, statistically based studies of the incidence of deafness in Nicaragua. All estimates of how many deaf people exist in the country or in a particular area, by any of these institutions, are simply guesses (sometimes educated, sometimes not). Even taking a random sample from registered members of the deaf association was not feasible: The registration list is not kept current, and there has never been any coordinated outreach effort to be sure that deaf persons in the country know about the association. Finding even those registered with ANSNIC was a challenge. The information that the deaf association had was not kept up to date, so an address might be twenty years old. It was common to arrive at a house only to find that the person to whom I wanted to talk had moved. Also, because Managua has no street names or building numbers, an address is simply a description of how to get somewhere from a familiar landmark and is, thus, very ambiguous.[9]

In spite of the impossibility of finding a statistically representative sample, it was clear from conversations and observation that members are a rather homogeneous group. They share very similar backgrounds and experiences that have shaped their worldview and how they understand events within the association and within the wider society.[10] Very few come from wealthy families or are educated. The commonality of members' life experiences influences greatly the group's cohesiveness, and it must be understood if readers are to comprehend the history of the deaf association in Nicaragua. Thus, I was left with the only alternative of gathering information from as many people as I could, making the sample as large as possible, and then drawing conclusions cautiously.

In this chapter, I describe the deaf community of Nicaragua as I found it in 1997. My presentation is biased toward the informants living around the capital, but I believe that is allowable because that is where we would expect the largest concentration of deaf persons. But it was possible to branch out from the capital, and thus, the sample is not limited to the capital only. While 46% of the deaf persons surveyed came from Managua, the Carazo area contributed 24%, Masaya 8%, Granada 9%, Matagalpa 11%, and Estelí 5% (see figure 2). My description is, naturally, heavily weighted towards those who have some connection to the deaf association, because those are the persons more likely to participate in any community.[11]

I base this description on three major sources. The first was an audiometric investigation I did to determine what level of hearing ability the then-current ANSNIC members had, in order to predict which persons having a hearing loss might be drawn to join the deaf community. The second, referred to as the "Deaf Survey," which I funded out of my own pocket, was a broader survey I wrote about home life, schooling, employment, and socialization preferences. The majority of those responses were collected by deaf members of the association who were paid as research assistants. The surveyors were encouraged to include "anybody who was deaf," and thus, the Deaf Survey was not limited to association members. The responses were generally categorical (respondents were asked to choose a category that represented their incomes) or specific (respondents were asked how many years they had been in school). Open-ended questions asking for opinions or feelings were found during the pilot study to be unusable because respondents felt uncomfortable with such questions or did not know how to answer them. I was allowed to copy the name, birth date, and membership card number of the 359 registered members of the association (as of May 30, 1997).

I bow to the limitations inherent in gathering this information (such as no ability to choose a representative sample), but I believe the trends from these three sources are in such accordance that they can, fruitfully, be used to describe which Nicaraguans are drawn to join the deaf association, and what their lives are like at the end of the twentieth century.

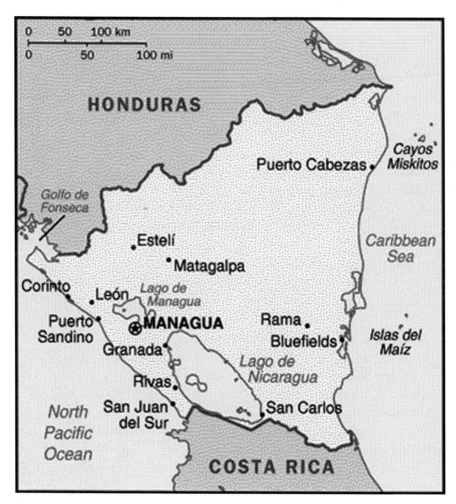

Figure 2. Map of Nicaragua

An Overview of Deafness

Even in countries where deaf communities have existed for generations, and where hereditary deafness is not unusual (the United States, for example) only a small percentage of deaf children are born to parents who are themselves deaf. The most typical figure cited is that 90% of deaf children are born to hearing parents and soon become communicative outsiders in their own families (Schein 1989). Mitchell and Karchmer (2003) have revised that figure to 95%. In Nicaragua, until recently, even fewer deaf children of deaf parents are known. In 1997, I found only one instance: a seventeen-year-old son of a deaf woman born in 1945.[12] Because she was never educated, and never learned either oral Spanish or any form of sign language, she also had no linguistic means, beyond home sign and gestures, of communicating with her son. This woman has been, and continues to be, very dependent upon her younger sister, and that sister took over the care of her nephew. So he, the deaf child of a deaf parent, actually grew up, as his mother had before him, in a hearing family.

Most humans are born with enough hearing (even if it is not perfect) that they acquire oral language as their primary mode of communication. Humans do not just have normal hearing or else no hearing. The typical human ear is tuned to perceive a broad range of auditory frequencies, and sensitivity to the different frequencies may vary selectively. A person does not need perfect hearing to rely primarily upon auditory input for language development and use. But there is a point at which the auditory signal becomes so degraded or inaudible that it cannot be the primary input. Generally, members of a deaf community have hearing losses in the severe to profound range, and their useable residual hearing is so restricted that they can detect only the loudest of sounds. These deaf people face serious communication challenges.

The age at which a hearing loss occurs is significant in determining whether a person will prefer oral language or sign language. The typical member of a deaf community experiences hearing loss at an early age, usually at birth or before the third year of life, and thus, acquires language primarily through visual, rather than auditory, input. Persons who acquire even profound hearing loss after adolescence usually retain their ties to oral language and do not identify with the signing community. Although some "late-deafened adults" may participate actively in deaf communities in other countries, none of the members of ANSNIC fell in that category.[13] All had their hearing loss when they were born or acquired it within the first three years of life.[14]

It is also notable that I never met any member of the deaf association who described a progressive hearing loss that took them from reliance upon oral language to a point where they preferred sign language.[15] Anyone who could remember being hearing (or had a relative tell them about how they became deaf) described sudden onset losses, such as those associated with meningitis, aminoglycoside ototoxicity, or measles, and the deafness occurred before they were school-aged.[16]

Like deaf people in many other countries, the members of the deaf association consider the term *deaf mute* to be derogatory (and I have observed how hearing persons do, in fact, use it that way), and they prefer to call themselves *deaf*. In fact, the hearing society of Nicaragua makes a linguistic distinction between someone who is deaf but speaks (and thus, probably lost their hearing after learning spoken language), calling them *deaf* and by referring to a deaf person who prefers sign language as a *deaf mute*. I often found myself caught up in this linguistic dilemma: If I used the term preferred by the deaf association and asked hearing persons to direct me to where a "deaf" person lived, I was usually sent to a late-deafened adult, who had absolutely no ties to ANSNIC nor wished to have any. When I explained that I was looking for someone who didn't talk, they would reply, "Oh, you should have said so. You're looking for a deaf-mute."

Although born apparently unaware of linguistic functioning, human babies from a very early age have proven to be receptive to sensory input that will later be used linguistically. Babies are able to recognize their mother's voices within the first few days of life and soon pay attention to the movements of caregivers' faces and their eye gaze (DeCasper and Fifer 1980; DeCasper and Spence 1991). The typical human infant begins life with several months of auditory learning, and approximately six months later will show signs of understanding and beginning to act on auditory input (Birnholtz and Benacerraf 1983). Six months after that, the typical human infant will begin to use vocal productions to express her- or himself linguistically.

Deafness, however, places serious obstacles in the way of this development, which is based on auditory learning. While deaf babies exposed to
visual language (i.e., sign language) have been documented to follow the
same linguistic milestones (Meier 1991)—understanding linguistic input
around six months of age and expressing linguistic concepts at approximately
one year—deaf children who have only auditory exposure are significantly
delayed linguistically compared with their hearing peers (Schow and
Nerbonne 1996). Without specialized training, it is not uncommon for a
deaf child to reach six years of age with less than a ten-word receptive or
expressive oral vocabulary. Even with intensive education, a deaf child's ability to understand auditory language and use oral expression, is very delayed
compared with the progress made by normally hearing children. Without
specialized training in oral language (and even with it), deaf children usually do not develop recognizable spoken language. They rely on a mutually
developed system of pantomime and referenced signs, known as "home sign"
(Morford 1996) to communicate with their families. The obstacle to oral
language learning, which deafness presents, is formidable.

Characteristics of the Deaf Community in Nicaragua
Hearing Status

Most of the members of the deaf association had little awareness of their
objective hearing status. As a certified audiologist, I offered in January
1997 to perform hearing evaluations for the members of ANSNIC who
wished to participate, and to provide a copy of those evaluations to the
association. In return, I was allowed to keep a copy of the evaluations and
quote the results in my writings.

The eighty-seven persons who were tested represent 25% of the total
membership list of the association. The youngest group (teenagers) is over-
represented, and the oldest members are underrepresented. This is because
the youngest members came regularly to the association for literacy classes
on Wednesday mornings and were thus, easily available, whereas the oldest group appeared only occasionally at the association and were thus,
more easily missed. There is no reason to believe, however, that there is
an age factor related to hearing ability that would make this difference
relevant.[17] All of the persons I tested told me that they had either been

Table I. Hearing Levels of Best Ear Tested. Hearing Testing by Author at Nicaraguan Deaf Association in 1997.

Description of Threshold Levels (as measured in dB)	Percentage of Members According to Level of Loss in Better Ear
Severe (60–79dB)	14%
Severe-to-Profound (80–99dB)	25%
Profound (100–109dB)	38%
Profound+ (over 110dB)	23%

born deaf or had been deafened by the age of three years. I never saw a late-deafened adult at the association, and was told that none came.

Hearing ability is described by hearing *thresholds* measured in decibels (dB) across a given frequency (pitch) range. Decibels are a measure of the intensity of sound, and a hearing threshold is the lowest intensity of sound that a person can detect (e.g., lower hearing thresholds mean that hearing sensitivity is more acute) at a given frequency. Descriptive terms (i.e., mild, moderate, etc.) are used to characterize the average of the thresholds across the frequency range most important for speech perception. No one in the test sample exhibited only a mild or moderate hearing loss (average of thresholds better than 60 dB), while the bulk of those tested had profound hearing losses. Looking at the averages for only the better ears (i.e., the hearing in their other ear was worse), we see that 71% of the test group averaged thresholds at 100 dB or more. (Normal hearing thresholds range from 0 to 20 dB. The highest output of an audiometer is typically 120 dB.) This group would *not* be expected to gain significant benefit for speech by using hearing aids, even if they were available.[18] Another 25% of the group, even under ideal circumstances, would be expected only to gain some benefit from amplification. Of the persons I tested at the association in 1997, only 14% would have been likely to understand speech with hearing aids.

When asked about their history of hearing aid use on the Deaf Survey, 72% of the respondents denied any previous use of a hearing aid, and 28% said that they had had access to one at some point in their lives. Only one or two respondents were using a hearing aid at the time of the survey. Hearing aids are not commonly used in Nicaragua, and they are expensive. In 1997, one hearing aid retailed for US$300, which was approximately equivalent to three-fourths of the 1997 per capita gross domestic product for the country (US$479.70). The high humidity, high average temperature, and other factors, such as dust, take a high toll on the hearing aids that are used. There are no repair facilities within Nicaragua, and the most common reasons given for not using a hearing aid were the high cost of batteries, the inability to get a broken hearing aid fixed, an earmold that was too small (and no way to replace it), and the loss of a hearing aid through neglect or thievery. Some persons also stated that the hearing aid "bothered" them and they preferred not to use amplification.

Age of Onset

On the Deaf Survey, 63% of respondents reported that they were born deaf, while 17% stated that they became deaf within the first twelve months of life. Seven percent stated that they were deafened between one and two years, while 13% reported that they lost their hearing after they were two years old, but before they were four years of age.[19] Only 2% stated that they were deafened after the age of four years. Thus, we would characterize the majority, 98% of the respondents, as prelingually deaf (i.e., they became deaf before they had learned to speak).

Most of the persons drawn to the deaf association have hearing losses in the severe-to-profound range, and have had those hearing levels from a very young age. However, there are deaf educators in Nicaragua who imply that the members of ANSNIC would be capable of using speech as their major mode of communication "if only they would try." Their claim is not upheld by either my hearing study or the Deaf Survey results. Hearing loss in the profound range and early onset of deafness are exactly the factors that provide the poorest prognosis for acquisition of fluent oral language skills by deaf persons (Schow and Nerbonne 1996). The majority of the members of the deaf association have been drawn to that group precisely because oral functioning is not a realistic alternative for them.

Language Use

Overwhelmingly, the preferred language of the members of the deaf community is a form of the sign language now called Nicaraguan Sign Language (NSL), which most members (at least at this point) learned as adolescents. Sixty-seven percent of the respondents in the Deaf Survey stated that NSL was their preferred mode of communication, while 25% listed oral Spanish as preferred. The remaining informants listed gestures only, or fingerspelling, or writing as preferred communication forms.

Before concluding that one-fourth of the respondents would rather speak oral Spanish than use NSL, it must be pointed out that 20% of the respondents said that they had not had the opportunity to learn sign language or had learned it only minimally, or their sign language skills were characterized as nonexistent by the surveyors.[20] The marking of "Spanish" on the surveys, in these cases, seemed to be a "default" option rather than a true preference.

Forty-four percent of the respondents said that they had learned to sign during their school years, while 26% stated that they had learned sign language at the deaf association. Nine percent credited their friends with informally teaching them to sign, and 20% either said they did not sign or were characterized as non-signers by the surveyors.

Competency in spoken Spanish is closely related to hearing ability. Only a very small minority of the members of the deaf community can carry on a conversation that is oral only, and most of these can do it only with difficulty. Those who can tend to have more residual hearing than most of the other members of the deaf community. Of those with intelligible speech, most would fall in a "hard of hearing" classification. Even most of these persons told me that they preferred to use sign language rather than spoken Spanish.

Of the approximately 400 deaf adults living in Nicaragua in 1997 whom I met or heard about, I could only document about 10 who probably had severe-to-profound hearing losses and who, at the same time, had intelligible speech and could understand an oral conversation. Two women who worked as secretaries fall within this category, and both exhibited excellent lipreading skills and highly intelligible speech. Both of them are bilingual in Spanish and NSL. There are about eight individuals who exhibit adequate intelligibility and lipreading ability in Spanish, and all of these persons also use sign language. These eight individuals found it difficult to state a preference between sign language and Spanish, and said that their preference would depend upon the context in which they found themselves. I only found two young men who had adequate capabilities in Spanish speaking and speechreading, but did not know any sign language, and who thus stated that Spanish was their preferred language choice at all times.

Communication within the Home

Ninety percent of the respondents stated that they were the only deaf members of their families of origin, while 8% had one sibling who was also deaf. Only 2% of the respondents had more than one deaf sibling. Seventy-eight percent stated that they were the only deaf person in their extended families, while 22% reported a deaf cousin, aunt, uncle, grandparent, or other relative. These responses parallel closely those obtained by Schein, who concluded that, in the United States, 90% of deaf children had hearing parents.

Sixteen percent of the respondents reported that they were the only sign language users in their present residence, 52% stated that there was one other person in the house who was competent in sign language, and 30% stated that there were at least two other persons besides the respondent who knew sign language in the house. It is my observation that deaf people in Nicaragua are very generous in their attribution of sign language skill to their relatives. A relative with an expressive or receptive vocabulary of fifty or so signs will be characterized by the deaf person as "able to sign." This level of "competency" severely restricts meaningful conversation.

When asked for preferred communication partners, 27% pointed to their mothers as the person with whom the most communication took place, while 12% indicated a sister, and 6% preferred to communicate with a father. Very sadly, the largest percentage of respondents—40%—stated that there was *no one* in their home with whom they communicated.

The majority of the deaf persons in this survey had very poor experiences in their attempts to learn oral Spanish (and *all* have made the attempt), with most of them, as adults, deciding that fluent oral functioning was beyond their abilities. All of them remarked at the relative ease of understanding sign language when comparing the experience to trying to learn oral language.

For most of those surveyed, the only free, unhindered, in-depth, punning, vociferous, eloquent, plaintive, mischievous, melodramatic, exuberant, or ironic conversations they ever have are within the deaf association. Within their homes, communication is very limited, and for most, has been that way since childhood. Only a very small minority of those surveyed can choose to initiate a conversation freely and at will with any member of their immediate families. For most, there is only one family member who has made the effort to adapt communication strategies (either learning sign language or accommodating in some other way to the deaf person's difficulty in understanding oral communications) to be able to communicate freely with the deaf family member; and thus, for the deaf person to communicate with other family members, the "adaptor" member must be present as a translator.

Perhaps the saddest answer recorded in the Deaf Survey is the fact that 40% of the respondents could not think of one person in their homes with whom they could communicate at will. Some of the respondents were in their teens, but most were in their twenties or thirties, and thus had families which had had decades to adapt to their hearing losses. Sign language has been in common use in the deaf association for more than ten years. The means for communication do exist, but it appears that many families do not avail themselves of this opportunity.

With home circumstances such as these, it is little wonder that deaf members are drawn magnetically to ANSNIC activities where all of the conversations and all of the activities are accessible to them. The majority of the respondents describe homes in which it would be very difficult for them to function as independent social actors. But that possibility is available freely at the deaf association.

Not all deaf persons in Nicaragua, or even all deaf persons at the deaf association, however, have complete fluency in NSL. (Remember that 20% of the respondents to the survey were non-signers.) Because of the social conditions chronicled elsewhere in this book, many deaf persons did not have access to sign language until they were adults, and there are others who still have no access. For these persons, being fully participating members of a social group, even when they join activities at the deaf association, is simply not a possibility.

Age

The most striking aspect of those who participate in deaf community activities is their youth. No old deaf people attend any deaf functions. There is no reason to believe that deafness is a recent phenomenon for Nicara-

Table 2. Deaf Association Membership Birth Dates by Decades

Age Range (n = 36) (Birth Date Listed in ANSNIC Files)	Number	Percentage of Total
40+ years (birth date before 12/31/57)	22	6%
30–39 years (1/1/58 to 12/31/67)	85	24%
20–29 years (1/1/68 to 12/31/77)	195	55%
15–19 years (1/1/78 to 12/31/82)	44	12%
Unknown birth dates	10	3%

gua; nor is there any reason to believe that deafness per se causes an unusually high mortality rate in Nicaragua. Elderly people are quite apparent in the general Nicaraguan population, so one is forced to draw the conclusion that a significant change in social dynamics occurred at some point because the age pyramid for the deaf community is extremely skewed. The birth dates from the list of registered members illustrates this fact well (table 2).

The Over-Forty Group

The oldest deaf person I met in Managua was a seventy-year-old woman who I will call Juana. I met her by chance in 2003. She was working at an auto parts store owned by an acquaintance. She mopped floors, made coffee, and ran routine errands. The store owner did not know how long she had worked for the business, because she had been there ever since he was a child when his father bought the store.

Her identification card (which she carried at all times with her) told us her name and birth date, but she was illiterate and did not use any standard signs, so we could only rely on her gestures and the owner's previous knowledge of Juana's life to interpret what she animatedly tried to communicate. It appeared she had a daughter, and that she evidently had attended school at some point. The store happened, by chance, to be very close to the house of Olga Tenorio, who taught at Nicaragua's first special education school from 1948 to 1976. From Juana's gestures, it appeared that Juana wanted to tell us that Olga Tenorio had been her teacher. Apparently Juana's daily walk to the store from her bus stop led past Olga's house, and she greeted the teacher when she saw her. Given her age, Juana may have attended the school, but it would only have opened when Juana was a teenager, and it is not likely that her schooling lasted long. (At that point, the pupils only attended school until they were fourteen or fifteen.) Olga Tenorio was ill and did not receive visitors during my 2003 trip, so I could not ask her. Juana was not registered at the deaf association, but other deaf members had previously told me of the existence of a woman named Juana who lived in the area where the store was located. Apparently this was the woman they meant; however, she worked in that area rather than lived there. Without any standardized language, it was impossible to ask Juana for more details about the school, or, as a matter of fact, about any details of her life.

The second oldest deaf person I met was Dolores Bustos Alemán, a woman born in 1945; but because she had never been educated, both her signing skills and Spanish literacy (for either fingerspelling or writing in Spanish) were nonexistent, and I could not communicate with her beyond gestures, nor could I gain any understanding of her history or life from her. Another man born in 1955, Roberto Cano, only had about six months of formal schooling; and although he is a capable artist, it was very difficult to converse with him because he knew no standardized sign language, and his ability to write Spanish words was very limited. He relied mainly on his mother to interpret his gestures. He could speechread a few words of his mother's speech, but the conversation did not go far.

Miguel Ángel Moreno (born in 1953) is a partner in a transportation cooperative. His signing ability is weak, but he communicates effectively by writing Spanish words and phrases on a notepad he keeps with him at all times. I met him at the deaf association, and he told me that he stops by there on Saturday afternoons "once every few months or so." He was one of the older students at the first special education school in Managua when some of the present association leaders were the younger students, and he maintains contact with them through ANSNIC. He is married to a hearing woman who does not participate at all in the deaf community, and in fact, denies knowing any sign language. Yolanda Mendieta and I visited Miguel Ángel's home and spoke with his wife and children. When I asked his wife if she used sign language, she burst out laughing. When I asked if she had considered learning sign language (there are classes for hearing people at the deaf association), she giggled while looking at me with a puzzled look, and did not answer. Neither she nor the couple's three children sign. To communicate with Miguel Ángel, they mouth words, use writing (they have a large chalkboard set up in their patio near Miguel Ángel's usual chair, so that he can write down Spanish words to indicate his intent), or use gestures. Miguel Ángel is a very resourceful person, having worked hard to become an associate in a transportation collective where all other members are hearing and only speak Spanish, and he has adapted marvelously to this communicative environment.

Salvador López, ten years older than Miguel Ángel, but a classmate of his at the first school accepting children with deafness, had similar language skills when interviewed in 2002, but lacked Miguel Ángel's literacy. He would mouth Spanish words while explaining with gestures. We were able to learn the basic outline of his life, but could not discuss how he felt about those events or his opinion of his upbringing and education. He was able to tell us that he had had two wives, both hearing. One, with whom he had two children, divorced him, and the other had just left. His son had died in an automobile accident, but he enjoyed playing with his daughter's children. When we talked with him, he was living in the house of a relative and communicated with his relatives via gestures.

Noel Rocha (born 1953) works on road crews for the city of Managua and is quite enthusiastic about communicating. He does not attend many deaf activities (although he is listed as a member of the association), but he maintains regular contact with various deaf friends, including Mauricio Zepeda, who accompanied me and Yolanda Mendieta, an NSL interpreter, to visit him at his home where he regaled us for hours with stories of the first special education school and his travels through Central America. Noel's signing was much more fluent than Miguel Ángel's, but it is not the standard sign language now commonly used at the association. Mauricio helped with translation, and Noel also used paper and pencil to write when the interpreter could not understand his signs. According to Noel, the students in the first special education school (also known as the Berríos school) invented a corpus of signs that they understood among themselves in the late 1960s and early 1970s. (His schooling ended with the 1972 Managua earthquake, when the Berríos school was damaged and thus, closed for a period. He found work during this time and never returned to school.) Although that small corpus of signs was used, there appears to have been little syntax or a formal language system. Noel vehemently denied that there was a "sign language" among the children at the Berríos school and described a combination of pooled home signs, gestures, and iconic references as the means of communication used among the students. He was adamant that he had learned what sign language he knew in the early 1980s at the homes of deaf friends, along with some self-study of a dictionary and by participation in a few of the meetings at Gloria Minero's house (see chapter 4), although he was not a regular attendee. He lamented the fact that he had never been able to attain the skill and fluency that some of his younger friends—like Mauricio—had. Noel's signature appears on the deaf association's Certificación de la Fundación document in 1987, (which I will refer to from now on as the certificación). It is one of the first legal documents that must be presented when requesting legal incorporation as a formal organization, so he evidently was, at least, an occasional (and early) participant when the deaf association was formed (his registration card number is 26), even though I never saw him at ANSNIC in 1997 and was told he came only very rarely.

Finally, one of the "elder" deaf women is a remarkable person who is one of the very few truly bilingual deaf persons in Nicaragua (Spanish/NSL). María Lourdes Palacios was born in 1954 and exhibited a profound hearing loss before she was two years old.[21] She is an only child of parents who moved from the countryside (Matagalpa) to the capital in order to find a school for her at an early age. She entered the Berríos school as a preschooler (not common at the time), and later her father sent her and her mother to live in Mexico City for five years so that his daughter could attend the Instituto Mexicano de Audición y Lenguaje (IMAL), an educational center with an oral philosophy that was responsible for most of the few trained teachers in Nicaragua in the 1960s and 1970s.

Upon her return to Nicaragua, María Lourdes attended a regular high school for a few years, but could not lipread the teacher's speech well enough to keep up. Through a friend of the family, she received training in hair dressing, and ultimately was trained in typing so she could look for work as a secretary. She had been employed as a secretary since 1977, first at the Centro Nacional de Educación Especial (a special education school in Managua) and later at the Centro Ocupacional para Discapacitados [COD]). She speaks with a voice and articulation pattern typical of persons with severe-to-profound hearing losses, but she is extremely intelligible, and her speechreading skills are astonishing. She is also a fluent signer, and on occasion, I observed her functioning as an interpreter between hearing and deaf persons. Although she did not learn any sign language while growing up (the IMAL's curriculum is strictly oral), María credits her interaction with a Peace Corps volunteer in 1979 and her attendance at the early meetings of what would become the deaf association for teaching her sign. She was one of the founding members of the association (registration card number 5), but later withdrew from active participation. She maintains contact with deaf friends, however, and appears occasionally at association activities where she participates fully. In reality, she is the only member of the over-forty category (as of 1997) capable of complete and easy communication with the rest of the sign-language-using members.

The Thirty-Year-Olds

Unlike the 6% of the membership represented by persons over forty years of age, the group of members born between 1958 and 1967 account for 24% of the registered membership. The majority of the founding members of the association were born in this period. (Eighty-four percent of those who signed the Certificación document were born 1959–1965). Many of them attended the Berríos school during the 1960s and 1970s, and it was this age cohort that formed half of the deaf students admitted to the new school, Centro Nacional de Educación Especial (CNEE), when it was founded in 1977. Likewise, this cohort contained a large number of the students who were sent on to be the first students at the COD, the vocational school for deaf and mentally retarded young adults, located in the section of Managua called Villa Libertad, when it was founded in 1981. Members in this age group appear to have learned sign language when they were teenagers or older, and generally belong to the group that Kegl and A. Senghas designated "first generation signers" (Kegl 1994; A. Senghas 1995). There are too many of them to describe individually.

The Twenty-Year-Olds

This is where the pyramid widens dramatically. Over one-half of the membership (55%) belongs to this age group. Only one or two of this group received any education at the old Berríos school, with first schooling at the new CNEE being usual. A large number of this group also went on to the COD until it was amalgamated with two other centers and ultimately privatized in 1992 (when enrollment of deaf students fell dramatically). The signing of this age cohort is qualitatively different (Kegl 1994; A. Senghas 1995), evidently because this group was introduced to sign language at a much younger age, some before six years of age. By the time this cohort reached late adolescence (seventeen to nineteen years), the deaf association was already formed, and most entered as regular, but not founding, members.

The Teenagers

The minimum age at which adolescents are encouraged to participate in association activities is approximately fifteen years. ANSNIC is an adult organization. Members are welcome to bring their children with them, and some elementary teachers of the deaf bring some of their students with them to celebrations so that the children are exposed to the sign language and adult signers; but children are generally not accepted as members. Forty-four youths belonged in this teenage category in 1997, although one-third of them had not applied for full membership in the association yet.[22] Most of the members in this group are no longer enrolled in the special education schools (which only offer an elementary school curriculum), and are either in vocational training courses or are staying at home. This group formed the bulk of the Wednesday morning literacy class. Many of these students were from outside of Managua. Thanks to a subsidy from the SDR, ANSNIC provided these students with roundtrip bus fare and a midday meal, which is what made the weekly trip possible for most of them. Some youths, in 1997, traveled to this class from as far as Jinotega (168 km. from the capital) and Rivas (about 120 km. from Managua).

The Future Association Members

In 1997, there were over 500 students ranging from four to twenty-four years enrolled in the eighteen special education schools throughout the republic of Nicaragua that have classrooms for the deaf and hard of hearing.[23] The deaf students are concentrated (e.g., 200 out of the approximately 500) in one school in Managua (built in 1977 as the National Special Education Center, it was renamed the Melania Morales Special

Literacy class at the headquarters of the National Association of the Deaf of Nicaragua in May 1994. Photo by Laura Polich.

Education Center in 1987 to honor a former teacher), and the older students at that school are very aware of the deaf association.[24] Some of those over fifteen years of age participate in association activities now, as do selected students from the Carazo (40–50 km. away), Nagarote (30 km. away), Rivas (120 km. away), and Matagalpa (130 km. away) areas.

Table 3. Deaf Association Membership by Age and Gender

Age Category	Total (N = 356)	Number of Males	Percentage of Males	Number of Females	Percentage of Females
Over 40	22	16	73%	6	27%
30–39	85	47	55%	38	41%
20–29	195	114	58%	81	41%
15–19	43	25	58%	18	41%
Unknown	10	6	60%	4	40%

Gender

Of the 356 members of ANSNIC whom I could verify from the membership list or through the hearing testing that I conducted, 58%, were male (209 of 356). This gender imbalance in the membership may stem from the slight predisposition that males seem to have for hearing loss over females, but is more likely due to the Nicaraguan social predisposition to encourage young males to explore the larger social environment and participate in activities and organizations outside of the home, while females are socialized to remain more within the confines of the home and to participate less in outside activities.[25] The gender imbalance remains across age in the membership (see table 3 on previous page).

Education and Transition to Adulthood 6

OVERALL, THE EDUCATIONAL achievement of all Nicaraguans is very poor. In 1995, the general population of Nicaragua over the age of twenty-five had an average of 3.8 years of schooling, and illiteracy was estimated at 35% in 1995 (IDB 1998). The average years of schooling for persons included in the sample of the Deaf Survey was 4.8 years. Literacy could not be tested, but my personal observations led me to believe that functional illiteracy is very high in the deaf community.[1] This observation is supported by the fact that the National Nicaraguan Association of the Deaf (ANSNIC) targets literacy improvement in the classes that it sponsors for members. Occupation and educational background are also commonly correlated, and this is true for the Nicaraguan deaf community also. Most of the members who are employed have jobs in the unskilled sector.

Twenty-six percent of the respondents to the Deaf Survey had never received any schooling, 8% had received one or two years, 35% had received from three to six years, while 25% had received from seven to twelve years. Five percent had more than twelve years of schooling, and less than 1% did not answer the question.

In 1997, the special education system consisted of twenty-two schools throughout the republic, which provided a curriculum adapted to mentally retarded, blind, or deaf learners. In this system, children are grouped in classrooms by disability and typically have an excellent teacher-to-student ratio averaging 1:10 nationally.[2] That same year, eighteen schools had at least one classroom for deaf or hard of hearing children, of which two were located on the Atlantic Coast (in Puerto Cabezas/Bilwí and Bluefields), and one was in the central western region (Juigalpa). Fourteen of the remaining schools were day schools, but a school in Ciudad Darío had a residential program serving approximately fifty deaf students each year.

123

The Boarding School at Ciudad Darío

The school is administered by the Roman Catholic Congregation of the Sisters of Saint Anne, which has its headquarters in Costa Rica. The school remains privately owned, but receives a national subsidy for teacher salaries and help with the children's room and board, and thus is required to follow the national curriculum set for special education students by the Ministry of Education (MED). Expenses not paid by the national subsidy (and it does not cover the residential costs for each student) are picked up by the congregation. The students themselves are not required to pay tuition or room and board, although they are required to provide their own clothing and school supplies.

At least five members of the adult deaf group that was gathering in 1997 in Estelí knew each other from their stays at the residential school for deaf children in Ciudad Darío (an hour by bus from Estelí), but it appears that they did not remain in contact after leaving the residential school, and, for some, their interaction with fellow classmates at the school had been superficial. This was especially true if they had not liked the school, evidently refusing not only to form affiliation with the school as an institution, but with anything or anyone that they identified with the school. They stated that it was long after they had left the school, through the invitations of a deaf shoe repairman to attend the gatherings at his house in 1996, that they had become reacquainted with their former classmates and begun to identify themselves as members of this small group.

Other Special Education Schools

Students in the special education day schools do not pay tuition (this is the nationwide policy for elementary education, extending to the sixth grade) although the parents are urged to "contribute voluntarily" to cover expenses such as materials and maintenance for the schools. At the largest special education school in Managua, the Centro de Educación Especial Melania Morales, the typical parental contribution of those who contribute is US$1 a month, although some contribute much more and some none at all.[3]

Since there is usually only one school in an area accepting special education students, transportation to the school is usually, although not uni-

Entrance to the Centro Nacional de Educación Especial Melania Morales in August 2003. Photo by Laura Polich.

versally, provided. For the city of Managua and its outlying suburbs, a conglomeration of 903,100 persons, comprising 25% of the country's 4,357,099-person population (INEC 1995), there is one special education school, which in 1997 had a total enrollment of about 700 pupils. Four large school buses set out in four different directions to pick up students, arriving back at 8 a.m. each morning filled to capacity. At noon, the buses are crammed again, each with over 100 children and teachers, as they repeat their routes dropping everyone off. Children from Tipitapa and Ciudad Sandino (at opposite ends of the capital) sit through the one-and-a-half-hour ride to the school in Barrio San Judas and the equally long ride on the return trip home.[4] The special education school in León had a school bus donated through a German sister-city program, but had to hold fundraising events to cover the cost of fuel and tires. In the smaller towns, students are dropped off at school by their parents or walk independently to school.

The vast majority of teachers working with deaf and hard of hearing children have "normal" teaching certificates, which means that they have completed nine years of education (six elementary grades and three years of *plan básico*) and a three-year teacher training course. For most of them, what they know about working with deaf and hearing-impaired children, they learned empirically—on the job.

In 2000, the Autonomous University of Nicaragua (UNAN) started a degree program in pedagogy with a major in special education. Like courses that some Nicaraguans received in the early 1980s at the Instituto Panameño de la Habilitación Especial (IPHE) in Panamá, this program consists of an overview of all areas of special education (mental retardation, deafness, blindness, motoric problems, etc.). The program includes one course dedicated specifically to the education of deaf children. The university graduated its first class with this major in 2003. The persons choosing to pursue a university degree with emphasis in special education are typically working as teachers during the day and pursuing their university degree in the evenings and on Saturdays. The additional credential allows them to rise on the pay scale and be in the pool of teachers vying for administrative positions. Still, no university training is required to teach elementary school, and until 2004, only elementary education was offered in the special education schools. In 2004, an experimental program was started in which some deaf students started their seventh-grade classes in a regular school, accompanied by sign language interpreters. The outcome of this program cannot yet be judged.

Though special education became a division of the MED in 1979, it is not compulsory in Nicaragua, and parents may choose or not to send their children to school as they wish.[5] The number of students enrolled in special education over the years hints at the serious educational shortfall which must be taking place, although it is difficult to point to many specific cases of children with disabilities who are being denied education by being kept at home or sent out to work. From 1982 to 1996, the total enrollment in special education (e.g., not just deaf, but children with mental retardation and visual impairments as well) oscillated between 0.25% and 0.47% of the total enrolled in primary education, or under 1% of the primary school population.[6] Children in classrooms for the hearing-impaired average only one-fourth of that population, or 0.06% to 0.11% of the children enrolled in elementary classrooms in Nicaragua.

Advanced Training

There are no deaf professionals in Nicaragua (e.g., someone practicing a profession requiring an advanced degree for admission, such as lawyers, doctors, or even certified teachers). In 1997 (nor up to 2003), I could find no deaf persons in Nicaragua who had graduated from a university program. There are a handful (I was able to make a list of approximately ten deaf persons) who have completed part or all of a high school course.

The educational system set up for deaf students in 1946 envisioned no more than six grades of academic education with vocational training to follow.[7] This same plan is in effect today, in that all the special education schools (except for the one experimental seventh-grade class started in 2004), which are now part of the public educational system, offer a curriculum of a possible (but not required) three years of preschool and six academic grades, which students may take anywhere from six to fifteen years to complete. It is expected that after completing the elementary education, children in the special education schools will progress to vocational training.

Up to 2004, there was no high school in Nicaragua that offered education beyond the sixth grade with accommodations for deaf or hearing-impaired students. That meant that there were no interpreters in the classes, no note-takers, no teachers with knowledge of deafness and the difficulties it presents to learning, and no special accommodations in regard to seating. Only students capable of excellent lipreading could hope to progress in this kind of atmosphere, and even those who did expressed how difficult it was. Parents and students have been quite vocal in their wish for more education, but the Ministry of Education has been hindered by lack of funds and capable teachers. In 2002, ANSNIC, teachers of deaf children, and parents of deaf children staged demonstrations outside the Ministry of Education's offices, which were covered by the local media. The Ministry agreed to work toward a full high school curriculum for deaf students. In 2004, a class of deaf students was located at a local secondary school with interpreters for the school's teachers! The year finished successfully, and the students will continue in 2005.

Vocational Education

With the closure of the one vocational school specialized for deaf and mentally retarded students (privatized in 1992 and closed in 1998 on charges of embezzlement), there are not many options for deaf youth. The Instituto Nacional de Adaptación Technológica (INATEC), which is responsible for vocational education for all Nicaraguans, usually opens a carpentry class for deaf students every few years, but because interpreters are not included and the instructors do not sign, most students drop out within a month or two.

The managers of the now-closed vocational center had complained that the deaf adolescents came to class with low literacy skills, and thus could not be accepted for the more "interesting" skills-training programs (such as computer training), but were only qualified to enter the most basic programs. (In 2002, however, through an international grant, a computer laboratory was set up at the elementary school, and some deaf students learned word processing.) Even when the former vocational school was functioning, the completion rate was very low. At the beginning of 1997, there was a workshop in carpentry, one in bicycle repair, one in baking, one in shoe assembly, and one in flower assembly that had deaf trainees. By the end of 1997, the deaf trainees in the bicycle repair, shoe assembly, and flower assembly workshops had all dropped out.

Prior to the center's closing, students complained that there was no communication with the teachers (most of whom did not bother to learn any sign language), that the classes were boring, or that they (the students) were being exploited. Students complained that while they were supposedly "learning" how to perform work in the assembly plants of the free trade zone (and thus, were not paid because it was a training period), the school's directors were selling the product to manufacturers and keeping the funds. Although the work took, at most, a week to learn, students were told that they had to spend at least six months "learning," and during this time, they had to pay for their own transportation to the center and meals. After the six-month training period, instead of receiving a letter of recommendation to a specific employer in the free trade zone, who, they had been told, had agreed to hire them, center officials simply told them to go to the free trade zone and apply for work as every other Nicaraguan did. But with the very high unemployment rate in Nicaragua, few deaf persons are hired from the hundreds of applications received weekly by these factories. Some, in fact, have a policy against hiring disabled workers. Thus, their six-month "training" turned out to be of little use.

In 1997, another institution, Centro de Capacitación Nicaraguense Alemán, which received financial assistance from Germany, initiated training workshops in cabinetry and automotive mechanics. The instructor in the cabinetry workshop learned some sign language, and seemed to be able to communicate adequately with his students, who in general, were making progress toward completion. In the automotive class, however, the instructor did not show any interest in learning any sign language to communicate with the trainees, preferring to rely on a hard of hearing trainee to translate. That trainee ultimately dropped out of the class because, as he told a teacher of deaf children with whom I was working, he did not want to be the translator, but rather wanted to learn to work on engines. Subsequently, the other trainees also stopped attending classes because they could not understand the instructor. By 1998, this program was also defunct.

The deaf association in Managua received a grant in the early 1990s from the Inter-American Foundation to build an addition to the meeting house, which would serve as a workshop to provide vocational training in industrial sewing, baking, and catering; however, it is unclear how regularly that training is provided and how training applicants are chosen. Traditional gender roles dominate in the deaf association as much as they do in the mainstream society, so training in these areas is directed more to the female membership, although some males are included. The association does run a business selling piñatas, which are made by both male and female deaf members. However, while this type of work is easily learned, it is not a marketable skill. For the male membership, the deaf association in Managua really has no vocational alternatives to offer.

Masaya is known as the handicrafts center of Nicaragua, and there are many small-family workshops in the area that produce traditional handmade items, which are sold in the markets of Masaya, mainly to the tourists. These items include woven hammocks, dolls, pottery, and wooden rocking chairs with caned seats and backs. The chapter of the deaf association in Masaya runs a workshop in which deaf youth are taught to weave the hammocks and do caning. These items are then sold, and the members receive a portion of the proceeds after the expenses of the association have been met (Meléndez 1999).

Other Training

The families of a few deaf persons have paid for their children to take art classes, but so far, as of 2003, only Roberto Cano Sanchez (who is not an active member of the deaf association, and who does not sign) has been able to sell his work on a regular basis. Another deaf man started a part-time job as an illustrator, but it is only for eight hours a week, and the remuneration paid only pocket money, not a full wage. At the instigation of various teachers, private individuals have trained groups of deaf youth to work painting pottery, doing leather work, or producing other *artesanía* (local handicrafts). One Managuan man, José Dolores Méndez, said that he supported himself making leather belts, which he sold in the marketplace.

Occupation

Nicaragua, overall, in 1997 had an estimated unemployment rate of 16% and an underemployment rate of 36% (CIA 1998). The gross domestic product for the whole country in 1997 was US$2,086,400,000,000. Per capita, this averaged out to US$479.70 (IDB 1998).

The members of the deaf community of Nicaragua are concentrated in the unskilled labor sector of the economy. The information obtained from the Deaf Survey indicated that 57% were working at the time of the survey, and 42% characterized themselves as "unemployed." Thus, while the country had an overall unemployment rate of approximately 13%, the surveyed deaf group had an unemployment rate of 42%. Of those who were employed, 30% stated that they worked a 40- to 60-hour week, 2% stated that they worked more than 60 hours per week, and 27% stated that they worked less than 40 hours a week, or in other words, held only part-time jobs. Forty-one percent did not respond to this question, mainly because although they considered themselves employed, the work was inconsistent (e.g., construction) or variable (e.g., when "helping," the work hours depend on the task to be done and are interspersed with other duties, so there is no definite work week). Thus, the country's underemployment rate in 1997 was approximately 36%, but for the surveyed deaf group it was 68%.

Income and Expenses

Income comparisons in Nicaragua are made through the annual computation of the "basic market basket," which is performed every August in a market survey done by the country's economic research institute, the International Foundation for the Economic Global Challenge (FIDEG), and published in reports in their monthly magazine the *Economic Observer.*[8] The basic market basket for 1997 was valued at 880 córdobas (US$88) a month (Renzi and Alaniz 1997). Members of a household with an income capable of buying more than two basic market baskets a month are classified as living "above the poverty line," the ability to buy two basic market baskets a month is classified as living "in poverty," and the ability to buy one or fewer basic market baskets is classified as living in "extreme poverty."Note that the calculation is for the household (usually defined as four persons: two adults, and two children), not individuals. If we hypothesize a typical household with two adults, each contributing a salary, then a salary of 440 córdobas (US$44) monthly from each contributor would be the minimal salary necessary to maintain the household in "extreme poverty." I shall characterize this as the minimum salary level necessary for financial independence.

For those who responded on the Deaf Survey that they were employed, incomes were reported over a very broad range. Fifty-three percent stated that they did not receive any income from their work. These are persons who are "in apprenticeship" (remember the youth of the community) or who "help" relatives with a money-making endeavor that provides income for the household, but does not provide individual salaries. Two percent stated that they were paid less than 100 córdobas/month, or US$10 (in November 1997, the exchange rate was 10 córdobas to US$1); 18% stated that they were paid between 100 and 400 córdobas/month (US$10–40); 12% claimed an income of 400–600 córdobas/month (US$40–60), 6% stated they received 600–1,000 córdobas/month (US$60–100); and 8% reported incomes of over 1,000 córdobas/month. The highest salary reported was 3,000 córdobas/month (by Miguel Angel Moreno, the member who belongs to the transportation cooperative), and the lowest was 0 córdobas/month. The median salary was 0 córdobas/month. (Of the 221 persons who provided responses to the question, 118 stated they received no regular income.)

Thus, of those reporting incomes, only 26% of the deaf respondents claimed wages that would characterize them as financially independent (e.g., over 400 córdobas a month, *assuming* they had a partner who contributed equally). Coincidentally, a person doing sewing in one of the assembly plants earns approximately 440 córdobas a month. And less than 14% of the respondents earned wages sufficient for them to be the sole wage earner and still maintain the household at the "extreme poverty" level (e.g., over 880 córdobas a month).

Questions about how the wages were spent turned out to be uninterpretable. Most of the respondents did not pay rent because they were living at home, and while they might contribute to the household's expenses, they had very unclear ideas of what the overall expenses of running a household were. For the respondents in Managua, transportation (bus fare) costs were an important expense, but in areas outside of Managua, respondents simply walked everywhere they needed to go.

The number of respondents receiving financial help or housing in addition to salary was very high. Only 11% stated that they did *not* receive any subsidy (provision of housing, food, clothing, electricity, water, or transportation help). Eighty-nine percent stated that they did receive some help, overwhelmingly from relatives. Typically, this help was in the form of a residence for which no rent was expected. When respondents lived at home, meals, electricity, and water expenses were included in the residence. When these respondents earned a salary, they would contribute a set amount (either a percentage or a given amount) to the head of the household, but the amount contributed often was only a nominal sum.

Employment of the Most Educated

Two of the approximately ten deaf persons I was able to locate, who had had education beyond the elementary level, are now employed as secretaries, interacting mainly with hearing persons, which makes great demands on their excellent lipreading skills. Only one of these participates occasionally in activities at the deaf association, but the other socializes regularly with deaf contemporaries in her home. Adrian Pérez finished a course as a dental technician in Spain, and was, for a period, employed in that field. His salary was so low (at first he was required to work without being paid to prove himself, but even after he was receiving a wage, it continued to be so low that he believed he was passed over for raises because he was deaf) that he chose to move to work in a warehouse. That wage never improved either, and when he was offered a position at the deaf association as a teacher of sign language and literacy skills in 1990, he gladly accepted. He, obviously, is fully integrated into the deaf community, as is the present president of the deaf association, who had attended classes in technical drawing and art, but is not presently employed in that area.

One man, who completed a portion of his studies at the National School of Fine Arts, began working part-time (eight hours a week) as an illustrator in 1997; but since then, he has been inconsistently employed. Another man, who spent most of his education "mainstreamed" in regular classrooms, was receiving training as a printer in his uncle's workshop. Neither of these two attended deaf activities in 1997, although one of them was listed as a member of the deaf association. One man, the son of two prominent teachers of deaf children, who was "mainstreamed" throughout his education, later acquired an office job with the national airlines; however, by 1997, he had emigrated from Nicaragua.

Steady Employment

Some deaf Nicaraguans have steady paying jobs, such as the older deaf man who is a member of the street repair crews of the city of Managua, as well as another who works at a soap factory, but these are unskilled jobs and pay very low wages. The man who is a member of a transportation cooperative has been previously mentioned. He regularly works on servicing the vehicles of the cooperative, and, at times, drives the route, which is an extra-urban route from a small town outside of Managua through various suburbs to a transportation node at the Israél Lewítes Market (also known as the Boer Market) in a southwestern portion of the capital.

Assembly Plant Workers

By far, the core of the members of the deaf community with steady employment are those who work at the assembly plants of the massive free trade zone on the extreme northeastern edge of Managua, which by the end of 1997 was composed of seventeen plants employing 12,000 people.[9] The majority of those so employed do sewing in the clothing factories, although there are also positions making gold chains in a jewelry assembly plant or assembling leather shoes in another plant. The wages are low, the hours are long, and the atmosphere is stress-laden. Most assembly plants operate on a piece-rate system, so whatever pressure the supervisors do not place on the workers, the workers assume for themselves in an attempt to raise, even if only a little, their very low wages. In 1997, sewing workers in the free trade zone assembly plants were paid an average of US$0.22 per hour (or approximately two córdobas per hour) for a forty-four hour week.

I was able to verify this rate because one Saturday afternoon (which is payday), the question of compensation came up in the course of free conversation at the deaf association. The question was asked: Do all plants in the free trade zone pay the same, or are there major differences? Various women produced their paystub for that week, and I calculated their per-hour wages. Others, men included, volunteered their paystubs for comparison, and by the end of the exercise, we had about twelve paystubs from the free trade zone to review. There was no significant difference between pay offered by the different plants. Out of curiosity, I asked how many deaf people were working at the assembly plants, and we began to make a list of who worked where. There were more than twenty-five working in five different plants. Twenty were doing sewing, while two were making chains, two were assembling artificial flowers, and one was assembling shoes. Periodically, over the next few months, I would ask about wages, and there was no change in rates during the time I was in Nicaragua.

This wage does not necessarily include transportation costs or midday meals. Only a miniscule portion of the workers at the free trade zone live close enough to walk to their jobs. Most must take at least one bus, if not two, to arrive. Bus fare one way in 1997 was US$0.15. Workers could spend, therefore, from one to three of the eight hours they were working simply paying for the bus fare to get to work. Some assembly plants provide a company bus. Many of the deaf workers told me they preferred the company bus because it was cheaper (evidently subsidized by the plant, but not free) and ride costs were deducted weekly from their pay (they didn't have to have change each day); also, because the company buses followed only one route, workers didn't have to change buses (and spend more on fares).

While working at the free trade zone provides the core of the steady jobs of the deaf community in Managua, it must be kept in perspective that deaf workers comprise only 0.2% of the labor force there. Most of the deaf workers are concentrated in two clothing assembly plants, and they noted that this was an advantage, since it gave them coworkers to chat with during the breaks.

A majority of the assembly plants have either an open or tacit policy against hiring "disabled" workers, but a spokesperson for the free trade zone stated that in the plants which had accepted deaf workers, the attitude was very positive toward hiring more deaf workers. There were few problems with the deaf workers wasting time in idle conversation because (as the deaf workers told me) they are carefully *not* placed next to each other. Any attempts at chatting by the deaf workers can be seen across the room, and thus, easily suppressed by the ever-vigilant supervisors. And in a piece-rate economy, chatting in sign language means diverting one's hands from work, and therefore, lowering one's output. Interaction between deaf and hearing coworkers seemed to consist of asking for more of a certain material or thread (by pointing to a sample), having one's output counted, and receiving the appropriate chits, which give one credit for the amount of output.

Many of the women of the deaf community had received training in sewing at the Centro Ocupacional para Discapacitados (COD), in Villa Libertad when they were younger, and some had been trained in the sewing workshop at the deaf association. The requirements for entry to a position at the free trade zone included the ability to operate industrial sewing machines and sergers, so some training before employment was imperative, and a knowledge of home sewing was not enough. Traditionally, sewing has been very much seen as an occupation for women, and the assembly plants at the free trade zone are overwhelmingly staffed by women. Some plants only accept women under the age of thirty. Given that the present government of Nicaragua has vowed to expand the present free trade zone and to open other such zones in other parts of the country, it is probable that assembly work will continue to provide an employment core for deaf people in Nicaragua.

Day Laborers

The men employed as day laborers usually work on construction projects. These workers are often referred to as *albañiles* or *ayudantes de albañile*, which might be translated as "masons" but the term does not cover the same semantic space as the English word. They might be expected to dig foundations, mix and pour concrete, construct walls of pre-formed concrete blocks, cover block walls with a cement finish, frame a roof and place the galvanized steel sheets (known as *zinc*) or roofing tiles, construct windows and glaze windows, build and hang doors, and so forth. The work is heavy and dirty, and lasts the length of a given project. Some deaf men are fortunate to work steadily as part of a regular crew (often because of family connections), with someone else in charge of finding and bidding jobs. Others work sporadically on jobs that relatives or friends refer to them.

These jobs usually pay a minimum wage. The highest monthly wage that I could find of a deaf man working on construction was US$100 per month (but compare that to the US$40 average wage in the sewing assembly plants). He was a regular member of a family crew and was also one of the very few deaf people who stated that he owned his own house. Average incomes for other men working as day laborers were impossible to calculate because of their sporadic nature. They might earn a reasonable income when working, but that must be averaged out over the period in which they are not working. And that is impossible to predict.

Maids

A few deaf women are employed as maids, but considering how common a source of employment this is in general for unskilled Nicaraguan women (Guerrero et al. 1993), the percentage of deaf maids is very low. The women I talked with who were maids had obtained their positions through the intercession of relatives, and had been in these positions for a long time. Likely, the difficulty in communicating with unfamiliar persons is the major deterrent to more deaf women being hired as maids. Deaf girls are certainly socialized to assume household chores as their given province, and many exhibited facility in cleaning and cooking at the deaf association.

Informal Employment

"Helping" relatives with their informal employment enterprises was, by far, the most common response for unskilled deaf Nicaraguans when they were asked how they supported themselves. One deaf woman, whose husband also works, helps her parents by serving customers in their small grocery store. In return, the profits from the dairy and ice cream sales are hers to keep. Other deaf people help with the baking of breads and tortillas, the products of which are sold door-to-door by another relative. Some did embroidery, knitting, or other handicrafts, which were sold by other relatives.

The Unemployed

There is also a group of deaf Nicaraguans who are not employed at all. They live with relatives, and thus have access to room and board, but beyond this are restricted to a gift of spending money from relatives or the earning of a small amount on occasion from some specific project. This group includes both men and women, but single mothers caring for one or more children are common in this category. When they can afford the bus fare, they come to the deaf association on weekends to socialize; but when they can't, they simply stay home.

Tipitapa and San Marcos

In 1997, a group of five to ten deaf persons, who otherwise do not have regular employment, was meeting regularly in Tipitapa, a town just outside of Managua, at the home of the most active member. They worked on crocheting and other handicraft projects, which they attempted to sell, but the market for such articles was (and remains) very poor because of fierce competition throughout the informal sector. Members of the San Marcos chapter of the deaf association are also taught to crochet and embroider, and the association works to sell finished products. The San Marcos chapter acquired a permanent locale in an old train station; and in 1997, they began to plant a vegetable garden on the premises, so that ultimately, the members would have access to the produce. The chapter was plagued by break-ins, though, and group projects languished. (By 2004, this chapter was defunct.)

Implication

One characteristic of an independent actor in society is the ability to be self-supporting, or contributing significantly to the upkeep of a household. This usually requires some schooling. Compared with the situation for deaf people fifty years ago, where hardly any deaf persons ever attained independent employment, the present deaf community is doing quite well: Seventy-five percent have had at least some schooling, and 26% receive a wage that gives them minimal financial independence.

But the outlook for the future is not bright. Educational achievement is low, illiteracy is high, and wages are low and in the unskilled sectors of the economy. The majority of the members of the present deaf community do not earn enough to support themselves independently, and they rely routinely upon (family) subsidies. Increasing the self-sufficiency of the members of the deaf community is a concern of anyone who works with deaf people in Nicaragua.

Marital Status

According to the Deaf Survey, 77% of the respondents classified themselves as single. The other 23% reported that they were married, cohabiting, or divorced. Twenty-eight percent of the single respondents stated that they had a girl- or boyfriend, and these were evenly divided between being a hearing boy- or girlfriend or a deaf boy- or girlfriend. Of those who were married or cohabiting, however, 84% stated that their spouse was deaf, while only 16% said that their spouse was hearing. Twenty-three percent stated that they had children, and all children were reported to be hearing. The ages of the children ranged from birth to fourteen years of age.

Residence

The Deaf Survey residence question indicated that 70% of the respondents lived at home (which was owned by the father or mother), while 9% stated that they lived with grandparents, 7% with sisters or brothers, and 3% with an aunt or uncle. Only 2% claimed to live in a house in which they themselves owned. (No one lived independently in a house they rented.) Six percent described various living arrangements in which they lived with friends or other non-relatives, but not independently.

The majority of respondents to the Deaf Survey live in their parents' homes, or in the case of the death of a parent, in the homes of sisters or brothers. It should be noted, though, that in Nicaragua, in general, it is extremely unusual for a person to live in a house or apartment alone. Until finding a domestic partner, most Nicaraguans take it for granted that they will live in the houses of their parents; but it is common for married or cohabiting couples to seek an independent residence. This seems to happen much less with deaf couples. Very few couples that included a deaf partner had independent residences. Upon settling down with a partner, most continued to live in their parents' houses, or they built a small house or an addition adjacent to their parents' homes. In the larger society, when

Table 4. Living Situations of Deaf Association Members

Age	Independent Housing	Independent Housing	No Financial Subsidy	No Financial Subsidy
15–19 years	5	10%	3	6%
20–29 years	7	5%	13	9%
30–39 years	4	12%	5	15%
40+ years	2	25%	3	37%

it becomes a burden for an aging parent to maintain a residence, it is typical for the parent to go live with a son or daughter, and thus, three-generational households are common. Deaf children, however, are more likely to remain in the family home, so that three-generational homes in the deaf community belong to the aging parent, rather than the son or daughter.

Age is significant here, of course. Younger persons in the general population are more likely to live with their parents, while older people in the mainstream are expected to establish independent living situations. In Nicaragua, it is a common expectation that children and young adults will continue to reside in their parents homes until they marry, at which time they are expected to establish an independent home. The majority of the members of the deaf association responded that they were single (a higher percentage than is true in the general population), and this will influence living arrangements too. Table 4 breaks down the listing "residence not in a close relative's house" and the category "not receiving financial subsidy" according to age. As can be seen in the table, the rates of "independent housing" and "no financial subsidy" increase with age, but the rates are still very low.

Social Class

Although social class was not a characteristic mentioned on the Deaf Survey, it is one that was apparent during the participant observation and interviewing. There is little social mobility within the deaf community because the vast majority of the members belong to the same economic class (lower) and have little potential for changing their financial position so as to enter a higher class. Except for one or two members, the community is homogeneous in terms of inherited wealth (none), present family incomes (generally low), and educational achievement (low).

I was told about various deaf persons who came from wealthier families, but I met very few of them. Most of them seemed to have left Nicaragua, either to be educated abroad, or to emigrate during the Sandinista period. I could only find about five in Nicaragua in 1997 who came from families of means. All of them had had extensive oral educations. One of the men, whom I characterized above as "assimilated," falls into this category. His signing skills are meager, and I believe that is the basic reason that he does not participate in the deaf association; but I also suspect that his upper-class upbringing also gives him very little in common with the majority of the members of the association. He was the only one of the respondents who mentioned having servants in the house. (When asked how many people lived in his home, he asked whether he should include the servants or not.) Likewise, one of the deaf secretaries comes from a wealthy, influential family. She has had disagreements with the leadership of the association, but I suspect that the fact that she comes from an affluent background is a greater impediment to her integration into the larger group.[10] I visited her at her mother's home where she lives. It is a very large, multistoried house with multiple patios on a large piece of land in a quiet suburb of Managua. It was a stark contrast to most of the houses of deaf persons that I saw, which were either simple one-story cinderblock houses with tile floors or basic timber structures with dirt floors.

The homogeneity of the present deaf community in economic terms probably has had a unifying effect. Coming from similar backgrounds gives members and potential members a common repertoire of experiences and common topics of interest. Importantly, where incomes are so low, there is little consumer competition or pressure to spend money in order to impress other members. Flashy clothes, cars, or gadgets are probably highly wished for, but are not evident in practice. Members can participate in deaf association activities without the need to spend a lot of money. This makes the activities maximally accessible to the greatest number.

Religious Affiliation

According to the Deaf Survey, 56% of the respondents claimed religious affiliation, while 44% denied practicing any religion. Of those who claimed a religious affiliation, 66% said that they were Roman Catholic, while 33% said that they were Evangelical Protestants (mainly members of the Assemblies of God). Of those who claimed religious affiliation, only 12% stated that the church they attended (the Assembly of God) provided an interpreter for deaf persons during religious services.

Although the majority of Nicaraguans are nominally Roman Catholic, and many deaf Nicaraguans give Catholicism as their official religious affiliation, the Catholic Church in 1997 did not appear to have any officially sponsored ministry for deaf persons. Since the late 1980s, interpreters for deaf persons have been allowed for church weddings and baptisms, but there isn't a single priest in the country who is even minimally competent in sign language, or who seeks to provide religious services adapted to the communication needs of deaf people. For the past three years, however, the archbishop's Sunday morning mass (which is shown weekly on national television) has been interpreted; the interpreter appears in a small circle at the corner of the TV screen. (Deaf members seem to be pleased with this addition, but they also state that the picture is so small that it is hard to understand.) I could find no deaf person who told me, now that the mass was interpreted, that watching the service on television or participating in person at the cathedral had become one of their Sunday routines. One of the interpreters told me that there may be one or two deaf persons at the mass, but she continued to interpret whether any deaf person was present or not in order to make the presence of sign language more familiar to typical Nicaraguans who might go to the mass or watch it on television. One deaf couple, who prefer to attend Catholic church services for the major ecclesiastical celebrations, rely on their seven-year-old hearing daughter to tell them what is happening and what the priest is saying. Some teachers of deaf children have assumed the task of teaching catechism so that young deaf children may make their first communion. During a first communion ceremony videotaped in 1997 in Ciudad Darío, one of the Sisters of St. Ann interpreted the whole ceremony so that the children could understand.

I called the Archbishop's office in Managua multiple times in 1997 to find out the Catholic Church's policy toward deaf people. The first time I called to ask what services were available for deaf persons, I was referred to a charity program that provided free food and clothing. I called back and was referred to a professor of theology (in this case a former priest who has been laicized) at the Catholic University of Nicaragua. When I explained to him that I wanted to know if the Roman Catholic Church in Nicaragua provided any kind of catechism classes for deaf people or adapted any of its services (mass, confessions, etc.) for use by deaf people, my question so stunned him that I thought, at first, that the telephone line had been disconnected. Ultimately, he admitted that he had no idea, and to his knowledge, there was nothing. (The interpreting of the one mass started three years later, at the insistence of the deaf association.) He could tell me, however, that in a survey conducted by the Catholic Church, 90% of Nicaraguans claim to be Roman Catholics, although a lesser number actually practice their religion regularly.

In 1995, a missionary couple from the United States, Matt and Eva Barlow, who are deaf and hearing, respectively, came to work with the Nicaraguan Assemblies of God in an outreach effort to the deaf community. They worked to learn Nicaraguan Sign Language (NSL) and began to invite deaf persons to a regular religious service in Managua, which Matt provided in sign language.[11] This couple was joined in 1997 by two women from Costa Rica and Nicaragua who had also learned NSL. The women provided interpreting and bible study instruction for a small group of approximately twenty deaf persons who gathered at one Managua church each Sunday. Matt and Eva started a school (on the edge of the capital on the road to León) that was originally intended only for adolescents, but which now accepts children of elementary school age. Religion is an integral part of the curriculum, and there is room in the building for some boarders. Unlike the Ministry of Special Education's schools, the teachers use Simultaneous Communication (matching signs to their spoken Spanish).

The Assemblies of God service that I observed in 1997 reserved the front three rows on the left-hand side of the church for deaf persons, and the regular service was interpreted into sign language by an interpreter who stood in front of those rows. After the sermon was interpreted, the group of deaf persons retired to a spot in the back of the church and a bible study class was given in NSL while the rest of the congregation continued with hymn singing and testimony.

The Jehovah's Witnesses have also targeted the deaf community for outreach, and they are careful to engage the services of an interpreter when they hold large rallies; but as of 1997, they did not have a regular meeting or service that was interpreted for deaf people. Various members of the group, however, attended sign language classes on Saturday mornings, evidently with the intention of proselytizing within the deaf community.

I interpret this high rate of ostensible religious affiliation as another instance of how deaf persons, even though cut off communicatively from so much information, are, in fact, acculturated into the majority culture. It is also a tribute to the desire of deaf people to be part of society. The majority of respondents claimed to be Roman Catholics even though there are only sporadic opportunities for them to understand any religious service or have any meaningful contact with religious personnel.

Social Preferences

Seventy percent of the respondents to the Deaf Survey stated that they were members of one of the chapters of ANSNIC. Thirty percent denied membership, but for most of these cases, that was because they lived in remote areas in which there was no deaf association chapter. Only 4% of the respondents stated that they belonged to some organization other than the deaf association, and in these cases, the organization was one in which identification of deaf children was a priority (usually it was the Association of Parents of Disabled Children [Los Pipitos]).

The final question on the Deaf Survey asked with whom the respondent preferred to spend leisure hours. Seventeen percent stated that they had more deaf than hearing friends (but that some of the friends were hearing), while 54% stated that they had no hearing friends, only deaf friends. Ten percent stated that they had more hearing friends than deaf friends (but some of the friends were deaf), while 10% reported that their friendships were evenly divided between deaf and hearing friends. One percent stated that they had only hearing friends, and sadly, 10% reported that they had no friends at all. Thus, 71% of the respondents described a deaf social circle, while 10% denied that they had any outside social contacts whatsoever. Only 11% reported that they socialized mainly in a hearing environment.

The interest in social participation is apparent in the answers to these questions. Most of the deaf persons interviewed were members of ANSNIC, and it usually was the only club or social organization to which they belonged. Likewise, 90% of the respondents described friends (usually deaf) whom they sought out for socialization.

A deaf community could definitely be identified in 1997, and it centered upon the deaf association: a place to meet and socialize with other deaf persons using a common linguistic system, NSL, which is prized by its members. Deaf adults have had some education, and many are employed. A significant number are either married or cohabiting, and own or manage an independent living space. These are persons who are active social members in an environment adapted to their non-oral needs. ANSNIC and its influences have provided great advances for deaf people in Nicaragua.

Adolescence, Language, and Community 7

DURING THE EARLY 1980s, Nicaraguan deaf people's behavior took a decidedly different path than it had in the previous thirty-five years. In 1979, Thomas Gibson found no deaf community in the country, but by 1986, there was a formal organization of deaf adults. Something was available during this time lapse that was not available earlier. Conversations consisting of home signs, gestures, and mouthed words must have occurred among peers, and between children and teachers, for a long time at the Apolonio Berríos Special Education School. Olga Tenorio, a teacher there from 1948 to 1976, said clearly that the students had used their hands to communicate outside of class, commenting that "it was impossible to stop them. And among themselves, they got a lot of information across."

All of her former pupils remember Soledad de Flores with fondness, and they comment spontaneously that she was a good person, so her students probably *did* want and did try to communicate with her in the same way at the Berríos school. The conversations with Soledad were probably not that different from the conversations Morena observed when former students visited Rúthy. While no community or communal language seems to have developed in the 1950s, 1960s, or 1970s, things changed for the better in the 1980s. We have to carefully compare these two periods to determine how such differing results could occur.

Nothing much changed from 1946 to 1992 in the lives of deaf children in the age range typical for elementary school in Nicaragua. Educational practices remained stable, although more special education schools were added in outlying parts of the country. The number of deaf students who were brought together daily at the special education school in Managua increased during this period from about 10 to about 200, and deaf children still were educated in schools that also contained students with mental retardation (who always outnumbered the students with deafness) or blindness.

In the late 1970s and early 1980s, however, enormous changes occurred in the lives of deaf adolescents. Many began spending more time with other deaf children on a regular basis and were required to remain in the educational system for more years. A vocational school was established that encouraged them to be independent and assume adult roles (like employment). This kept adolescents and young adults together at a time when they were carving out their identities and craving a peer group in which to try out and enact their abilities to be social actors. Additionally, a regular meeting time outside of school fostered a sense of communality, and provided a group to which to belong.

In other words, increased opportunities for adolescents and young adults was what made the 1980s different from the 1950s. Based on the Nicaraguan example, I hypothesize that adolescents and young adults, then, appear to play important roles in the formation of deaf communities and their sign languages.

We know that Berríos school students would stop attending classes when they turned fifteen, but we have no way of knowing what percentage actually followed this practice.[1] We know that some exceptions were made: While Salvador López left school when he turned fifteen, Noel Rocha was nineteen when he left. (This age policy was not made especially for the students at the special education school. From 1946 to 1992, most Nicaraguans only expected to obtain an elementary education and then leave school to work at approximately age fourteen or fifteen.) Yet, when the deaf pupils were transferred to the new school in 1977, nearly half of them were fifteen to nineteen years old. And in 1981, a training school was opened to accommodate students fifteen to twenty-five years of age. Clearly, deaf youth were encouraged to spend more years in school, and that allowed them further socialization opportunities just at the point that parents were likely to allow them to ride the buses independently, and where seeking out school friends at their homes was possible and important to them.

In 1981, the vocational workshops were moved from the elementary school to the new site in Villa Libertad, and a radically different method of learning reigned there. Everything emphasized employability. Arriving independently, on time, every day, was part of the curriculum. Classes had didactic portions, but most of the work was hands-on practice, a method that allowed a good amount of banter and dialogue throughout the day. Classes were held during traditional work hours, rather than only in the morning hours (which had been the practice for the elementary school from 1974 to 1980). This kept the adolescents and young adults in contact longer. And they were expected to find their own way home, rather than being delivered by a bus. This new schedule kept the students together longer and held them to more adult-like behavior.

There were more socialization possibilities outside of school also. There is no evidence of significant contact among deaf pupils outside of school hours during the 1950s, 1960s, and early 1970s (and note, no evidence of the development of a sign language either). About the time that Rúthy Durán entered the picture, parties and social gatherings began to be routine. The athletic teams and the folklore group brought students together outside of classes, and the athletic trips gave them prolonged periods of peer interaction. The opening of the Vocational Center for the Disabled (COD) in 1981 seemed to encourage even more contact (visiting each other at home, or making plans for activities in small groups), and the scheduling of regular meetings at Gloria Minero or Rúthy Durán's houses starting in late 1983 was mentioned by nearly every older deaf person interviewed as having been a crucial source of socialization. By 1986, when the small group voted to organize a deaf association, out-of-school contact among the young deaf adults was common.

The heterogeneous system of communication adopted in 1981 at the COD was an early fusion point in which the typical gestures of Nicaraguan oral conversation were combined with

• the various systems of home signs that students brought with them
• the shared home sign pool and signs invented at the Berríos school and at the National Center for Special Education (CNEE)
• and occasional Spanish, Costa Rican, and American signs picked up from dictionaries, courses at Programa Regional de Recursos para la Sordera (Regional Resource Program on Deafness) (PROGRESO), or from Mayra or Adrián.

All of these components were melded into a language in common use at the COD in 1986, the first year that Dr. Judy Kegl began her study of Nicaraguan Sign Language (NSL).

Linguistic evidence available to us implies that the group that clusters around the 1962 rubella cohort is the first generation of signers in Nicaragua, and that the sign language emerged only in their lifetime.[2] Most members of this cohort, and some members born earlier, are available to interview today in Nicaragua, and they have said that although they used gestural forms to communicate among themselves when they went to school, the sign language which they now use as their preferred mode of communication did not develop until they were young adults. These same persons, whose birth dates cluster around the 1962 cohort, happen to be the founding members of the National Nicaraguan Association of the Deaf (ANSNIC). If we look at the first fifty registration cards issued by the Association to Help and Integrate the Deaf (APRIAS), 8% belong to members born in 1953–1958, while 62% were born in 1959–1965, and 26% were born in 1966–1973.[3] Likewise, the certificación document, one of the first required documents to be presented when applying for formal status as an organization, was signed on December 21, 1987. Eighty-four percent of the signatures (twenty-seven out of thirty-two) belong to deaf persons born in the 1959–1965 period, with only 12% (four out of thirty-two) belonging to those born before 1959. I do not believe this linkage is coincidental.

What is striking about the Nicaraguan case is that as adolescents and young adults remained longer in the educational system and began to increase their out-of-school contact, the communal use of sign language also increased. Something about being at an age when participation as an independent social actor is important appears to interact with the formation of a group whose identity is based upon deafness, and both of these interact with the need for a communal sign language. All three elements seem to be needed, and they do not appear to arise one at a time, but as a "fuzzy" system that develops together.

The age distribution of the members of the deaf association also gives us indirect evidence that language and group membership are linked. ANSNIC's age distribution does not mirror that of the general Nicaraguan population. (Although half of the general population of the country is under the age of fifteen, and life expectancy is lower than in other countries, Nicaragua does have its fair share of middle-aged and old members.) But, in 1997, the deaf association had very few members in their forties

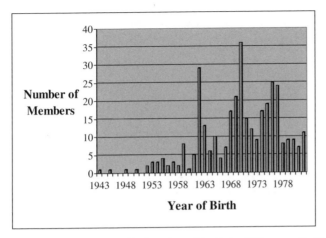

Figure 3. Graph of birthdates (1943–1980) of members of the National Nicaraguan Deaf Association (*N* = 321).

or older, more in their thirties, many in their twenties, and a large number now in their teens.[4] What accounts for this skewing? Figure 3 is not even across all years. There are decided peaks that probably represent cyclical rubella epidemics.[5]

Note the peaks for 1962, 1970, and 1976–1977. Not all of the members born in these years are deaf due to rubella, but, because other common causes of deafness (e.g., heredity or meningitis) occur at a constant, not cyclical, rate over time, we can conclude that the variation obvious in the graph reflects the long-term effects of recurring rubella epidemics. The graph is striking in that the first upswing in 1959 leads to the 1962 peak. There is no reason to believe that rubella cycles only began in Nicaragua in the late 1950s. But where is the peak that would have been expected in 1956? Or the one that should be there in 1950? Or those that should have been exhibited in the 1940s or 1930s?

One explanation given to me for this sudden occurrence of deaf people born around 1959, with nearly none born before that year, was that previously all disabilities in children were very stigmatized. Parents simply did not bring deaf children out into the light of day to be seen as members of society if they were disabled in any way. (This is the "Eternal Child" model.) Such children were kept at home and either treated well with their own private nurse or mistreated horribly by being chained in a back room, depending on individual circumstances. Thus, the deaf persons who would now be in their seventies and sixties and fifties were kept at home and never allowed to become part of society, and that is where they are today. But, here, ANSNIC figures by themselves are simply not enough.

Looking for a parallel group in Nicaraguan society, I went to the blind association. Blind persons were just as stigmatized as deaf persons. Like deaf children, blind children were also seen as a punishment for their parents' sins. They were kept at home and not educated. The first school to accept blind children was also the same school, set up in 1946, to first accept deaf children. Thus, if being kept at home, not socialized to the larger society, or not allowed to go out was what was keeping older deaf adults out of the deaf association, then we should see this same pattern in the membership list of the blind association. But what is striking is the number of persons in their seventies, sixties, fifties, and forties who attend blind association activities along with the younger members that are listed (table 5). The blind association has elders! And the deaf association simply does not. I hypothesize that language is the cause of this discrepancy.

Consider the case of a blind person, male or female, who hypothetically spent the first sixty years of her or his life shut up at home, not allowed to go to school, not allowed to go out on the streets, not allowed to work, but kept at home being a member of society only through the stories overhead from other family members. Finally, in 1989, the first organization specifically for blind people, the Marisela Toledo Association for the Blind, is founded, and a friend or a relative offers to take this pre-

Table 5. Comparison of Membership by Birth Years for Blind Association and Deaf Association.

Birth Years for Members	Marisela Toledo Association for the Blind: Managua Chapter only (N=253)*		National Nicaraguan Association for the Deaf: Membership list (N=315)	
	Males***	Females	Males	Females
1966–1979	60	36	127	95
1936–1965**	89	29	57	36
before 1935	29	10	0	0

*The count for the Managua chapter was made by the Marisela Toledo Association for the Blind in May 1995.
**The earliest birth year for the deaf association is 1943.
***Note the predominance of male members over female members in all categories, a characteristic also true of the deaf association (cf. chapter 3).

viously isolated person there. That person arrives and finds a group of people with similar stories, sits down to chat and share, and, if offered the chance, probably is happy to fulfill the membership requirements to become a part of the group.

Now consider a hypothetical deaf contemporary of sixty years of age who has also spent her or his whole life at home. Overhearing stories is not in that person's repertoire. She or he has probably managed to arrange a common code for basic functions with one or two family members, but I have yet to find a hearing family of a deaf person who has evolved a family code that could talk in depth about abstract concepts or displaced events, such as those in the past or the future. The language skills of a sixty-year-old deaf person who has never received any schooling, and has lived at home all his or her life, are rudimentary. Even if, in 1986, when APRIAS, the first organized group of deaf persons, was organized, a relative or friend offered to take that person to the deaf association, the isolated deaf person's ability to enter that group and communicate would have been nearly nil.[6] One certainly *can* learn language beyond the critical period for language learning, which is agreed to taper off around puberty, but it becomes harder and harder to do so. And when there has not been a fully functioning first language by some time in the twenties or thirties, it is only the rarest of individuals who manages to learn one later. Thus, if older deaf Managuans, who I am certain do exist, although I was able to find only very few of them, had arrived at ANSNIC meetings without language, they would not have been able to communicate and would have had little reason to continue visiting the association, and even less reason to sign up. In that case, the membership rolls of the deaf association would have a decided scarcity of older members, exactly the situation encountered.

Or consider an alternative hypothesis. What if there *were* a sign language that *did* form among the schoolmates of the 1950s, 1960s and early 1970s, but it wasn't *passed down* to the generation of those who are now in their thirties? What if we hypothesize the existence of a *different* sign language than that which is used now? Perhaps that could explain the lack of older people in the membership rolls, because if deaf people went to the deaf association and didn't understand the newer sign language, they may not have joined.

But note again that there *is* no other organization for deaf persons in Nicaragua. Yes, there are private homes where deaf people meet, but as much as I searched, I never found any clue of someone older who wasn't already on the membership rolls who went to those homes to socialize. I was also told by Noel Rocha, born in 1953, that a few "older" deaf persons in Managua (i.e., older than he is) occasionally met in a specific corner of a downtown park, but he said that the meetings were not regular (i.e., he couldn't tell me when I should go in order to find them). He denied vigorously that any of those persons used a standardized sign language, saying that the communication at those meetings was by gesture or fingerspelling of Spanish words (using the two-handed alphabet which was used at the Berríos school). If older deaf people did come out of their homes and participate in private socializing, they would certainly be known (especially to the older members of the present deaf association that we sought out), because their ages would cause them to stand out.

So, because there is *no other place* to go, even if these older people had arrived at ANSNIC with a different sign language—that is, with a linguistic base—they would have everything to gain by learning the new sign language and nothing to lose. So a little effort put into learning a second language would open up the *only* organization that presently exists in Managua for deaf persons. And *not* learning the new sign language would mean that unique opportunity would be closed to them.

Anyone who has observed the elation that two signers experience when, each having been mired in a hearing world, meet up, and are able, even if only for a while, to communicate freely with their hands, would not doubt that any older deaf person who had the capability to learn the new sign language would not have hesitated to do so. Furthermore, the members of the present deaf association are extremely adept at cross-communicating with signers of other sign languages. They have received signing visitors from the United States, Canada, Sweden, Germany, Japan, and many other places, and there has always been a sense of camaraderie even if not everything is immediately understood. Both sides adapt.

The present deaf association regrets its lack of elders. In multiple conversations from 1997 to 2002 association president Javier López Gómez stressed that then-current association members had no role models to follow. If there had been older deaf people who had used a different sign language, and who attended association activities, they would have been welcomed, and ultimately linguistic differences would have been overcome.

With one exception, the oldest fluent signers in 1997 were thirty-four to thirty-eight years old. The one exception was María Lourdes Palacios, a forty-three-year-old woman. But she was a secretary at the CNEE and later at the COD also. She says she did not know sign language as a child, but she remained in contact with the students who had been in the oldest class in 1977, and she participated as one of the founding members of the association (registration card number 5). It was through that contact that she probably learned the sign language.

Of the twenty-four registered members born before 1959, Yolanda Mendieta and I were able to locate twelve, and María Lourdes was the only one who signed fluently. Two of the pre-1959 group are hard of hearing and prefer to identify with the hearing community. Five communicate only through gesture and fingerspelling or writing of Spanish words. Four (all men) occasionally come to the deaf association for activities, but they sign with great difficulty and must often supplement their meanings with writing or fingerspelling in Spanish. No one could tell us about the whereabouts of the other twelve older members.

Beyond the linkage between language and community provided by the membership figures at ANSNIC, it has simply been impossible to find any evidence of an older, standardized NSL or the use of any standardized sign language before the 1980s. (Home signs appear always to have been present, but a standardized language goes beyond the level of home sign.) One hypothesis that has been articulated in the literature is that there was no sign language or community before the early 1980s in Nicaragua because there were no schools, and it was only after the revolution that education for deaf children was available.[7] The lack of proximity was responsible for the lack of a language.

But there *was* education for deaf children before the revolution. Among other facts, the special education school used in 1980 was built in 1977 and probably opened with fifty deaf students at least two years before the revolution. Education for deaf people has been available in Nicaragua since 1946, when the first special education school opened with ten deaf pupils. By 1952, at least, the number had increased because Soledad Escobar de Flores, who taught the deaf class for twenty-two years, remembered that her class usually averaged eighteen or so throughout her tenure at the school. In 1975, it is certain that there were at least twenty-five deaf pupils divided into two classes. If just bringing previously isolated deaf children together in a school is sufficient to produce a sign language, we really must ask why a sign language did not develop forty years earlier. The children's pooling of home signs, and then grammaticization of the result into a language, should have begun in the late 1940s and continued through the 1950s, 1960s, and 1970s. When the school was first opened, as Dr. Berríos's sister, María, points out, it targeted children in the ten- to fifteen-year range. Over time, younger children were admitted (e.g., María Lourdes Palacios was six years old when she attended in 1960), and by the 1970s, entrance at five or six years of age was not unusual (e.g., Mauricio Zepeda, Douglas Vega, Julio César García, etc.).[8] Also, by the 1970s, some pupils (Miguel Ángel Moreno or Noel Rocha) were remaining past the original upper-age limit. In 1976, pupils fifteen and over were common. The age range widened, but the school did not close (even after the 1972 earthquake).

So there was never a point where one class graduated and a whole fresh group of deaf students started over. The "chain of transmission" has been unbroken from 1946 to the present. But there is no evidence of a sign language developing among students in the old school. We have interviewed nineteen deaf adults who attended the Berríos school and asked each of them what the sign language was like at the old school. Their replies have always been the same: "There was none. We just used gestures and mouthing of Spanish words and writing. The sign language didn't come until the meetings at Gloria's house started [1983–1989]."[9]

The hypothesis (that simply bringing young deaf, previously isolated children together will produce an eruption of a language) also shows some limitations when other groupings of deaf children in Nicaragua are considered. At least twenty-four previously isolated, young deaf children were brought together in 1975 at the special education school that Jilma de Herdocia founded in Nicaragua's second-largest city, León. Rúthy Durán and María Teresa Castillo, both recent graduates of the Instituto Panameño de la Habilitación Especial's (IPHE's) deaf education training, taught four hours in the morning in Managua at the Berríos school and then took the bus to León, where they taught for three hours in the afternoon, and then returned home to Managua. (They both say it was a rather grueling routine that year, which was not repeated in 1976.) The León children were together about three years before the Sandinista Revolution interrupted classes (versus only two years together in the new school in Managua before the revolution), and their post-revolutionary classes started again at the same time as those in Managua. No sign language has been reported as a result of bringing those children together.[10] There are also no reports of spontaneous languages developing in Chinandega (which typically has had three classrooms for deaf students—around twenty to thirty students each year), nor at the boarding school at Ciudad Darío (which has had a constant enrollment of approximately fifty deaf students, living together all day long as boarding students, from 1982 to the present). Simply placing deaf children together in one spot does not seem adequate for the formation of a sign language. Furthermore, if proximity was all that was necessary, we would have expected multiple sign languages to develop in Nicaragua, because all of these groupings of children were isolated from each other as well.

Numbers also seem to be important to the process: A language is not generated among children until there is a "critical mass" (so far undefined). All researchers (and all Nicaraguan deaf people, for that matter) agree that the sign language developed first in Managua, so let us consider the Managua pupil counts from 1946 to the present. The first special education school (the Berríos school) started with ten students, and within a few years, that number increased to twenty (and possibly spiked to twenty-five pupils at some points).[11] In 1975, the deaf class was divided into a younger group and an older group, so that there were twenty-four to twenty-five deaf students for two years before the school closed. All twenty-five transferred to the new school in 1977, and another twenty-four previously uneducated students were added to the mix, making a total of, at least, forty-nine children at the new school in 1977 divided among four classrooms. Before the revolution, one more class appears to have been added, so that in 1979, there were approximately fifty-seven to sixty-one deaf students. In late 1980, after Popova and other members of the technical team finished their training courses, the school opened with ten classrooms for deaf children, each with approximately twelve students, so the total enrollment of deaf children climbed to 120. From 1981 to 1984, teacher positions were added, so that by 1984, total enrollment of deaf children in the school was approximately 200. That total enrollment remained constant until 1997. In the past five years, class sizes have increased (but no new teacher positions have been added), so that by 2003, the total of the deaf population at the school was 251.

The sign language did not develop at the Berríos school, so evidently twenty children do not constitute a critical mass. If, as other authors suggest, the sign language first developed in 1977, then fifty *would* be a critical mass. Why, then, did the fifty students brought together from 1982 at Ciudad Darío not spontaneously produce a sign language also? The Ciudad Darío students would have had "critical mass," and in fact, had the advantage of spending all their waking hours together because they were boarders, so they had even more intense interaction than the students at CNEE in 1977. But no one reports an emergence of a sign language at Ciudad Darío, and we have no older signers who use that language. When asked directly, former teachers and previous students deny such a claim.

Another hypothesis is that it was not the number "50" in 1977 that was sufficient, but the 120 when the number of classrooms for deaf children was doubled in 1980. This does provide a larger critical mass and many more possible conversation partners; it, too, is unlikely. Remember that the Ministry of Education took over the school in 1979–1980 and the National Welfare Institute (INSSBI) planned to place the older students in the COD, but the building was not ready in 1980. Thus, the twenty-five students in the oldest class no longer attended academic classes in the morning, but they did continue to come to the workshops at the CNEE to learn vocational skills. According to Nora Gordon (who taught a class of deaf preschoolers during the 1980 school year), they came, however, in the afternoon, when the younger children had already left.

The cohort centered on the 1962 rubella epidemic is universally acknowledged as the first users of sign language in Nicaragua. They did not attend class at the same time that the increased enrollment of 120 was on the school grounds. In 1980, they attended class when the younger children were not at the school; by 1981, the members of the cohort had all been transferred to the COD, which was located on the other side of the city from the special education school, and where deaf students only totaled fifty-five.

So what changed between 1946 and 1986 that encouraged both the language and community to blossom? Some authors have hypothesized that the 1979 revolution brought a change of educational philosophy, an opening and freeing of previous strictures that allowed deaf children the freedom to sign with each other, something that had not been possible before because severely oral teachers had previously punished any use of sign language.

The revolutionary Sandinista government certainly did espouse universal literacy and did increase the number of schools with classrooms for deaf children. (But, most of the new classrooms for deaf children were built in the "countryside," where deaf education had previously not been provided, and the numbers of deaf pupils in these countryside schools were small.) After talking with many teachers, administrators, and deaf persons who went through the schools, I concluded, however, that the situation for deaf education after the revolution was not one of openness, but actually the reverse: The pre-revolutionary schools in Managua were much more eclectic and open to sign language than the post-revolutionary schools for deaf children, which were severely, adamantly, and dogmatically oral.

The first source for deaf education had come from Dr. Centeno Güell, who was influenced by Spanish oral teaching; but the first special education school also received technical assistance and advice from Argentina, pre-revolutionary Cuba, Mexico, Honduras, and the United States. Other than the directive to teach the children to speak, a teacher of deaf children, up to 1980, could use any method possible that might further that goal. Soledad Escobar de Flores said that, in 1952, Dr. Berríos essentially introduced her to her deaf class, and then left, leaving the education of the pupils up to her. María Teresa Castillo and Rúthy Durán had the advantage of studying deaf education in Panama, but they state they were free to use any method they chose in the Berríos school. Likewise, in the new CNEE, teachers were encouraged to be creative. There was an evaluation of the school in 1979 done by Carmen Ortíz (originally from Puerto Rico) as a representative of the Bank Street School in New York. She gave inservices during her stay in Nicaragua, encouraging the teachers to use all modalities and methods; and she sent a large selection of academic games after she left. The rumors drifting in from Costa Rica on the Total Communication methodology were met with interest. Some representatives from Nicaragua attended a workshop in

Costa Rica; and later, at least one workshop on the topic appears to have been held in Nicaragua.

According to Luz María Sequeira, who was the vice principal of the new special education school in Managua in 1977, (and who went to a Total Communication workshop in Costa Rica) use of sign language (along with oral speech, of course) was quite acceptable: "We weren't against signing. In fact, we found the kids blossomed a lot when they were allowed to use their hands. We didn't want to stop that." The school *must* have been open to signing because they requested a volunteer for two years from the Peace Corps to instruct the teachers in the Total Communication method. Thomas Gibson knew from the time that he accepted his assignment (in other words, before he had started his language training) that he would be working with teachers of deaf children at a special education school.

The picture changed significantly after the insurgent forces overthrew the Somoza dictatorship on July 19, 1979, and recreated the whole educational system in Nicaragua. Jilma de Herdocia became director of special education, and she appointed Natalia Popova to be the coordinator for deaf education. Popova was trained in strict Soviet oral methods, and she did not leave anything up to chance. The curriculum was rewritten, and the teachers were required to use the same methodology: Comunicación Verbal (Verbal Communication). In the 1980 workshops, Popova delineated in a step-by-step fashion the following: the classes that were to be taught, the concepts that were to be introduced, the order in which topics would be introduced, and the accompanying vocabulary words.[12] Popova did not tolerate any deviations from her methodology. The teachers of deaf children either used her Verbal Communication method exactly as they were taught, or they didn't continue as teachers of deaf children. The Verbal Communication method had no place for sign language, or even gesture. In fact, signing of any sort, whether with or without speech, was considered a hindrance to oral language learning, and teachers were prohibited from using it at any time or any place (in other words, also during recess).

If bringing deaf children together from 1946 to 1979, when sign language was tolerated (and even encouraged after 1978), did not facilitate the emergence of a sign language, it is hard to understand why a language would suddenly emerge among the students at the school precisely at the moment that sign language was declared taboo. Popova may have been unable to influence anyone on the playgrounds during recess, but during instructional hours, she made sure sign language was not allowed. For four-and-a-half years (1980–1985), while Popova was coordinator of deaf education, sign language was a dirty word. Only when she left could the possibility of sign language be introduced into the discussion of educational methods, and it was not until 1992 that teachers were allowed to use sign language in the classroom if they wished. I am aware that instructional method is typically irrelevant to language usage among deaf children outside of the classroom; however, it is still problematical as to why sign language would not appear when it would have been tolerated, but *did* appear at the same time that it was banished as a possible teaching tool.

When interviewing the older members of the present deaf community, there is a striking linguistic chasm between those born before 1959 and those born in the 1959–1966 period.[13] One difference between these groups is that the older ones were not at the Berríos school after the 1972 earthquake, while most of the younger ones did continue their schooling.[14] And all thirteen who were enrolled in the older class in 1975–1976 (and who were all transferred to the CNEE in 1977) are considered founding members of the deaf association. In other words, they were at the Berríos school during at least some of their "linguistically sensitive" years, which is the age at which we would most expect them to invent a visual language system to which they had full access when nothing else but the oral language was available from teachers.[15]

The linguistic divide is noticeable for Salvador López, Miguel Ángel Moreno, and Noel Rocha, all born in the 1940s and 1950s, and who left the Berríos school before 1973. (Salvador left in 1963, while Miguel Ángel and Noel did not return to the Berríos school after the 1972 earthquake.) All three cannot be counted as fluid users of sign language. Multiple means (gestures, fingerspelling, writing, and some signing) are necessary to interview them, and there are questions (abstract) that they simply cannot understand. If there were some form of language developed in the 1973–1976 period, then they missed it.

Moreover, Noel attended school from the ages of nine to nineteen, Miguel Ángel from seven to nineteen, and Salvador from ten to fifteen. Thus, all three were at the Berríos school during at least a portion of their linguistically sensitive periods, and were interacting with other deaf children who ranged from ages seven to fourteen. If simply bringing deaf children together during their linguistically critical years is enough for a language to form, then why do Salvador, Noel, and Miguel Ángel not exhibit a secure grasp of sign language now? Why, when they are asked directly if they use sign language, do they all reply in the negative? Noel states openly that he is somewhat envious of the generation of his friend, Mauricio Zepeda (a member of the 1962 cohort), who, according to Noel, "can say anything they want in the language, not like me for whom signing is very hard."

Was there perhaps some linguistic ferment, the beginning of a sign language occurring between 1973 and 1976 that the transfer pupils carried with them to the new school? If that were the case, it should have been evident to Adrián Pérez when he visited from Spain in 1976, and it should have been noticed by Thomas Gibson in 1979.

When interviewed in 2002, Adrián was definite that Rúthy's pupils did not use a sign language at that time, and as far as he knew, it was the only group of deaf persons who socialized in Managua. If there had been a deaf community in 1976, it seems most likely that the adolescents to whom Rúthy Durán introduced Adrián (her pupils at the Berríos school) would have known about its existence and, at least, *told* Adrián about it. Rúthy's pupils at that point ranged from thirteen to seventeen years of age, and they maintained ties with Noel Rocha, who was twenty-two and working.

Noel is a sociable person, which is evidenced by the fact that he had regular communication with Douglas Vega (until Douglas left in 1986), and still keeps up with (at least) Javier López Gómez, Mauricio Zepeda, and Josefa Gutiérrez. Noel is also very independent and has a curiosity about new information. He persuaded Douglas Vega to travel with him to Honduras and Guatemala in the early 1980s, and he says they made contacts with deaf persons in those countries.[16] If there had been a deaf adult group anywhere in Nicaragua, especially in Managua, Noel would have known about it, and would have had no reason not to tell his younger friends about it; and they, in turn, would have had no reason to keep that information from Adrián.

If the adolescent group had known about any larger group meetings of deaf persons, it is also most likely that they would have *taken* Adrián to one of the meetings during his three-month stay. There was plenty of time to find out about an upcoming deaf community event and invite Adrián along, or to communicate to any deaf community that Adrián was in town and to present him to the group, or at least to some group members. And if there had been any deaf community, it is most likely that they would have *wanted* to meet Adrián, and thus, gone out of their way to invite him. (Adrián was certain in his interview that he met no other deaf people besides Rúthy's pupils during the 1976 vacation.) Remember that Adrián in 1976 was not just any old deaf adolescent, he was receiving an education in Europe on scholarship. (In my research, I have come across less than ten deaf scholarship recipients for the period 1946–1997. Getting scholarships and going away to study is not routine for deaf people in Nicaragua.) Adrián, thus, was an unusual and exotic visitor who could potentially share a lot of information not easily available to any Nicaraguan deaf group in 1976.

If there had been any such group, it would have been small, had few resources, and been almost secretive in its dealings, because absolutely no one, deaf or hearing, remembers it today. However, if it had existed and heard about Adrián's presence, it would surely have made some kind of contact with him. As the common Nicaraguan saying goes, a deaf community (a regular gathering of deaf adults in Managua) "gleams by its absence."[17] Thus, I am forced to conclude that there probably was no adult deaf group, or a sign language either, in 1976. Gibson in 1976 also found no deaf community nor a sign language.

Julio César García, who was born in 1962 and attended the Berríos school during 1971 and 1972, also had to stop his education, like Noel, Miguel Ángel, and Salvador, because of consequences of the 1972 earthquake. He says he had no contact with other deaf persons until he independently entered the COD in 1981, and later attended the meetings at Gloria's house. (Salvador and Miguel Ángel never attended any meetings at Gloria's house, and Noel attended only sporadically.) While conducting the interviews for this book with Salvador, Miguel Ángel, and Noel were very challenging, the interview with Julio César was conducted uneventfully in normal NSL (i.e., that which was in common use among ANSNIC members in the 1997–2003 period). Yolanda Mendieta, the Spanish/NSL interpreter, noted that Julio César's language use was similar to that of the other deaf persons born in the 1960s.[18] Juan Leiva gives an even starker example. Born the only deaf child in a poor hearing family, he never had any education, but helped his father and brothers with manual labor from as far back as he can remember. When he was about twenty years old, someone told his mother about a school that he might attend, and Juan found his way to the COD where he was especially drawn to carpentry. Unfortunately, after less than six months, he quarreled so much with the teachers that he was expelled. Later, he did regularly attend the meetings at Gloria's house. So Juan was never at the Berríos school or at the CNEE; but he told us his story in sign language, and Yolanda characterized his language to be like that of Javier and the first cohort of signers. The fluency of Gerardo, Julio César, and Juan make it unlikely that attending the Berríos school in the 1973–1976 period or the CNEE between 1977 and 1980 was necessary to be among the first users of the sign language.

During my research, I found a decided lack of linguistic models for deaf children before, perhaps, the late 1970s: They did not have sufficient access to oral Spanish for it to be their language model, and neither could anyone tell me of another person living in Managua who was a *fluent signer* of *any* signed language.[19] The Total Communication influences from Costa Rica in the late 1970s brought in some linguistic models through the use of signs along with speech (e.g., Thomas Gibson), but they were fleeting and not sustained. New signing models were not welcomed after 1980 at the schools, and it does not appear that any fluent signer of another signed language moved to the capital to live either. When Adrián Pérez returned from Spain to Managua for good in 1982, he would have been the most fluent signer to whom the first NSL signers were exposed.[20] Adrián was a founding member of the deaf association, but he was not, at first, as involved as he would later become with the organization. The initiation of the meetings of deaf youth at Rúthy's and Gloria's house seems to have had nothing to do with Adrián's homecoming, but it is interesting that the first generation of signers talk about the transition from the home sign/gesture/writing/mouthing system to one with more grammar *after* Adrián returned from Spain, and not before.

The lack of a standardized sign language in Nicaragua before the 1980s has other implications too. Language is the medium through which social agency is realized, and if most deaf persons did not have sufficient access to oral language to perform as social actors in the majority society, the formation of a deaf community would imply the need for a linguistic alternative, such as a sign language, to form, more or less, concurrently. The glaring absence, then, of a sign language during the 1946–1980 period provides support to informants' remembrances that a deaf community did not form during this period even though education was being provided to deaf persons. Its absence also casts doubt on the assertion that wherever schools for deaf children are formed, sign languages appear and deaf communities spring up.

The first documentation of the use of sign language in Nicaragua occurred in 1986 when Judy Kegl, and her student, Cyndi Norman, recorded the fact that the adolescents in the COD were using a sign language among themselves.[21] Kegl and Norman came upon a group already using a shared sign language, which tells us that the sign language had to have developed before 1986. However, when this process began is unknown. Cyndi Norman also knew that the students at the COD met regularly outside of class, even though she does not appear to have known about the regular meetings at Gloria's house. Cyndi, who was Kegl's student, stayed in Nicaragua five more months, continuing to go to the COD after Kegl had left and documenting a list of everyday signs, which she later included in her master's thesis.

Exactly what the sign language looked like in 1986 is problematic. Kegl chose not to record any videotape in 1986, but only made written notations, which appear to have been essentially a list of nouns. Cyndi Norman collected single signs, and her thesis consists of descriptions of how each sign in the list of concrete nouns or enactable verbs was formed. No one has yet published any description of the grammar used in 1986, and it would have been a formidable task to have accurately recorded a sufficient corpus for later analysis using only a paper and pencil. Some spontaneous conversations were recorded in 1987, but, to my knowledge, none of them has been analyzed in depth, nor published. A few sentences, collected in 1988, have appeared in publications (e.g., Kegl, Senghas, and Coppola 1999). The majority of the published grammatical analysis of NSL comes from Ann Senghas's work, which dates from the 1990s to the present.[22] Every deaf person we spoke with emphasized that NSL has evolved significantly from the days of "the meetings at Gloria's house" to the present, especially after Javier returned from Sweden in 1992.

While post-1986 documentation of what the sign language in Nicaragua looked like has been fragmentary, there is absolutely nothing to tell us what it looked like earlier. No one recorded it, and no linguist observed it. And it is an impossible hiatus to fill. All we know is that Adrián Pérez did not recognize it as a language in 1980, yet did recognize an increase in single signs in 1982; and his subjective impression is that the language did not develop until the meetings at Gloria's house had been underway some time. Other deaf members, who do not know another sign system as Adrián does, also relate the same subjective impressions that Adrián does: The eclectic, heterogeneous, and pragmatic communication was slowly standardized during the 1980s, and great changes occurred in the language after Javier became president of the ANSNIC in 1990.

News of sign language reached Nicaragua in the 1970s and the 1980s. Costa Rica was encouraging sign use in its educational system. Mayra Mena, a member of APRIAS with a very low identification card number, evidently spent time in a Costa Rican school for the deaf, and shared her knowledge with Javier when she returned. Gibson was well received in 1979, as was Adrián during his visits. Yet members like Juan Carlos Alemán and Edda Salguera emphasized the fact that the sign language they were used to when they first started attending meetings at Gloria's house (for Juan Carlos, 1985, when he was fifteen years old) went through a great deal of development, being rather "primitive" in 1985, but more capable of deeper expressions in 1999: "Now you can say more with sign language than you could before."

It appears, however, that it was only *after* APRIAS formed, probably not until 1989 or 1990, that the idea that sign language could become the major medium of communication among deaf persons (rather than being used as a secondary system while placing primary emphasis upon oral communication) occurred to Javier and others. Javier López Gómez was a founding member of APRIAS and designed the group's logo, which was adopted in 1986. The logo, which illustrates a hearing voice breaking down the isolative wall of deafness, is integrationist in perspective. Javier was an officer of the group from the beginning, meaning that he participated in discussions around the writing of the bylaws (although it appears that the actual composition was done by Rúthy Dúran and Gloria Minero), and was well aware of, and evidently approved of, the assimilationist goals of the association.

But any APRIAS project connected to sign language found Javier an enthusiastic participant (e.g., the sign standardization workshops in the late 1980s and early 1990s), and he was one of APRIAS's first "sign language teachers." Javier stated that his interest in sign language had begun in the late 1970s when he was given a sign language dictionary during an athletic trip to Costa Rica.[23] Javier, through his early enthusiasm for sign language, his dedication to making it a functional communication system for himself and his friends, and his commitment to share his knowledge with the other deaf persons in Nicaragua, must be considered a catalytic personality for the nascent deaf community in regard to sign language use. Other students at CNEE were exposed to sign language (they went on the same trips that Javier did and met with the same representatives of deaf organizations in other countries), but it did not seem to spark the enthusiasm or curiosity among them that it did for Javier. Remember that Thomas Gibson only found one young man (this was Javier) capable of holding a non-home sign conversation at the deaf gathering in 1979. Javier was famous among his contemporaries for seeking out anyone who knew sign language or had access to a dictionary of any kind in order to improve his vocabulary. He also became the core leader behind the group's post-1990 move away from the integrationist perspective and a fervent champion of NSL.

After all, the evidence suggests that a sign language developed and was adopted for standard use in Nicaragua in less than fifteen years. And while NSL exhibits some lexical influences from Costa Rican, American, Swedish, and Spanish Sign Languages, it is not simply one of these languages adopted across the board by deaf Nicaraguans.[24] I have been told by linguists that NSL shows enough variance in syntax and vocabulary that it can be classified as a separate sign language.[25]

Although not directly connected to the founding of the deaf association or the use of sign language there, a movement to incorporate sign language into the teaching methodology had the support of American, Swedish, and Finnish educators who were volunteers in Nicaragua in the 1988–1993 period. At the same time that sign language became a possible tool for the schools, the use of sign language as a major mode of communication (rather than an adjunct) at the deaf association gained popularity.[26] Yana-María Graver and Sheila Hougan, U.S. citizens working as volunteers from 1988–1992 with the León/Minnesota Project, ran an experimental kindergarten using a Total Communication approach in León (Hougan, 1993). Their success favorably impressed the Ministry of Education and paved the way for more use of signing in classrooms.[27]

Multiple "sign standardization workshops" took place in the late 1980s and early 1990s. Javier Gómez López, the president of ANSNIC in 2003, could not recall the exact number over the years, but remembered attending at least three. Gloria Minero remembered that the first workshop was held after the meetings at her house had become routine, but before the deaf association had formally been founded (i.e., after 1983, but before April 22, 1986). During a workshop, members of the association worked in small groups discussing which variations of signs should be adopted as the "standard" versions that members should use, and then a vote was taken.[28] Yana-María Graver worked with members of the deaf association in Managua on the production of an early (dated 1992) hand-drawn and mimeographed dictionary of NSL.[29] The signs represented in the dictionary were ones that had been discussed during one or more of the standardization workshops held during that period.

A retired teacher of deaf children, Anna Scott from Sweden, a volunteer with the organization Svalorna, traveled to Nicaragua for multiple stays over a ten-year period and spearheaded a campaign in the late 1980s to encourage sign language use in classrooms in San Marcos and Managua, while at the same time encouraging the formation of a San Marcos chapter of ANSNIC.

Tuula Jaaskelainem, an educator of deaf children from Finland, worked as a volunteer in the Ministry of Education's main office in 1992 and 1993. She also encouraged the use of sign language in both the formal and informal (home visitor) educational programs, participated in activities with the deaf association, and provided inservices to teachers of deaf children to encourage the use of sign language.

The 1990 visit to the deaf association by Anders Andersson and Kerstin Kjellberg, members of the executive council of the Swedish Association for the Deaf (the group which was responsible for the funding funneled through the Swedish International Development Association (SHIA) to the association) and advocates of a "cultural" model of deafness, had a profound impact, as noted earlier, on ANSNIC's direction and its attitude toward sign language.[30] Andersson had long talks with the leading members of the association, urging them to be proud of their deafness and see the beauty of their sign language.[31] According to Sebastián Ferrar (he was the SHIA administrator at the time, and arranged the logistics for the Swedish visitors), Andersson and Jenifer Grigsby (who was president at the time) did not hit it off as well as might be hoped, probably because Andersson had no appreciation of Grigsby's oral talents, for which Grigsby usually received compliments.

Up until 1991, interpreting between oral Spanish and NSL had been done strictly on a volunteer basis, but the budget under the new administration included a salary for an interpreter for the organization, as well as a receptionist to answer the telephone (who obviously had to be hearing). María López Gómez was appointed interpreter, and Sandra López Gómez became the receptionist, and later secretary. Both are Javier López Gómez's sisters. Two courses have been offered in the country over the past ten years to teach hearing persons to interpret oral Spanish to NSL (and vice versa). The first was given by Carolina de Drueta, the wife of Juan Drueta. She gave a six-month course in 1995 during the time that her husband was acting as a consultant for the first printed dictionary. The second was taught by Isela Palacios over a longer period, 1999–2000. Isela had been a teacher of deaf children in Nagarote (a village about an hour's bus ride from Managua). She won a scholarship (1997–1999) to study sign language interpreting in the United States. The scholarship included a promise that she would work with the deaf association for at least two years upon her return. Isela fulfilled her promise by teaching an afternoon class for a small group (essentially the same people who had attended Mrs. Drueta's workshop earlier). There are presently about ten persons in the country who function as oral Spanish/NSL interpreters.

The deaf sign language teachers in 1991 appeared to have worked more on teaching sign language to their own members, but in 1992, when signing was allowed in public school classrooms, deaf teachers from the association went weekly or biweekly to give classes to the teachers at the special education school in Managua (now known as the Escuela Melania

Morales). In later years, they branched out, traveling to other towns (within an hour's bus ride) with special education schools (such as Granada or León) to give weekly classes to the teachers. In the 1990s, literacy was also targeted, with deaf education teachers from the public schools giving classes for young adults once or twice weekly.

The Swedes continued to visit periodically over the years and provided funds for Noel Lam (the father of a deaf son) and Javier López Gómez (president of the deaf association) to travel to Sweden for a conference in 1991. Javier remained in Sweden ten months (fall 1991 to summer 1992, at the home of Ingvar Ekvall), learning skills that would help with the composition of the dictionary. Without the Swedish support (which continues to the present), it is unlikely that as many activities would have been carried out, or that the general public would have come to know the deaf association. The Royal Swedish Deaf Association later provided funds for two deaf persons and two hearing persons to attend an international congress on deafness in Europe. Since 1990, they have also provided funds for the officers of ANSNIC to travel multiple times to other Central American countries for regional meetings of deaf people.

Thus, the sign language in Nicaragua did not develop in a vacuum, but owes a debt to multiple influences. The language and the community appear to have grown in tandem, and they grew most rapidly among a group that was not composed of children, but looking toward adulthood. As a "fuzzy" system (just like the language), the exact point at which the friendship circle expanded to become a community is not clear-cut.

By the time the first constitution was written in 1987, the group was described as a national organization, and its purpose was defined beyond socialization. Importantly, membership was made available to any deaf person in Nicaragua, a significant departure from the earlier group of friends that gathered in each others' homes in 1977, 1978, or 1979. Until the group obtained the permanent meeting house in 1989, it met at Durán's or Minero's houses or other locales they could arrange. To participate, one still had to be invited by an active member in order to know where to go. After 1989, however, news of the meeting house spread throughout Managua, and by asking for the *casa de los sordos,* one could ultimately be directed to the meeting house without the need to have prior acquaintanceship with other deaf persons. Personal invitation continued to be an important recruitment method, but this reification of the deaf association through the presence of a permanent location was an important step in the process of becoming a community because it made the group available to anyone, simply on the basis of deafness.

Significantly, in the period of the late 1980s and early 1990s, the founding members of the association began to take on adult roles: They found partners within the group and began to set up households and have children; they began to seek employment that not only provided pocket money, but also allowed them to feed their children and to contribute significantly to their own maintenance. In 1986, there was only one deaf couple, Gerardo Lezama and Damáris Robles, who had a child (a one-year-old daughter, Aura) attending the meetings.[32] By 1994, the majority of the founding members were in committed relationships, married, or even divorced, and the presence of children at association events was commonplace. As members were now functioning as societal adults, being taken seriously as social actors was a significant issue.

Increasingly, from 1992 onward, ANSNIC has become the "voice of deaf persons" in Nicaragua, participating in various educational and social work coalitions and work groups as the representatives of the deaf community. Since approximately 1996, the association has used the name National Nicaraguan Association *of* the Deaf, as opposed to Association for Integration and Help *to* the Deaf, the official name adopted in 1986. This is a significant change in philosophy that reflects the different way ANSNIC members expect to be a part of Nicaraguan society in the twenty-first century.

Afterword

It is another hot, dusty, August afternoon, this time a Sunday, but five years after I heard Natalia Galo's story. Yolanda and I are out looking for the older deaf adults, the ones who remember the time before the sign language and before the Association had a house. We have an address, but we are not sure it is right, and anyway, like any Managua address, it is ambiguous. We are in Primero de Mayo, a not-so-desirable section of the capital: the streets are not paved, and there is good evidence that this section is not on the public sewer system. Stray dogs and chickens wander the same street we do. The sky is darkly overcast, and we walk in drizzle, which we know means that a downpour is only minutes away.

We find our landmark, the gasoline station, and discuss which direction is north. "From the gasoline station, three blocks to the north" says the slip of paper; there is no other indication. Now we're on our own. So we walk one, two, three blocks. There is nothing that looks like a house here, but a helpful passer-by suggests that we should have first crossed one of the bridges over a deep ditch, and then started counting. We cross the bridge and count again. The drizzle is now definitely rain. We ask for help from a man who is sitting on a broken-down lawn chair in the front door of his cement block house: "We are looking for a deaf man who lives in this area, you know, someone who doesn't talk."

"Sure," he nods, "that house there. Both the man and his wife don't talk."

As we approach the open front door of the designated house, a man sitting in a wooden rocking chair just inside the room watching a silent TV set notices the movements of our walking toward him, looks up, and recognizes Yolanda. It is Juan Leiva, a man born in 1962. She greets him with a big hug and a greeting, hoping he and his family are well. He thanks her and offers us a place to sit down, and Yolanda introduces me. I have met Juan briefly five years ago and recognize him, and he remembers the meeting as well. He tells us that Christina Guevara, his wife, is at a funeral and will not return until nightfall. No matter, Yolanda tells him. We have come to learn your story. We would like you to tell us what it was like for you when you were growing up.

171

Juan invites us in (before the downpour hits) and offers us a glass of plain water, the common courtesy given any visitor, which we most gratefully accept. It is just about to rain, but it has been a hot, dusty walk to find the house. We drink the water all at once. Then, when the glasses have been returned to the kitchen, and we are settled, our host sits again in the rocking chair.

Then Juan in his logical, carefully formed Nicaraguan Sign Language, in an almost laconic manner, but preserving details, tells us what it was like to grow up in Nicaragua the only deaf child in a hearing family, to be unaware until he was a teenager that any other deaf persons like himself existed, to discover then a language that was completely accessible to him, and to find a group where he could make friends and find a wife.

He tells us of his life performing manual labor, of the birth of his hearing children, and of the life he has carved out centered on his family, and on his friends, who, like him, are deaf. His wife thinks he drinks too much, and he wishes he earned more, so that he could live in a better neighborhood. But, overall, he tells us, he is satisfied with his life. Things have changed dramatically for deaf people, he signs, in the last forty years. It is much better now. He tells us that, as a child, unable to communicate with anyone around him, he never imagined, he would grow up to have close friends and a family. He never thought he would have this kind of a life.

"With sign language, you can learn so much."

Appendix
Interviewees Consulted 1994–2003

This project would have been impossible without the willingness of these people to share their time and search their memories. I thank them all, and wish to acknowledge their contribution here.

Name of Interviewee	Date of Interview[1]	Relationship to Topic
Abrego, Victoria	16 June 1997	Mother of deaf son
Aburto, Jacqueline	12 September 1997*	Mother of deaf son
Arevalo, Esperanza	2 July 2001	Mother of deaf daughter
Acuna de Isabá, Alma	26 May 1994*	Audiologist
Aguado, María Eugenia	24 September 1997	ANSNIC[2] member
Aguilar, Azalia	9 June 1994	Administrator, "Los Pipitos"[3]
Aguilar, Ivette	12 August 1997*	Deaf educator
Aguilar, María Teresa	21 October 1997*	COD[4] director; social worker
Ahlers de Cuadra, Aneli	12 August 1997	Audiologist
Alemán, Juan Carlos	15 September 1997	President; ANSNIC member
Altamirano, Verónica	7 June 1997	ANSNIC member
Alvarado, Thelma	30 October 1997	CNEE[5]/COD teacher
Amador, Juan José	10 June 1997	Epidemiologist
Araica, Danelia	18 July 2002	ANSNIC member
Artola, Humberto	5 March 1997	ANSNIC member
Avilés, Sócrates	20 October 1997	CNEE teacher
Ayón, Silvia	10 June 1994*	Deaf educator
Balladares, Jilma	14 October 1997	Director, special education
Balmaceda, Lisette	19 October 1997	ANSNIC member
Baltodanos, Jimmy	5 March 1997	ANSNIC member
Baltodanos, Marvin	22 April, 1997	Deaf educator
Barbosa, Carmela de	15 October 1997	Director, special education
Barcénas, Soybeda	2 September 1997	Community educator
Barlow, Eva	3 July 1997*	Assembly of God missionary
Barquedano, Ervin	15 June 1997	ANSNIC member
Barríos, Melba	28 July 2002	ANSNIC member
Barríos Mayorga, Angela	14 August 2002	Sister of Dr. Berríos
Barríos Mayorga, Maria	14 August 2002	Sister of Dr. Berríos
Bohmer de Selva, Rosemary	16 October 1997	Director, CNEE
Bolger, Robert	21 August 2003	Deaf visitor to ANSNIC

Cano Sánchez, Roberto	3 July 2002	Deaf man
Cano, Mario	23 May 1994	Deaf educator
Cardosa, Gioconda	4 August 2001	ANSNIC member
Carrillo Cruz, Nelys María	22 August 1997	CNEE educational team
Carvajal, Socorro	24 October 1997	Director, INSSBI[6]
Castillo, Francisco Javier	22 March 1997	Deaf educator
Chamorro Morales, Dina	26 June 2002	Deaf educator
Chavarría, Soledad	10 July 1999	Director, PROGRESO
Cuarezma, Alejandro	24 February 1997	Statistician
Cortéz, William	27 April 1997	ANSNIC member
Gonzáles, Camila	16 June 1997	Deaf woman
Delgado, Gilbert	21 October 1998	Administrator, Gallaudet College
Díaz Luna, Arcadio	10 May 1997	ANSNIC member
Díaz Varela, Gerardo	24 June 1997	Director, INATEC[7]
Durán Collado, Rúthy	1 August 1997*	Deaf educator
Elizondo, Ruth	7 October 1997	Director, special education
Escobar de Flores, Soledad	22 September 1997	Deaf educator
Estrada, María Dolores	3 September 1997	Deaf educator
Ferrar, Sebastián	15 September 1997	Administrator, SHIA[8]
Filena, Kasta	20 October 1997	Deaf educator
Fletes, Ruth Danelia	2 June 1997	Deaf educator
Flores, Rosa Adelina	10 June 1997	Deaf educator
Galo, Natalia	16 July 1997	ANSNIC member
Galo, Milagros	22 May 1997	Deaf educator
García, Isaura	19 August 2002	Educator
García, Julio César	16 July 2002	ANSNIC member
García, Salomón	7 July 1997	ANSNIC member
García, Zoila	21 August 1997	Deaf educator
García, Maria Jose	12 June 1997	Deaf educator
Gonzáles, Luís	1 November 1997	Interpreter for the deaf
Gonzáles, Marisela	18 August 1997	Educator
Gonzáles, Mercedes	18 August 1997	Educator
Gonzáles, Rosario	7 July 2000	Educator
Gordon, Nora	2 November 1997	Deaf educator
Gozebruch, Guillermo	4 March 1997	Administrator, "Los Pipitos"
Grigsby, Jenifer	30 September 1997	ANSNIC member
Guadamuz, Nancy	17 October 1997	Deaf educator
Guevara, Christina	16 July 2002	ANSNIC member
Gutiérrez, Josefa	21 July 2001	ANSNIC member
Gutiérrez, Patricia	18 July 2002	Deaf educator; interpreter
Hanssen, Gören	5 May 1997	Administrator, SHIA
Hernández, María Antonieta	13 July 1997	ANSNIC member
Jeréz Martínez, Manuel	20 July 1997	ANSNIC member
Joffre, María Elena	3 August 2001	Deaf educator

Kegl, Judy	10 May 1995*	Linguist
Lam Herrera, Noel	27 May 1994*	Deaf educator (RIP)
Lara, Socorro	13 March 1997	ANSNIC member
Leiva Rostrán, Juan Eluterio	16 July 2002	ANSNIC member
Leiva, Martha	27 July 2002	CNEE/COD educational team
Lezama, Gerardo	19 October 1997	ANSNIC member
López Acevedo, Ingrid Carolina	2 July 2001	ANSNIC member
López Gómez, Javier	25 May 1994*	President, ANSNIC member
López Gómez, María	13 June 1997	Interpreter for the deaf
López Gómez, Sandra	14 March 1997	Secretary for ANSNIC
López, Mario	2 July 2001	Father of deaf daughter
López, Salvador	11 August 2002	Deaf man
López López, Marcos	27 August 2003	Chauffeur to Dr. Berríos
Lugo, Mariana	9 April 1997	Social worker at COD
Luna, Guillermo	28 June 1997	ANSNIC member
Malespín, Violeta	17 August 2000	Representative, MECD
Malespín, Dr. Omar	11 October 1997	Epidemiologist
Mántica, Carlos	27 August 2003	Historian; businessman
Marcos Frech, Suad	14 February 1997	Activist for disabled
Marín, María de Soledad	14 August 1997*	Deaf educator
Mejía, Gerardo	18 July 1997	Geneticist; physician
Meléndez, Narcisa	15 October 1997	Deaf educator
Membreño, Dalia	21 October 1997	Deaf educator
Méndez Berríos, Patricia	29 August 2003	Niece, Dr. Berríos
Mendieta, Yolanda	15 July 1997*	Deaf educador; interpreter
Mercado, Gregorio	1 June 1997	Father of deaf son
Meynard, Yolanda	15 May 1997	Deaf educator
Midence, Mabel	16 July 2002	ANSNIC member
Minero, Gloria	15 October 1997*	Deaf educator
Miranda, Yadira	27 September 1997	Deaf educator
Morgan, Guillermina	July 28, 2003	Educator
Mójica, Javier	22 February 1997	ANSNIC member
Morales, Carlos	1 July 1997	Deaf man
Morales, Enrique	22 October 1997	Statistician
Moreira, Miriam	4 April 1997*	Deaf educator
Moreno Vallecillo, Miguel Angel	31 May 1997*	ANSNIC member
Murrillo, Mercedes	19 October 1997	ANSNIC member
Obando, Ángela	12 September 1997*	Mother of deaf son
Ortega Bojorge, Elbia	28 June 2002	ANSNIC member
Ortega Bojorge, Mercedes	6 July 1997	ANSNIC member
Ortíz, Amy	13 March 1997*	Deaf educator; interpreter
Palacios, María Lourdes	29 June 1997*	ANSNIC member
Pallais, Chantal	24 September 1997	Educator
Pérez, Alex	15 February 1997*	ANSNIC member

Pérez Castellón, Adrián	7 July 2002*	ANSNIC member
Pilarte, María Teresa	17 October 1997	Educator
Popova, Natalia	25 May 1994*	Deaf educator
Preda, Serenella	24 October 1997	International volunteer
Quesada, Carmen	20 July 1997	Mother of deaf son
Ríos, Napoleón	9 November 1997	Lawyer; public notary
Rivas, Mayela	19 October 1997	ANSNIC member
Rivas, Jasmina	16 June 1997	ANSNIC member
Rivas, Rosario	31 May 1994	Deaf educator
Rivera, Blanca	20 May 1994	Director, special education
Rivera Rostrán, Johana	10 July 1997	ANSNIC member
Rivera, Josefa	18 September 1997	Social activist
Robles, Damaris	19 October 1997	ANSNIC member
Rocha, (Maulio) Noel	14 September 1997	ANSNIC member
Rodríguez, Yesenia	22 July 1997	ANSNIC member
Rojas, Maritza	26 September 1997	Deaf educator
Román, Desirée	5 February 1997*	Director, special education
Romero, Auxiliadora	28 April 1997	Director of COD
Romero, Irlanda	19 June 1997*	Mother of deaf daughter
Rostrán, Soledad	2 June 1997	Deaf educator
Rugama, Susana	7 April 1997*	Deaf educator
Ruíz, Armando Majíro	19 October 1997	ANSNIC member
Ruíz, Ileana	22 May 1994*	Audiometric technician
Ruíz, Raúl	7 April 1997	Education researcher
Salguera, Edda	15 September 1997	ANSNIC member
Salmerón, Gloria	5 July 1997	ANSNIC member
Sánchez, Daysi	26 September 1997	Deaf educator
Sánchez, Luisa	30 June 2002	Mother of deaf son
Sequiera, Luz María	21 October 1997	CNEE Vice director
Sequiera, Oscar	10 August 1997	ANSNIC member
Scott, Ana	20 October 2000	Swedish deaf educator
Silva, Coralia	8 July 1997*	Educator
Tablado, Tulio	30 October 1997	Administrator, MECD
Tenorio Hernández, Olga	20 July 1995*	Deaf educator
Tijerino, Iris	15 May 1997	ANSNIC member
Tórres, Marcia	17 September 1997*	Deaf educator
Tórres Minero, Morena	12 June 1999	ANSNIC member
Vargas, María Luisa	31 May 1994	Deaf educator
Vasquez Picado, Sergio José	6 July 1997	ANSNIC member
Vega, Ivonne	13 September 1997	ANSNIC member
Vega Correa, Lesbia	27 June 1997	Representative, Managua Free Trade Zone
Zamora, Daysi	4 October 1997	ANSNIC member
Zamora, Edelma	2 June 1994*	Deaf educator
Zamora, Rebeca	9 July 1997	Fuerza/Futuro Director
Zepeda, Mauricio	14 September 1997*	ANSNIC member

Notes

Introduction

1. A free trade zone (Zona Franca) is an industrial park with multiple plants in which products are typically assembled from pieces manufactured elsewhere. Although some of the companies running plants in these zones are Nicaraguan, most have headquarters in other countries, such as China or South Korea. As the Internet website entitled Free Trade Zones explains: "According to the legally accepted definition, the free trade zones . . . are those parts of the [host country's] territory that are managed according to special laws and bylaws and are excluded from the laws of the governing motherland. These zones are excluded from the domain of the custom authorities and enjoy the full freedom for the in and out flow of goods and commodities. Unique geographical locations, sufficiently developed infrastructure and the foreign investment incentives have provided ample opportunity for internal as well as foreign investment in the zones." (http://www.salamiran.org/Economy/FreeZones/FTZ.html, no date given for last update. Consulted on February 19, 2005). Since workers in the free trade zones are paid only the minimal wage of the host country, it is economically feasible to send components manufactured elsewhere for assemblage to a free trade zone in a country such as Nicaragua, and then return the product to other countries where it can be sold for a much higher price. Nicaragua is only one of many countries with this type of arrangement. The Internet website, EscapeArtist, for example, lists information about the free trade zones in 33 countries (http://www.escapeartist.com/ftz/ftz_b.htm, last updated in 2004, consulted on February 19, 2005). For many years, there was only one free trade zone in Nicaragua, in northeastern Managua, but more zones have been set up in Sébaco and Ciudad Sandino, and more are envisioned for other parts of the country in the future. In 2002, the Ministry of Labor signed an agreement that the minimum wage for workers in the free trade zones would be 730 córdobas (equal to US$52.00 at that time) per month (Castillo Zeas 2002).

2. This is a Nicaraguan affectionate term referring to small children, perhaps translatable as "The Kids." The name of the association is significant in that it is definitely an association FOR disabled kids. The "kids" themselves have no voice in the organization's agenda.

3. Unfortunately, he left Nicaragua during the 1979 revolution, and his present whereabouts, if he is still living, are unknown, so I was never able to interview him.

4. While denying vehemently that the membership list was "confidential" and or that the association had any policy against releasing this information, the president of the deaf association nonetheless took a long time to give me the membership list, which I finally obtained in May 1997 after several formal requests starting in February. (All requests were granted, the problem always consisted of finding a time convenient for the member in charge of the records to show me the files.) According to the then-vice president (who cared for the files), no master list existed. I was finally given access to two drawers, one containing the files for all the male members, and a separate one for the files for the female members. I read each file individually, copying by hand the name, birth date, and registration card number listed. Thus, all references to number of members of the deaf association are current only as of May 30, 1997. Obtaining access to this data was onerous and time-consuming. I have not had the opportunity to bring these numbers up to date in my subsequent visits to Nicaragua, which have all been shorter than the 1997 fieldwork. After organizing the information into a database, I gave the president of the deaf association copies of the list arranged by last names, first names, birthdates, and registration numbers. He appeared pleased with the lists, and at that point noted that it was a worthwhile task, and that the association would benefit from having a master list. He was not interested, however, in obtaining a copy of the database so that it could be kept current. From subsequent discussions with him from 1997 to 2003, I am led to believe that the rolls have not been updated regularly, or been made in any way comprehensive.

5. As will be explained in more depth in later chapters, I hypothesize that it was the large number of rubella babies born around 1962 (1959–1965) who formed the first group which deaf members refer to as the "deaf community." Their language abilities mark them as late language-learners. Demographic information indicates that the next rubella epidemic peaked in Nicaragua in 1970. Members born in the 1966–1972 period exhibit linguistic characteristics which suggest that they learned sign language earlier, either as preteens or adolescents. Yolanda and I were searching specifically for deaf persons who had been teenagers before a recognized deaf community existed. Thus, we looked for persons born before the 1970 rubella epidemic. Naturally, we also interviewed persons born during and after that time, but these younger members were much easier to find because they participated regularly in deaf association events. The older deaf adults had to be searched out painstakingly.

6. For example, I leafed page-by-page through each volume of *La Gaceta* from 1946 to 1990, because there is no index, either comprehensive or for a particular year.

7. The interviews were mostly done by deaf interviewers, who were paid.

8. The first two trips were financed by summer research grants from the University of Redlands, the second two through a Fulbright Foundation teaching/research fellowship, and the last trip was self-financed.

9. In 2004, I was informed of various re-groupings and reorganizations that were contemplated, but not yet completed. These are not included here because I closed the data-gathering phase of my research with the information I collected during my last trip in August 2003. A continuation of the present book will be needed some time in the future, and I hope Yolanda Mendieta will take up the task of documenting the history of deaf people in Nicaragua.

Chapter 1: "Eternal Children"

1. A substance that poisons the inner ear and causes hearing loss.

2. I wanted to be sure that my characterizations of attitudes of parents of deaf children, or community attitudes about deafness, were representative of the region (and not just local to Managua). I was able to verify this myself with interviews in Carazao, Estelí, Ocotál, Juigalpa, and Bluefields. But time ran short, so I hired Luís Gonzáles, a former teacher for the Ministry of Education, to interview parents and teachers in Matagalpa and Jinotega. He wrote out a summary of each interview, and on November 1, 1997, we sat down and reviewed the notes together, and I augmented details he described but had not written down. Luís and his wife, Marcía, (she is a teacher of deaf children) are friends of the Matagalpa chapter of ANSNIC, and helped in obtaining a place for the group to meet. Luís visited the families of active members of the deaf association in Matagalpa and interviewed them about their experiences. He then interviewed the deaf members to gain their perspective. As the interviews show, parents and their sons and daughters view many things, including quality of communication, differently.

3. This section is based upon information received from Dr. Napoleon Ríos, a practicing lawyer in Managua. Dr. Rios's wife was involved in special education in the 1980s. He is the lawyer who drew up the deaf association's original papers applying for judicial recognition as a legal entity in 1986. On November 9, 1997, I paid him for a legal consultation (for which he had previously prepared) in which he explained to me Nicaraguan law as it relates to deaf persons. At that time, the "reglamentation" for Law 202 had just been published, and Dr. Rios said that he had not observed its influence in any legal matters.

4. It was published in number 180, the September 27, 1995 edition of the official newsletter, *La Gaceta*.

5. In August 2002, the president in office, Enrique Bolaños, accused his predecessor, Arnoldo Alemán, of diverting state funds to his private use. Alemán, through retorts to the press, dared Bolaños to prove his accusations, and Bolaños promised the press that his government would provide irrefutable proof. On the evening of August 8, 2002, Francisco Fiállos, a top member of the government, gave an impressive Powerpoint presentation proving the allegations to a live audience, which was simultaneously broadcast by all the national television stations. The diverted funds were referred to as the *guaca* or "buried treasure." I watched the presentation with everyone else, and saw that there was no interpreter for the deaf present.

Chapter 2: Special Education

1. These are the Vilchez sisters who lived in Managua for many years. Although both are identified as deaf in the articles in *La Gaceta* about their scholarships and their appointments as teachers, many persons remembered them and noted that they could speak. Since there was no audiometry in those days, and because they were able to function as home economics teachers in regular schools, I believe that today they would be classified as "hard of hearing," and not deaf.

2. Dr. Berríos's sisters, María and Ángela, stated unequivocally (in a personal interview in August 2003) that psychiatry was Apolonio's emphasis while studying in Mexico, but the doctor's first job was working with miners (who mostly had lung diseases). He is also mentioned by others as a pediatrician, and he evidently had a contract with the national railroad company to take care of their workers. In other words, he practiced as a general physician, and his study of psychiatry should not be interpreted to mean that he practiced psychiatry as it is generally interpreted today.

3. Dr. Pedro Berruécos and his wife María Paz gave a set of lectures in Nicaragua in 1961 about deafness. Silvia and Antonio Ayón went to the lectures and stayed afterward to talk to the speakers. Ultimately, they both went to Mexico to enroll their son, Antonio, in the IMAL's school while they both took the training course in speech therapy. The parents of María Lourdes Palacios also went to these same lectures, and the result was that Mr. Palacios decided to send María Lourdes and her mother to live in Mexico City for five years, so that she could go to the IMAL school. María Lourdes and her mother never returned to Nicaragua during these five years, and her father could only afford to visit them twice. Both parents felt the sacrifice had been well worth it.

4. The decree in *La Gaceta* authorizing the funds for the school's first-year expenses gives an address that is close, but not the same, as the location across the street from the Mántica house. The school probably moved one other time in the earliest years, but by 1952 when Dr. Berríos took over as the director, the school was where the future post office would be.

5. For example, the question of education for children with disabilities also seems to have been a concern of various members of the Rotary Club at the time. When the first school was established, the Rotary Club donated the furniture. The Berríos sisters also remember Carmen Huembes and Amelia Debayle as key members of the group concerned with special education.

6. I have certainly been unable to find any such records. Olga Tenorio Hernandez taught for many years at Special Education School Number One. She took over the directorship of the school in 1974 when Dr. Berríos died and ran it until it was closed in 1976. The pupils were absorbed into the new National Center for Special Education in 1977. In a 1997 interview, when I asked her about the enrollment over the years, she told me that she had kept the "*libro de matriculas*" (the enrollment register) for many years after the school closed, but in the early 1990s, in a fit of housecleaning and decluttering, she had burned it "because I couldn't see it would be of any use to anyone." She states that she has forgotten the number of students at the school, saying, "I'm an old lady. Why would I keep that kind of thing in my head?"

7. The Nicaraguan currency is the *córdoba*, which for many years, including 1949–1950, was equivalent to the dollar. In the 1980s, there were periods of superinflation with revaluations, and there is now a floating exchange rate.

8. Olga Tenorio told me this in 1995, and the Berríos sisters corroborated this in 2002. The doctor's sisters say that he wrote about the Montessori method in his letters home while he was in Mexico, and they believe he was responsible for its influence in the first special education school.

9. Dr. Elías Corea Fonseca dedicates a whole page (p. 118) to Dr. Berríos in his history of medicine in Nicaragua, and refers especially to the doctor's charity work among the poor. As for deaf education, I have, in fact, had many Nicaraguans tell me that there was no schooling for deaf children until "Doña Hope [de Somoza] opened her school [in 1977]." In regard to this particular issue, many Nicaraguans are wrong.

10. In 2003, I interviewed the doctor's former chauffeur, Marcos López, who said that the car was a large station wagon-like vehicle. Marcos says he made three trips a day, picking up and delivering about seventy students. He said there were other children who were brought to the school by their parents, and he estimated the total enrollment of the school in the 1960s to be "around 100 children."

11. Olga Tenorio is the only one who remembers that the name was officially changed. I could find no announcement of the change in *La Gaceta,* but everyone I talked with during my research did commonly refer to it as "the Berríos school." She also showed me an undated newspaper clipping that evidently was written in 1974, which was a letter to the editor from Tenorio. She signed the letter as "director of the 'Apolonio Berríos Special Education School.'"

12. Olga Tenorio says that she turned in the Libro de Actas for the first special education school along with her written report to the Ministry of Education in 1986, and that none of the material was returned to her. The typescripts of the reports are in the Ministry of Education's Documentation Center, but there is no trace of the Libro de Actas. This would have been a ledger with numbered pages containing a description of all official actions, and should have been kept current from 1946 to 1976. Any group that has *personería jurídica* (legal recognition) is expected to keep such a ledger.

13. The portions that I needed were not open when I was in Nicaragua in 1997 or 1999 (they were not unpacked from wherever they had been before). When I visited Nicaragua in 2000, the Archive was "in transit" (and therefore, unavailable) from its old location in the Social Security Building to renovated quarters in the National Palace (which used to be used by the National Assembly, but which now houses museums, the National Library, and the National Archive). It was open and functioning in 2001, and I spent many stifling August afternoons looking through dusty boxes, which had no internal organization. That was fortunate because when I returned in 2002, it was closed again, due to lack of funding.

14. Any astute reader, at this point, is going to wonder why I did not just ask Olga Tenorio for the approximate numbers in 1950 as well as the number enrolled in 1962. I interviewed Olga in 1995, when I still had only a vague idea of the history, and she is the first person who told me definitely that there had been a special education school before 1979. Then, I had three conversations with Olga in the first six months of 1997, one of which was long and tape-recorded (but at that point, it hadn't occurred to me to ask about enrollments). I told her I would transcribe it and give her a copy. In all of these conversations, it was very easy to get her to reminisce about the school, and she was proud of her ability to remember details (the founding date of the school, for example). When I returned with the transcript of the taped conversation in June 1997, however, she told me that someone had told her I was "writing a book." "Well, yes," I explained, "I am writing a dissertation, which is essentially a book." "And anybody can read this book?" she asked. "Yes," I replied, "The rules are that one copy goes into the library of the University of Texas at Austin, and anyone can check it out, and

anyway, I intend to send at least one copy back to Nicaragua for everyone to read." At that point, Olga said she would take the typescript home and "correct" it. When I returned to pick up the corrections, I found that her memory had taken a significant turn for the worse. I did ask her about the enrollment and other details, but alas, Olga "couldn't remember." I have seen her on most of my subsequent trips, and have continued to ask about the old school. Her memory continues to be weak. I was quite puzzled by the change in attitude until I found the partial budget for 1963, which is discussed in the text. I believe that Olga Tenorio does not care to have certain irregularities that occurred in the old school brought to the notice of the public.

15. The Instituto Panameño de Habilitación Especial is an establishment in Panamá devoted to training teachers of children with special needs. It includes a laboratory school, where trainees do teaching practica. In the early 1970s, Guillermina Morgan, Melania Morales, and Blanca Rivera finished the training courses for teaching children with deafness, mental retardation, and blindness, respectively. Rúthy and María Teresa studied there in 1972–1974. Immediately after the revolution in 1979, eight persons already involved in special education received a government scholarship to study at IPHE. These graduates held important positions in special education during the 1980s. Among them were Noel Lam Herrea, Sister Edelma Zamora, and Ruth Danelia Fletes. All of them were later either administrators in special education or principals of special education schools.

This was the year that Rúthy and María Teresa taught mornings in Managua and afternoons in León. After Dr. Berríos died, the school day at the Escuela Especial No. 1 was cut from a full-day program to one that ran only in the mornings. The lunch program was also cut out, and the children were returned home after classes at noon.

16. The 20–30 Club was described to me as a social club with a strong service component, first set up for young people between the ages of twenty and thirty, hence its name. I believe it is similar to the Junior League clubs in the United States. This club has played a philanthropic role in special education for many years. The Managua chapter helped with donations at the first special education building in 1946, and later, it provided Antonio Ayón with a scholarship to cover the cost of his studies in Mexico. In 2002 and 2003, it was involved in raising funds through a telethon for the Instituto Medico-Pedagogico, which the organization, Los Pipitos, plans to build.

17. This is how Marcos López described the buildings during an interview in 2003. His description agrees with that of María, Ángela Berríos, and Dr. Berriós's niece, Dr. Patricia Méndez Berríos.

18. In 1995, Dr. Ann Senghas videotaped a photograph album at the home of Olga Tenorio, which included a water-stained photograph of a teacher and students using that kind of hardwired auditory training system. From notations on other pictures, the album appeared to date from the 1960s. Ms. Tenorio worked mostly with mentally retarded children during her years at the Berríos school, and most of the photographs are of those classes. There was only one photograph specifically labed as the class for deaf children. When I asked about the photograph in 1999, Ms. Tenorio told me that she had destroyed it and, thus, could not show it to me.

19. The Ministry of Public Education (MEP) designates someone with a teaching certificate. Not all of the personnel at the school were certified.

20. Both Mercedes's sister-in-law, Ángela Berríos, and Ángela's daughter, Patricia Méndez Berríos, in 2003, stated unequivocally that Mercedes Berríos only had one sister.

21. I have met with Silvia Ayón many times, and she has been most helpful, especially in 1997. She told me this story in one of our many 1997 interviews. (During that year, I lived only six blocks from her house, and in the evenings, I would go to her house, and we would sit on the porch while she reminisced about the old days. Her husband had died only a few years earlier.)

22. I first interviewed Silvia Ayón in May 1994, and the whole interview was about how important oral education was, and how much she had fought over the years to teach deaf children to talk. She was especially upset with the Ministry of Education at that time because teachers in the public special education schools had been allowed to use sign language with speech for the past two years. When I saw her again in March 1997, she was transitioning into retirement and still advocated oral education, albeit with much less passion. She surprised me completely in July 1997 when she said that "sign language is good for the deaf." Something had changed her mind between 1994 and 1997! As it turned out, the son whom everyone told me was a model oral deaf adult, the son whom Silvia had shielded so effectively from sign language, and who had held a "regular" job with Aeronica, the national airlines, which showed how good his oral skills were, had met a deaf American woman who taught at an oral school but who came from a deaf family. He had married her, learned sign language, and was living in New York. According to Ms. Ayón, her son had told her how much he valued sign language and how much it had enriched his communication opportunities. "It makes him happy, which is what I want, so I have been reevaluating whether deaf children should learn sign language or not," she said. Still, in Nicaragua, Silvia and Antonio Ayón continue to be identified as model educators of the oral deaf, and their son was often cited to me as a deaf person who had successfully learned to speak. I have never met him, and cannot judge.

23. The cancellation was published in *La Gaceta,* on May 23, 1983.

24. Because the special education system has always been so small in Nicaragua, many parents have either not known about it, or it was not easily accessible to them. Many times, parents would make arrangements for a developmentally delayed child or a blind or deaf child to be placed in a regular class. Typically, these arrangements are not very successful. Gary Miron, a student from the University of Stockholm, did a very interesting doctoral dissertation (Miron 1996), collecting his data in 1988–1990 on the number of unofficially integrated children with disabilities who were in the public education system. The phenomenon he studied was not new in the 1980s. One of Guillermina Morgan's tasks in the 1970s had been to find children who would benefit more from education within the special education schools, rather than sitting through regular classes from which they could not benefit.

25. This club had chapters in both Managua and León.

26. There are rumors that Hope Somoza, herself, had a disabled child whom she kept hidden, but I can find no support for that rumor. Others, such as Rosemary Bohmer de Selva, believe that Hope Somoza had contact with the persons from the Kennedy Foundation, and had been inspired by them to improve education for children with disabilities in Nicaragua. Remember also that Amelia Debayle had been interested in special education in the 1960s. Anastasio Somoza's mother's family were the Debayles, and Hope could have come across the topic through contact with her husband's maternal relatives. Unfortunately, Doña Hope has passed on, and I cannot ask her directly about her motives.

27. Because of the continued high earthquake risk, the old center of the city was not rebuilt. Even up to 2000, there were wide stretches of uninhabited land among the ruins of old building in the "downtown" section. This decentralization is the most striking characteristic of the city—it is a network of suburbs, rather than one urban center.

28. I say "probably" because no records of enrollment exist. Through five years of interviews, I have reconstructed a list of the students who were probably enrolled in the first year at the new school. Starting from photographs taken in 1977 by Rúthy Durán (she unfortunately only took pictures of her own class, not of all of the classes), I made a list of names and have asked teachers and administrators who were at the National Center for Special Education (CNEE) in 1977 to inspect my list and make corrections. My most recent reconstruction is of forty-nine deaf students in four classes, but it is, after all, based on my asking people to remember what had happened nearly twenty years before.

29. There is a widespread impression that the school was elite, charged a hefty tuition, and prior to 1979 was only open to the rich. One woman who worked

as a teacher's aide at the school at the time told me "the parking lot was always filled with cars—rich people dropping off and picking up their children." But I cannot find much objective support for that impression. Both Rosemary Bohmer de Selva and Luz María Sequeira, the director and vice director in 1977, as well as Guillermina Morgan, the liaison between the school and the Ministry of Public Education, deny the allegation and say that schooling was free. Looking at the reconstructed list of pupils (gathered through the memories of five former teachers), I find that none of them have remarkable last names, and the ones I can find today (at least 80% of the 1977 enrollment) are certainly not rich. No one has ever commented on the economic well-being of the ones I cannot trace, although the ones who emigrated during the 1980s may have been families of means. Jenifer Grigsby, who definitely does come from a prominent family, is *not* on the list. She had been a pupil at the Ayóns' private school and was then placed in a regular school with daily tutoring. The fact that people were turned away (and I have talked to parents who did try to enroll their children and were turned down) seems to be due more to lack of space than to any discrimination according to financial status.

30. Clustering of pavilions is the typical layout for schools in Nicaragua and other Central American countries. Four to eight classrooms laid side by side are covered by a common roof with large window banks on opposing walls. Because of the tropical climate, the windows are typically left open to catch any breezes, and each pavilion has a broad porch along one side that is useful during the rainy season. In the countryside, two-classroom pavilions are common, but at the CNEE, each pavilion has eight classrooms.

31. Exactly what "the" Total Communication methodology was has been a topic of debate for many years. Here I am referring to the practice in which a speaker speaks in Spanish while signing signs from the local sign language.

32. There is a photocopied document in the files of the office of the Programa Regional de Recursos para la Sordera (Regional Resource Program on Deafness) (PROGRESO) called *Pasantía,* or Practicum, which appears to have been the handouts and readings provided to teachers (it does not say that the practicum was limited to Costa Ricans, but it also does not mention visitors from other countries) who attended the training given on October 15–26, 1984, at the Virgin Poderosa School in San José, Costa Rica. The training was led by Professors Gloria Campos and Ana Isabel Rodrigúguez. The training was sponsored by the Associación Mima Bravo, and the unsigned introduction was written by someone from that organization. The Introduction begins, "Costa Rica has been a promotor of the use of Total Communication since 1976."

33. Note that this is twelve years before a similar association was organized in Nicaragua. All of the information about Costa Rica comes from the archives of PROGRESO in San José, Costa Rica, which I was able to consult in 1999, courtesy of Dr. Soledad Chavarria.

34. Rúthy Durán's brother lives in Costa Rica and is married to Grace Jara, a top administrator in deaf education at the Costa Rican Ministry of Education, and an early advocate of the Total Communication methodology. It is impossible to imagine that Rúthy, who is very close to her brother, would not have heard through her sister-in-law about the new trend in 1975–1976, or about the workshops in 1978.

35. Mima, who everyone remembers as an extraordinary person, was an enthusiastic and forceful advocate, but she was killed in a car accident a year later. In her memory, the Asociación Mima Bravo ("a not-for-profit private organization with the goal of providing programs to benefit the deaf population of Costa Rica") was founded to continue her work in January 1979. Among other projects, the association sponsored training workshops in Total Communication. (Information taken from the archives of PROGRESO in San José, Costa Rica, during a research trip in 1999, courtesy of Dr. Soledad Chavarria.)

36. There is a letter to PROGRESO (in its archives in San José, Costa Rica) from Gallaudet College's International Center on Deafness, dated July 8, 1978, and signed by Dr. Gilbert Delgado who proposes "a training seminar of one week for two representatives from each Central American country to be exposed to the philosophy of Total Communication."

According to Soledad Chavarria, while the workshops for teachers working in Costa Rica started in 1976, the ones intended for representatives from other countries did not start until after Dr. Delgado's letter on July 8, 1978. Hence, the Nicaragua workshop could not have been earlier than this, and it could not have been later than June 1980, because by that time, Natalia Popova de Jiron was the active supervisor for deaf education in the Department of Special Education, and she would certainly not have allowed such a workshop to be held in Nicaragua. Two teachers specifically mentioned "1980—before Natalia took over," which could have been January or February 1980, the last part of the year-end holidays before classes resumed in March. Teachers would have had the free time to attend a workshop, and Popova does not appear to have been in charge until the academic year started.

37. Ruthy says that Adrián's amazing expressive style with gestures caught her eye at a family baptism party when Adrián was three or fours years old, and she was fascinated to learn that he was deaf. She intended to be a teacher, and did

help Adrián when she could, but she says she decided to be a teacher of the deaf only after visiting the Guadalupe school in Costa Rica (the one founded by Dr. Centeno Güell). Adrián, by that time, had already gone to Spain.

38. There were many new things to learn in Astorga, but he remembers that one of the biggest shocks was the fact that there were deaf adults in Astorga. He had never seen a deaf adult in Nicaragua.

39. The academic year in Spain runs on a schedule similar to that of the United States (starting in autumn and ending in the spring), whereas Nicaragua's, at the time Adrián was in school, started in March and lasted until the end of November. These visits home were made during his summer vacation, and paid for by a very generous couple in Spain who essentially treated Adrián as their son during his time in Spain. Both Adrián and his father are eternally grateful that this couple made it possible for Adrián to visit his family during his years of schooling in Spain.

40. By complete accident, I acquired a copy of *La Sordera* by María Infante, which contains a history of the Costa Rican deaf community. She noted that a Peace Corps worker named Thomas Gibson worked in Costa Rica in 1980. I wondered if this might also be the "Tomas" so often referred to in Nicaragua. The Peace Corps Returned Volunteer office had no records of any Peace Corps volunteers in Nicaragua in 1979 (the official count was evidently done in October, and all the volunteers had left by then), but there was a record of Thomas Gibson's Costa Rica stay in 1981. The office forwarded to him my letter asking if he was the same person, and he responded affirmitively.

41. I interviewed Mr. Gibson by telephone on March 30, 1998.

42. It is a logical impossibility to prove definitely that there was no deaf community or no regularized sign language in 1979. (This was carefully pointed out to me by Dr. Madeline Maxwell as I was doing the field research in 1997.) We can only show that accumulated evidence makes it unlikely. The fact that Gibson met no deaf adults definitely does not mean there were none—we are certain that they existed at that time, but probably were socially isolated. If there had been any deaf group to receive the notice of Gibson's presence, it is most likely that a representative, at least, would have shown up. Gibson was the talk of the town in May 1979 in deafness-oriented circles.

43. Rúthy Durán was adamant that Douglas Vega was the first student to see the linguistic opportunities of signed languages, and, at first, was more enthusiastic than Javier. But everyone else mentions Javier as the first to pick up on sign language and to be the most diligent in learning signs from any source he could. Douglas Vega had registration card number 1 when the deaf association was for-

mally organized in 1986, so he obviously was very active in the deaf group at that time (Javier has card number 2). But as of 1981, Douglas was working full-time, while Javier was not. The deaf association was founded in April 1986, and, according to his sister-in-law, Jacqueline Aburto, Douglas emigrated to Mexico (and later to the United States) "right after Christmas in 1986, soon after [Jacqueline's son's] first birthday." In 1987, Douglas sent his sister, Ivonne, a dictionary of sign language he found in Guatemala. Both Jacqueline and Ivonne say that that dictionary was photocopied and widely distributed at the time, but later came into Javier's possession and he did not want to continue to photocopy it. Douglas did not return to Nicaragua, so his influence on the deaf community and sign language ended as of 1987.

Gibson did not remember this young person's name. But blondish hair is not that common in Nicaragua. And Javier's hair is one of the first traits people notice about him. His name sign, in fact, refers to the kinky, curly hair, which is of a blondish color (it was probably lighter twenty years ago when Mr. Gibson was in Nicaragua). Javier's family comes from Chinandega, and other people told me that the hair type is characteristic of that region of the country. The reference to that hair type and that hair color of a young, deaf man in 1979 Nicaragua can only refer to Javier.

Javier's knowledge of signs at that time probably came from Costa Rican sources (whatever information the teachers brought back from the Total Communication workshops, as well as Javier's trip with the athletic team in 1978). Dr. Soledad Chavarria of the University of Costa Rica noted that there *was* a heavy American Sign Language (ASL) influence on the sign language used in Costa Rica in the late 1970s and early 1980s, because Gloria Campos had learned Signed English in New York, Mima Bravo was studying at Gallaudet College, and the first dictionary pictures were photographed on the Gallaudet campus. Dr. Chavarria said that Rafael (Ralph) Valverde was especially enamored of ASL, and as an officer of the deaf association, his opinions were respected. Thus, Dr. Chavarria said, if Javier had learned from the Costa Rican dictionary published in 1979, he would have seemed to Gibson to be using many ASL signs. Chavarria also commented that the Deaf Association of Costa Rica had slowly rejected that influence, and by the 1990s, were using many more indigenous Costa Rican forms, considering their language, LESCO, to be a different language than ASL. Gibson also told me in his telephone interview that when he arrived in Costa Rica, he had no difficulty at all communicating with the young deaf adults he met, a situation he characterized as "the opposite to what I had found in Nicaragua."

Chapter 3

1. Specifically, the Special Education Schools No. 1 and No. 2 in Managua, the special education schools in León and Chinandega, and the program in Puerto Cabezas. The school in the Barrío Candelaria (Managua) accepted only blind students, and the residential school in Ciudad Darío at that time only accepted children with motoric handicaps. Olga Tenorio insists that the nuns in Jinotepe also ran a school, but I have not been able to find any evidence of it. Marlene Stadthagan, the person most knowledgeable about special education in Jinotepe, denied that there had ever been such a school in Jinotepe.

2. In the late 1970s, this position was held by Guillermina Morgan. I was able to interview her by telephone in 2003.

3. The *equipo técnico,* or technical team, was composed of six specialists who oversaw different areas of special education. In 1980, the team was composed of Natalia Popova de Jirón, Guillermina Morgan, Magda Santamaría, Blanca Rivera, Melania Moncada, and Melania Morales. (This was the Melania Morales who would later be accidentally killed on a coffee-picking brigade, and for whom the CNEE was renamed in 1987.) All of them spent most of 1980 training the new special education teachers who would staff the expanded school system.

4. I was told by Esperanza Salvador (a teacher with twenty-five years of experience) that the traditional academic year in Nicaragua started in March and ended at the beginning of December. (December 8, the Feast of the Immaculate Conception, is the most celebrated holiday in December, although Christmas is also important.) From the year 2000 forward, however, the school year has started in February and finished early in November. The Nicaraguan sign for the month of March is a stylization of placing books in a school bag, a reminder that it used to be the month for starting school.

5. Nicaragua has cities such as Managua, León, and Granada. Everything that is not city is considered rural, and called the "countryside" (or in Spanish, *el campo*). Life in the countryside is typically more primitive, based on ranching or farming, and *campesinos* (those who live in *el campo*) are assumed to be unsophisticated (in terms of education). However, I also noticed a tendency to compare Managua (the capital) to everywhere else in the country. So, at times, my interviewees would talk about all of the teachers of the deaf from the countryside coming into Managua for a workshop. This would include the teacher from Rivas, from Ocotal, from Matagalpa, and so on, which are small towns. The special education schools draw their populations from the towns, and maybe a few farms on the edge of the towns. None of the special education schools outside of Managua and León provide transportation for the pupils. There is no special

education in the truly rural areas. Deaf children from rural homes are boarded at Ciudad Darío (where their parents are still responsible for dropping them off and picking them up at specified times of the year), or else they go without education.

6. One of the first acts of the new government was to set up a literacy crusade with the goal of universal literacy for Nicaragua's population. Beginning in March 1980, students from twelve years of age were sent to the countryside to work alongside farmers during the day, and teach the family to read at night. The crusade did bring an amazing increase in literacy to the country in 1980, but the pressures of the Contra War and the deteriorating economy did not allow sufficient follow-up. Governments since 1990 have only paid lip service to adult education, and the illiteracy rates in Nicaragua today are comparable to those when the literacy crusade began. Although many teachers in regular schools did go with their students to the countryside, the teachers at the CNEE were part of the crusade's "rear guard" and devoted a part of each day to tutoring urban children in lieu of going to the countryside.

7. For example, another branch of the government or even another part of the Ministry of Education might requisition the school's buses for a specific purpose (such as to transport Literacy Crusaders to their destinations, or to retrieve them), and so classes would be suspended because the children could not get to the school without the buses.

Among the 1980 activities of the new Department of Special Education was a census of children who needed special education and their recruitment into schools. Many parents simply did not know what was available, so the classes started out with small numbers, and the pupils trickled in all year as their parents became aware that schooling was possible for their children. The pupil counts for that year are from the end of the year, not the beginning.

8. See Kegl, Senghas, and Coppola, "Creation through Contact," p. 200: "By 1980, schools for special education had sprung up across the Pacific Coast, the largest being in Managua. Here, over 500 deaf children came together over the course of a few years."

For the increase, see, for example, Kegl and McWhorter, "Perspectives on an Emerging Language," where on page 19, they write: "When hundreds of deaf students came together in the school in the early 1980s, their individual homesign systems were brought into contact on a large scale."

9. I have spent much time collecting enrollment figures for children in deaf education classrooms, both nationally and locally. Over the period from 1977 to 2003, deaf children have accounted for 17–30% of the total enrolled in special education. Deaf children have never been the majority population of special

education schools. Usually 75% of special education schools' populations are listed as "mentally retarded."

10. In fact, I have also never seen 500 deaf *adults* ever gathered in one place in Nicaragua. During my 1997 fieldwork, I was present at the ceremony for the first published dictionary of Nicaraguan Sign Language (NSL), and for the elections of officers of the association, both of which were the most-attended events that year at the deaf association. There were about 200 deaf adults at each of these events. Remember, Nicaragua is a *little* country.

11. Escobar told me that she found the alphabet in a French book and adopted it for teaching in her classroom in the 1950s. But given that the British use a two-handed fingerspelling system, and the French presumably continue to use the one-handed system which Laurent Clerc brought to the United States in 1815, I suspect that the book was British. I don't believe Escobar read either English or French, so the distinction could have been lost on her. What is important is that she, the teacher, did incorporate fingerspelling. Some of the oldest deaf adults today are more comfortable with the two-handed system, although they are also familiar with the one-handed system introduced with the Total Communication influence, and reinforced by Popova.

12. This teasing strategy to encourage verbalization did not originate at the CNEE. Most deaf adults who remembered this remark attribute it to Olga Tenorio and date its use back to the first special education school. As I have explained, I believe it did have some impact on what the children perceived as linguistic.

13. To be fair to Popova, behaviorist psychology, including operant conditioning, heavily influenced language training throughout the world in the 1970s and 1980s. I learned a similar approach for teaching language when I worked as a school speech pathologist in the early 1980s. Teaching language through naturalistic settings, either to deaf or otherwise language-impaired children, did not become common until later.

14. Here, I mean on a larger scale. Individual wealthier families may have taken their children to the United States or Europe earlier for hearing aids; but those were isolated cases, and those children did not attend the special education schools. Olga Tenorio, Silvia Ayón, and Dr. Alma de Isabá all characterize the hearing aids given out by the SS Hope as "the first hearing aids in Nicaragua."

15. Ileana Ruíz, at first, was employed on a full-time basis by the Ministry of Education. Later she chose to work part-time for the Ministry of Education and part-time for the audiological center run by Los Pipitos. In 1999, she accepted a full-time position at the audiological center, and the Ministry of Education has had no audiometrist since. Ms. Ruíz never had an audiometric booth for her work with the Ministry of Education. When the Department of Special

Education was moved to new offices in 2001, there was no space for any audiometry. But then, in the move, all the audiometric equipment was "lost." At present, Los Pipitos, is the only resource for low-income children (the majority of the public school children) in regard to audiometry, and testing there is not free.

16. This figure was estimated by Noel Lam Herrera, the coordinator of the hearing impaired/deaf program at the Department of Special Education in the Ministry of Education in a personal interview in July 1994. In another interview in 1997, Lam stated that he did not believe the situation had changed from 1994. Over the course of five trips made in 1999–2003, I also could discover no reason to believe that there was any significant change from Lam's 1994 estimate.

17. This was still the practice in August 2003.

18. Because Morena was integrated into a regular classroom at the Clementina Cabezas School at the beginning of the school year in March 1983, this would place the visiting that Morena remembered as happening between approximately June 1980 (when classes at the CNEE resumed after Natalia's training) and November 1982 (the end of the 1982 school year).

19. Or any other sign language either (e.g., ASL). Even when members of the deaf association would use standardized signs slowly and in simplified sentences, Rúthy did not understand. I observed her greeting some of the leaders of the deaf association during a conference at Los Pipitos in 1997. All parties were glad to see each other, but when the deaf members tried simple sentences in standardized NSL, she could only understand the more iconic signs. Most of the conversation was gesture, because by 1997, the deaf association had made it clear that, as a matter of pride, they wanted to communicate in NSL, and that they did not consider lipreading oral words to have a place in sign language. It was actually quite sad to witness the awkwardness in this meeting between parties that twenty years earlier had been quite fond of each other.

20. We know that Rúthy was active through December 1987 because the Certificación meeting was held at the preschool where she worked. She must have been the one to arrange permission to use the building and the one with a key, etc. She appears to have retired from association activities sometime in 1988, because she says that she definitely had nothing to do with writing the grant to the Swedish Deaf Association or buying the house (c. May 1989).

21. Remember that we are talking about a "fuzzy" system here. As Bart Koscko explains, a fuzzy system can be both in a certain state and not in that state at the same time. Dr. Koscko uses clothes driers which use a computer chip functioning under a fuzzy logic system as an example. At any moment, the clothes in a dryer will be wet to a certain extent while also being dry to a certain extent.

The dryer will continue to blow hot air on the clothes until the extent of wet reaches a certain low point and the extent of dry reaches a predetermined high point, and then the dryer shuts off. From what I have been able to observe, NSL also developed as a fuzzy system, one of the endpoints on its gradient being gestures and homesign, while the other end was standardized sign language. But I find no evidence of a sharp disconnection point where homesign ended and standardized sign emerged. Rather both coexisted in changing quantities for a long period, although what is accepted as NSL by deaf adults today is weighted heavily toward standardized signing, while gesture/homesigns are considered "primitive."

22. And there are many. See O. Aguirre Heredía, Los Gestos Como Forma de Comunicación. Also, some of the most "Nicaraguan" words in the 1997 Sign Language Dictionary are based on non-verbal gestures common in the discourse of hearing Nicaraguans. This point was underscored for me in an interview in 2003 with Robert Bolger, an American deaf man who began to visit Nicaragua regularly in 1987. He said the sign language he encountered in Nicaragua in 1987 to be quite distinct from the ASL he knew. He gave me a list of some of the signs whose differences had amazed him in 1987, and most of the Nicaraguan versions are gestures commonly used by all Nicaraguans, not just the deaf.

23. Though some sustained memory-poking of my informants, I have reconstructed a probable enrollment list for 1977 (nothing official survives), and it is interesting that all birth years are not equally represented. The youngest deaf student in the school was four (born 1973) and the oldest deaf students were seventeen (born 1959). Half of the students were in two classes with students in the twelve- to seventeen-year range (with 60% of the twenty-three students in those two classes born in the year 1962 alone). The other half of the deaf students were in two classes with pupils ranging from four to ten, with 35% of those classes born in either 1968 or 1969. The five-year span from 1963 to 1967 (one-third of the possible birth years) accounted for only five students (10% of total enrollment), and no one at all from the birth year 1965 was included. This uneven pattern (which I believe mirrors rubella epidemics peaking in 1962 and 1968–1969) is found again in the 1997 registration list of the deaf association. The teachers with whom I reconstructed the list did not notice this pattern.

24. Remember that this is immediately after the revolution, and there were many young men who had sustained injuries that left them paraplegic or hemiplegic. These were the focus of the Gaspar García Liviana Center, not the more traditional motoric problems, such as those associated with polio or cerebral palsy, which special education schools had seen before, although youths with those problems were certainly included. This center continued to receive an influx of

new para- and hemiplegic trainees throughout the 1980s as a result of the Contra War.

The Occupational Center for the Disabled (COD) took over the unused Casa Comunal, a community center, in Villa Libertad, a suburb in the eastern section of Managua. Thus, the center came to be known as the "school in Villa Libertad." All of the deaf persons I interviewed seemed to think that the center's name was "Villa Libertad." Only hearing people referred to it as the COD, its official name.

25. This is an area that is still a problem in Nicaragua. There are a large number of students who, because of low testing scores or the inability to progress academically, have been labeled "mentally retarded" when in other places or times, they might simply be called "slow learners" or "learning disabled." Educational psychologists are few in Nicaragua, and educational testing is still in its infancy.

26. The Costa Rican signs were taught by Marta Granados de Avilés, a speech therapist who had learned them during her training, which probably focused on Total Communication. Her master's thesis on special education, which lauds oral education, is available at the library of the Universidad Centroamericana (UCA). It is undated, but from internal evidence, it appears to have been done in the 1976–1978 period. Marta had a deaf child, who inspired her to look further into education for deaf children. The staff of the COD state that Marta received training in sign language in Costa Rica (which would probably have been the Total Communication method advocated by PROGRESO at the time). Marta was one of the first Nicaraguans to emigrate after the Sandinista Revolution. Her ex-colleagues believe she went to Canada, some say Toronto, but I have been unable to trace her.

27. Remember that this is Nancy Guadamuz's subjective impression, but it was corroborated by other colleagues who worked at the COD at the same time, including Dalia Membreño and María Teresa Aguilar. Later, I note that deaf persons in Nicaragua rate the signing skills of any hearing persons very generously. My point here is that the use of homesigns, mimicry, gestures, and signs was widespread at the COD from its inception. I am not saying that it began as a regularized language.

28. The years 1983–1984 marked the serious onset of the U.S.-backed Contra war. Health and education budgets were cut in order to make resources available for military defense.

29. These years are showcased because classes accepting deaf students began in 1946, and the use of sign language was first officially permitted (but not required) in classrooms for the deaf in 1992. In the intervening period, education was strictly oral in philosophy.

30. Keep also in mind that there were others described as "successful" who informants also spontaneously labeled as hard of hearing. I include here only those who I have reason to believe had at least a severe-to-profound hearing loss, and thus, would usually be termed "deaf." But audiometric documentation in this period is rare.

31. These are terms used spontaneously by my informants in talking about the oral goals for the deaf, and I reflected these terms back to them in my questions.

Chapter 4

1. In particular, she showed me a set of five or six pictures taken at a party celebrating Mother's Day (a holiday that is taken very seriously in Nicaragua) in 1975.

2. Mentioned specifically by informants (including, but not limited to, Rúthy) were gatherings before 1979 at the homes of Javier López Gómez, Mauricio Zepeda, Uriel Cuadra, and Roberto Useda.

3. She has some wonderful pictures of her three- and four-year-olds marching in a 1980 parade.

4. All three of these teachers remain fundamentally oral in their educational perspectives today. They see the usefulness of signing, but none of them advocates signing alone. Speech is still the ultimate goal of deaf education for all of them.

5. Some of the early, large gatherings for the group that would become Association to Help and Integrate the Deaf (APRIAS) were held at the Roberto Vargas Batres Preschool, which Rúthy could get permission to use without having to pay a fee.

6. Indirect evidence of the presence of this attitude at that time among deaf association members (it changed later), is provided by Cyndi Norman's comment in her thesis that during her six months living in Nicaragua in 1986, there was a younger group of signers (those enrolled at that time in the COD) whom she characterized as the "signing deaf" and an older group (those who were former students at the COD—those who had entered in 1981 and left by 1986) whom she named the "speaking deaf." While the younger deaf (with whom she interacted on a daily basis) always signed to her, the older group (those who would have been the founding members of the deaf association, and who she met only occasionally) insisted on speaking to her, even though she could barely understand them and had to ask constantly for clarification. Cyndi's impression was that while the older group watched the younger group sign with her and knew that she understood at least some signing, that they were proud of their oral skills and wanted her to know that

they were capable of more than signing. The same persons named as "speaking deaf" by Norman in 1986 became strong advocates in the 1990s of using Nicaraguan Sign Language without voicing for communication.

7. Dr. Napoleón Rios, the lawyer mentioned previously, acted as the notary at that meeting and filed the original with the proper authorities. He is required by law to keep a copy of all official documents that he draws up and make them available for public inspection. I was able, therefore, to copy the names of those present by referring to his archive. I had already copied the vital statistics of the registered members of the deaf association.

8. I was informed by the archivist at the National Assembly that all the papers from the period in which the Sandinista Party controlled the government (e.g., 1979–1990) had been "taken by the Sandinistas when they left," and she had no idea of their present whereabouts. These are documents that, by law, are required to be permanently archived for future reference. Someone did not want those papers available to future historians, but which side that might have been is speculation at this point.

9. The *Gaceta* is the official organ of the Nicaraguan government. Decrees ratified by the National Assembly do not legally take effect until they are published in the *Gaceta*.

10. Probably the closest United States equivalent would be the Department of State.

11. All deaf informants stated this unequivocally. Many said that they had learned to sign by going to APRIAS meetings. Gloria Minero and Yadira Miranda also stated that sign language was more used during the meetings than oral Spanish. Robert Bolger, a deaf American, who first went to Nicaragua in 1987, also noted that the APRIAS meetings were held in sign language. Although he was familiar with ASL, he says that the signing used at the APRIAS meetings was different, and that it took him a while to learn it.

12. The Swedish International Development Association is known in other contexts as SIDA, but this acronym in Spanish is also used to denote Acquired Immune Deficiency Syndrome (in English AIDS), so in Spanish-speaking countries, the organization is known as SHIA. The organization administers programs worldwide, especially in Africa.

13. Saying that the house of the deaf association was near the UCA was the most useful indicator until 1998. A small shopping center closer to the deaf association underwent an enormous renovation to morph into Metrocentro. It includes one of the few multistory buildings in Managua and its first escalator. This is now the most useful landmark for finding the deaf association.

14. I don't know who was counting that day, but members on the Certificación list two years earlier already had membership cards numbers 60 and 66.

15. Jacqueline corroborates this and said she is sure the meetings to which she accompanied Ivonne took place in 1984 because at that time she was madly in love with Ivonne's brother, Sergio, and was willing to do any favor to impress him or his family, including taking his little sister wherever she wanted to go. Jacqueline and Sergio married in early 1985.

16. Ferrar said that Gloria translated, but Gloria denies this and says that Sebastián probably had her mixed up with Yadira Miranda, whose coloring and hairstyle were similar. According to Gloria, she had stopped participating in APRIAS activities by this time. She did translate for the visit of Anders and Kerstin in May 1990 (she is listed in a report written by Kerstein to SHIA as the only translator during the visit); but in the latter part of the year, ugly rumors that she was misappropriating funds led her to reduce her participation significantly. Yadira says that she does not remember anything about such a meeting, but agrees that Sebastián regularly asked her to help him by translating during this period. Gloria was busy arranging her move back to El Salvador, which she did in 1991.

17. Jenifer Grigsby, who had been president up to this time, and who headed the assimilationist slate, said that she, personally, did not vote because her daughter decided to be born on that day.

18. Richard Senghas includes it in his dissertation (1995). I heard the exact same story from multiple deaf people in 1997, and it seems to have become a metaphoric story of how deaf members came to demand their rights from hearing persons who treated them patronizingly.

19. Although only one volume appears to have been envisioned originally, funding continued after 1997. In 2003, a colorful children's dictionary was published.

20. But, the association has evidently not changed the name officially, a procedure that would require a petition to a court and the modification of much paperwork with resultant expenses.

21. None of this is formally articulated, but must be inferred from association actions or interpreted from the president's statements and explanations.

Chapter 5

1. The governmental agency responsible for demographic information is the National Institute of Statistics and Census. Figures used in this chapter are taken from the last census, which was published in 1995. The planning for the next census is under way, and there are rumors that the next census will in-

clude a "disability" question, but it is not yet certain how specific the question will be.

2. There is no agreed definition for "deafness," and the impact of severe-to-profound hearing loss is different depending upon the age at which it first occurs. Thus, we have few guidelines for estimating how many people in a given country are "deaf." The National Institute on Deafness and Other Communication Disorders places the prevalence of deafness at approximately 1% of the U.S. population. Figures reported by the World Health Organization (many countries do not even collect this data, so the rates given by WHO are only from the countries who did give a report) range from 0.1% to over 5%, but deafness has a different meaning for countries in which different treatments are available. I have chosen to be very conservative and am estimating that 0.5–1.0% of the population of Nicaragua would be classified as deaf. In this work, we are concerned only with the subpopulation who would most likely be drawn to join a deaf association. Naturally, the number of persons in Nicaragua with hearing loss of a degree less than severe is much greater.

3. Thirty-eight percent of the Nicaraguan population is concentrated in the western part of the country in the capital or in a set of towns (e.g., Masaya, Jinotepe, Granada, etc.) that are within a one-hour bus ride from the capital. Many live in one of the smaller towns and commute to work in the capital.

4. But he gave no reasoning for how he arrived at this estimate, although he was asked. The number 600 is simply his best guess.

5. This is an administrative region similar to a "county" or "parish" in the United States.

6. Travel to the Atlantic Coast is something else. There are no reliable roads, the bus-boat trip takes two days and is, at times, beset with bandits. Whenever possible, travelers between the capital and the Atlantic Coast fly. Once on the coast, travel between towns and villages is by boat.

7. In 1997, there was only one deaf man who told me he could drive (Miguel Angel Moreno). He was a partner in a bus collective and drove a certain route each day. It was not clear whether he had obtained a license.

It can easily take an hour or more to cross Managua by bus in non-rush hours. A two-hour bus ride each way is considered a reasonable amount to travel to attend deaf association events. Those coming from Jinotega, (168 km. to the north), travel four hours each way.

8. Usually referred to in Spanish as *la casa de los sordos* or *el sede* (headquarters) *de los sordos*.

9. This was made especially apparent to me when I tried to write a chronology of education for deaf children in Nicaragua. During different interviews,

I was given more than six addresses for the location of the first special education school in the 1952–1962 period. When I sat down with my friend, Noel Gómez, a lifelong resident of Managua, he pointed out to me that they all indicated the same place, but each began at a different landmark (some landmarks had been destroyed in the 1972 earthquake and had been replaced with other buildings, so they meant nothing to me, a person who had only seen the city post-earthquake) and simply appeared to me to be different; but in reality, they were all consistent.

10. For example, one Saturday afternoon in chatting with a group of about six members, I mentioned that a friend was coming to visit me (from the United States), and I asked them what they thought the most interesting parts of Managua would be for me to show my friend. The question was patently absurd to them, but then I realized that all of their social life revolves around the deaf association. None of them had ever had a friend who didn't know just as much about Managua as they did, and the idea of showing a friend the sights of the city was meaningless.

11. But it is not limited to members. By instructing the surveyors to survey "anybody who was deaf," some very isolated individuals were included.

12. This was not a stable union, and the whereabouts of the father are unknown. Although not completely certain, it is believed that he was hearing.

13. The example that immediately jumps to mind is that of Dr. I. King Jordan, president of Gallaudet University, who grew up with normal hearing and was deafened when he was in his early twenties. Dr. Jordan states, however, that his situation is unusual, and he should not be considered a typical member of a deaf community.

14. When the deaf association was founded, there was at least one person who lost her hearing at age eight, but she calls herself "hard of hearing" and stopped attending association events around 1990.

15. I have met members of deaf communities in the United States who describe being "slowly edged out of the hearing world" to a point where communication with sign language is more comfortable. But that was before cochlear implants were common. Many of the persons with progressive hearing loss who in past years would have come to identify with deafness, now are considered excellent candidates for cochlear implants, and thus, continue to be users of oral speech.

16. The aminoglycocides are a family of antibacterial drugs which are known to be poisonous (ototoxic) to the inner ear (Stach 1998). Most of the members of the family have names ending in –myacin, such as streptomyacin, gentamyacin, kanamyacin, and so on. These drugs were first given to civilians after World

War II. In the 1950s, their effect on inner ear function began to be noted. At present, aminoglycocides are usually used as a measure of last resort in the United States and Europe when an infection does not respond to other antibiotics. All of the aminoglycocides, but especially gentamyacin, are readily available without prescription at all pharmacies in Nicaragua. Some aminoglycocide use in Nicaragua is self-medication (one woman told me that taking a regular preventive dose of gentamyacin would ward off ear infections), but physicians routinely prescribe them too. I spoke with multiple physicians in Nicaragua who were unaware that any of the aminoglycocide antibiotics were ototoxic. Gentamyacin is easily available in generic form, and is thus one of the less expensive antibiotics for physicians to prescribe in Nicaragua. Just how the inner ear is poisoned is not yet well understood. Some of the aminoglycocides cause more damage to the vestibular portion of the inner ear, some more to the cochlear portion, and some cause problems throughout the inner ear. When there is damage to the cochlea of the inner ear, hearing loss results.

17. Neither noise-induced hearing loss nor age-related hearing loss (both of which do include age factors, but also are associated with certain audiometric configurations) was found to be the likely cause for anyone's hearing ability at the deaf association.

18. Among many others, both Stach (1998) and Schow and Nerbonne (1996) discuss the criteria for hearing aid fitting and the expected benefits from amplification.

19. I report their responses here, but I doubt some of those who set the age of their hearing loss as three or four years of age. If they had been hearing well up to that date, they would have had a very good grasp of oral language when they were deafened, and that should be mirrored in their present grasp of oral or written Spanish, or fluency in NSL, which would then have been a second language. I don't see that ability, though. Adrián Pérez's hearing loss is well-documented as occurring at eighteen months of age, and his grasp of Spanish is superior to nearly every other deaf person; but he was educated for eight years at a school in Spain, so the reason for his better Spanish skills is not clear. However, one person who told me he was four years of age when he was deafened (and his family confirmed that age) shows all the signs of congenital hearing loss. If he had actually been deafened at four, he would have had a very good grasp of Spanish grammar; but this person does not demonstrate this either in his ability to read and write Spanish. His behavior is typical of someone born deaf. I believe that those surveyed who gave three or four years of age as the date of onset of their hearing loss are actually telling us of *when the hearing loss was noted* by family members. Congenitally deaf children do not know that they are deaf and assume that everyone experiences the world as they

do, so they don't complain about not hearing. I have tested some three-year-olds who were so visually alert that they had managed to confuse their parents into thinking they heard, when they did not. Usually, parents suspected something earlier, but a child could have passed unrecognized. Only in thinking back did the parents realize that the "homemade" tests they had tried on their child had incorporated some visual component to which the child was very sensitive, and that was what the child was responding to. There are some hard of hearing members at the deaf association, but I believe that everyone with a profound hearing loss there was deafened before the age of two.

20. When questioned closely, the surveyors stated that these surveys had been administered in a combination of sign language and gestures, and that the surveyors had relied on family members in the home for information to fill out the survey or to act as translators using home signs more familiar to the respondent. At times, a respondent might be able to understand some familiar speech from a family member, but the same words would not be understood when said by an unfamiliar person.

21. Probably meningitis, because her mother said she had an extremely high fever when she was six months old.

22. Observation of the fifteen- to-twenty-five-year-old group attending activities and classes at the association in 2002 indicates that this "generation" will be even larger than the same-age group described in 1997.

23. The numbers of children in special education have continued to increase since 1997, and this includes children in *audición* (deaf education). In a personal communication in March 2003 as the new school year was starting, Yolanda Mendieta wrote that the incoming classes were overflowing and the schools were having great difficulty accommodating the increased enrollments of first-year deaf children. Rubella epidemics still are unchecked in Nicaragua, and to me this indicated that there had been another rubella epidemic approximately six years earlier. These children will one day probably be members of the deaf association.

24. Melania Morales was a teacher of developmentally delayed children at the CNEE. On a volunteer coffee-picking brigade in 1986, she was accidentally killed. The CNEE was renamed in her honor the following year.

25. Note later the comparison of membership between the deaf association and the blind association. The blind association also has a preponderance of males over females in its membership list.

Chapter 6

1. Only a very small number of the members who were active in association activities (in other words, those I saw regularly at the association) could read

Spanish at the level required to understand the sentences in the Deaf Survey. I found less than ten of them, and not all of them were interested in the work of finding deaf people to survey, so the majority of the surveys were conducted by five deaf persons.

2. This is especially noteworthy in light of the fact that in regular primary education, the teacher-to-pupil ratio is 1:40.

3. This information is based on an interview with Susana Rugama, who in 1997 was the head of the deaf education section of the special education school in Managua. It was confirmed in 2000 by Rosario García, principal of the school and Ivette Aguilar, vice principal of the school.

4. When the bus for a particular section of the city breaks down, the pupils from that section of the city simply do not go to school until the bus is repaired (the wait varies, but it is usually *not* the day after the bus breaks down). When I was visiting in Tipitapa in 1997, I was told that the bus had not come for about two weeks, so the children were not in school. Each bus usually transports about 100 pupils, and since most people belonging to the low-income sector do not have telephones, there is no official announcement that the bus isn't coming, nor any notice that it has resumed. After the children have waited about an hour at the bus stop, they just return home. Parents find out that the bus is running again by word of mouth.

5. Quoted from required class reading packet (photocopied, no author, no date, page 28) for the UNAN course, Educational Administration, in 2001: "The curriculum for the education of minors with disabilities lasts 9–10 years, with liberty on the part of the student to leave the educational system during this time, because in the country [Nicaragua], special education is not obligatory in character" (my translation). I had earlier heard this from Noel Lam in 1995 when he was the head of the deaf education section in the Department of Special Education in the Ministry of Education. This is one of the reasons that the Ministry of Education does not make a concerted effort to find all disabled children who could benefit from education; another is that they couldn't handle the enrollments if they did. Special education receives less than 1% of the budget for the Ministry of Education in any given year.

6. Education officials in the United States routinely estimate that approximately 10% of the primary school population will require some form of special education.

7. See Ministry of Education, Department of Special Education, "Introducción a la Educación Especial."

8. There is a list of items considered necessary to support a four-member family (in other words, one with two parents and two children), and prices for

these items are checked monthly at different shopping centers and then averaged. The total averaged cost for the items would be the value of one "basic market basket."

9. From a personal interview with Lesbia Vega Correa, Public Relations Representative, Industrial Free Trade Zone "Las Mercedes," June 27, 1997.

10. In 2003, however, while she still did not appear at any of the deaf association events, she was socializing with a small group of the older deaf adults who met at private homes. In my interview with her, she said she never went to the deaf association, but yes, was quite definitely a member.

11. Matt and Eva do not appear to have any wish to introduce ASL as a competitor to NSL. They did attend the Saturday NSL classes for the general public on Saturdays in 1996 with the intention of learning the language; but it is probably very difficult for Matt not to use ASL when he wants to explain himself and there is no equivalent in NSL. Eva uses Simultaneous Communication, so her signing mirrors the oral language. (She uses English with me, but I have seen her sign while speaking Spanish too.) With the prestige ASL enjoys in Nicaragua, it would be difficult for them not to be influencing the sign language use among the deaf people with whom they associate. But, it must be noted that they are not the only ASL users who regularly come to Nicaragua, and are certainly not responsible for the ASL influence that was obvious before they arrived. Bob Bolger, a deaf man from California, has been visiting Nicaragua every year since 1987, and he must have had some influence on language usage over the years.

Chapter 7

1. I heard this expectation in interviews with Soledad Escobar de Flores (teacher of the deaf, 1952–1974), Olga Tenorio Hernandez (teacher and later director, 1948–1976), María and Ángela Berríos (sisters of the director, Dr. Apolonio Berríos) and Isaura Garcia (teacher at the school, 1960–1962).

2. There was an apparent rubella spike in 1962, so that of the seventy-two registered deaf members born between 1959–1965, 40% were born in 1962 alone. Those born between 1959 and1965 are what I refer to as "the 1962 cohort."

3. Fifty is chosen as a purely arbitrary number. The registration files did not have the date on which the registration was filed, only the member's birth date and registration card number. Thus, I could not determine how many members had joined in a given year.

4. In 2003, mostly younger members attended deaf association events.

5. Even today, there is no universal vaccination for rubella in Nicaragua. The same cyclical variation is seen when the birth dates of the children enrolled in

classrooms for the hearing impaired in special education schools in 1997 are graphed, indicating that rubella epidemics are continuing in six- to eight-year cycles. Rubella is a disease that if contracted by a pregnant woman results in the child being born with severe-to-profound hearing loss, or visual abnormalities (Johnson and Whitehead 1989).

6. The deaf association gives April 22, 1986, as its founding date.

7. For example, see Kegl, "The Nicaraguan Sign Language Project"; Kegl and McWhorter, "Perspectives on Emerging Language"; or Kegl, Senghas, and Coppola, "Creation through Contact."

8. Indirect support for the youngest children probably being six years old came from Ivonne Vega and her mother, Ángela Obando, when they reminisced in 1997 how Douglas had wanted Ivonne to come to his school with him when she was four year old (in 1976). She did go once, but hated it and screamed and tantrumed until she was brought home. Asked why she didn't like the school, Ivonne replied, "They were all big kids; there was no one my age." She was one of the first enrolled in the new school in 1977, however, and didn't have to have her name on a waiting list because Olga Tenorio told Ivonne's mother to simply take her to the school and say she was one of the transfers from the Berríos school, all of whom were being accepted. When questioned, Ivonne said that she did enjoy going to school in 1977 because she was in a class with children her own age.

9. I specifically say "we" because I could not have done the interviews alone. Yolanda Mendieta's fluency in NSL, her interest in the deaf, and her wide knowledge of and friendships with deaf people in Nicaragua made the interviews possible. She started as a paid interpreter in 1997, but by 2003, we were collaborators in searching out the older deaf people to hear their stories. I thank her heartily for her help and encouragement.

The nineteen adults who we interviewed were Liseth Balmaceda, Melba Barrios, Roberto Cano Sanchez, Arcadio Diaz Luna, Natalia Galo, Julio Cesar Garcia, Cristina Guevara, Josefa Gutiérrez, Manuel Jerez, Socorro Lara, Gerardo Lezcama, Javier López Gómez, Mabel Midence, Mercedes Murillo, María Lourdes Palacios, Noel Rocha, and Mauricio Zepeda. The interviews were done between 1997 and 2002.

10. In fact, the socialization opportunities were still sparse for deaf people in 1997. I spoke with one woman at one of the Saturday afternoon gatherings who told me that she was from León, and that she regularly made the trip on Saturdays to Managua just to be able to visit with friends in sign language. She told me there was no equivalent group in León.

11. Olga Tenorio implied in some of my interviews with her that there were up to fifty deaf pupils at the Berríos school, but since she told me bluntly that

she burned the enrollment book for the Berríos school, and since no statistics from the school survived in the Ministry of Education's papers, there is absolutely no way to verify the numbers. I detail in this work the investigation I did to determine how many classrooms for deaf children the Berríos school had, and I could never get past one class. Considering the size that the school rooms had to be to fit on the land where the school was located, even twenty-five in a class would be very crowded.

12. Mimeographed copies of instructions elaborating the Verbal Communication method are still available in the small library maintained by the Ministry of Education. All have been given brown packaging paper covers to preserve them. The covers include the titles of each section, but most of the mimeographed documents are anonymous. A few include "Natalia Popova" or "Natalia de Jirón" (her married name) as the author. The anonymous mimeographed copies all use the same typewriter and paper, and it is obvious that they all came from Popova's office at about the same time. None are specifically dated, but from internal evidence, they appear to have been typed in 1983 or in 1984. (Each year, the revolutionary government designated an official slogan which was to appear at the beginning of any document. None of the documents apparently from Popova's office were dated, but all have the slogans. By knowing which slogans were used in which years, information I gained from other documents that had both dates and slogans, it is possible to date documents written between 1979 and 1990.)

13. With the exception of María Lourdes Palacios, who was born in 1954, but her case must be considered separately.

14. The Managua earthquake on December 21, 1972, destroyed a major portion of the city, killing a large number. There were multiple students from the Berríos school who did not return after the earthquake either because their families needed their earnings, or the families migrated to other areas of Nicaragua permanently or temporarily when their homes were destroyed. The school itself was not damaged in the earthquake.

15. Children are known to be especially adept at learning whatever language is used around them. There is agreement that children from birth to three years are particularly sensitive to language learning, and this language acquisition facility remains great up to puberty. The ability to learn language remains a possibility throughout an individual's life, but it becomes more difficult with age. Language-learners past puberty usually retain an "accent," even if they acquire excellent mastery of the language, and the grammatical repertoire seems to be reduced in late language-learners. None of the deaf persons discussed here had complete access to a standardized language system during their most sensitive

years (birth to three), because their families spoke Spanish and they did not have full access to the oral system. Most entered school at six or seven years of age, and had only oral Spanish and the communal gesture system used by the pupils in the school as linguistic input.

16. Douglas is now living in the United States, but when he left Nicaragua, he went first to Guatemala, then to Mexico, and finally to the United States. Maybe some of the contacts he made with Noel on that trip helped him when he first left Nicaragua.

17. *Brillar por su ausencia,* or literally "gleams by its absence." In Nicaragua, this expression is commonly used to note the absence of someone or something expected, but not present. For example, "Joe Doe must be angry with us, because he didn't come to the party. He gleamed (or shined) by his absence."

18. All of those born in the early 1960s appear to be late language-learners, and there is a qualitative difference between them and those born in the 1968–1976 period.

19. Mr. Perezalonzo, who was educated in Spain, may have been a fluent signer, especially if he went to the same school as Adrián did, where signing outside the classroom was common. But he does not seem to have shared this knowledge with anyone. Remember, only hearing persons remembered him; none of the deaf did.

20. Unless we count Thomas Gibson's influence in 1979, which I don't. I believe Gibson was crucial because he was testimony to the linguistic-ness of sign language, its usefulness as a social tool, and its social acceptability in other places. But three weeks of teaching has limits as a linguistic model.

21. During Kegl's three-week stay, she concentrated on the COD.

22. For example, see Senghas, "Children's Contribution to the Birth of Nicaraguan Sign Language" and Senghas and Coppola, "Children Creating Language."

23. Javier is vague about the details of this trip. In one interview he implied that he had gone to Costa Rica with family members but Rúthy Dúran says her understanding was that when Javier went with the athletic group that it was his first trip to Costa Rica. (Rúthy said: "When we went to Costa Rica he never mentioned to me that he had been there before!") The dates written on the backs of the photographs Rúthy took on the trip are clear that the group from CNEE went to an athletic contest in May 1978. Soledad Chavarria, of PROGRESO in Costa Rica, said that by 1978, copies of the Costa Rican Sign Language Dictionary (Hacia una nueva forma de comunicacion con el sordo) were available (this is corroborated by a letter from Dr. Delgado to Dr. Chavarria), although the publication date of the copy I examined said April 1979. According to Soledad, Javier

could have obtained the dictionary on the athletic trip, or it could have been given to him by Mayra, or could have been brought back to him by one of the teachers who went to Costa Rica for a Total Communication workshop in 1979. Rúthy Dúran is also very clear that Douglas Vega and Javier López Gómez obtained some form of a dictionary from Thomas Gibson in 1979, because they immediately showed it to her with elation, and began to practice the signs.

24. Many folktales exist of deaf Peace Corps volunteers transferring ASL to other countries and either imposing ASL over an indigenous sign language or introducing ASL where no previous sign language existed. There is no evidence that this happened in Nicaragua. Perhaps it was the Sandinista Revolution that blocked Gibson from performing his agreed-upon term of Total Communication teaching, which is responsible for saving Nicaragua from this fate.

25. Specifically, by Dr. Judy Kegl and Dr. Ann Senghas.

26. According to Noel Lam, who in 1995 was in charge of deaf education at the Ministry of Education, use of sign language in classrooms was allowed on an experimental basis beginning in 1988. In 1992, any teacher who chose to do so, was allowed to incorporate signing as a methodology. No teacher was required to use sign language, however, and knowledge of sign language is not a prerequisite to be a teacher of the hearing impaired. The official educational philosophy of the Ministry of Education is integrationist—to produce graduates of the primary curriculum capable of functioning in the oral mainstream. In practice, very little speech is used in instructing deaf pupils (at least in the classrooms at the Escuela Melania Morales, which I observed in August 2003).

27. Although he had long talks with Anna Scott and Tuula Jaaskelainem about using sign language, Noel Lam Herrera told me that his personal visits to Yana-María's class convinced him that sign language could be a useful educational tool. The directors of special education (there were four in the 1988–2002 period) relied on him to set the direction, and he urged the teachers in Managua to investigate sign language and agreed that instructors from the deaf association should give afterschool classes in sign language to the teachers of the deaf. The spread of sign language for instruction in the schools was much slower than in the capital, but the outlying schools have followed the capital's lead.

28. Richard Senghas was present at one of the workshops, and he describes the process he observed in his dissertation (1997).

29. The *Diccionario del Lenguaje de Senas de Nicaragua* is dated March 1992 and states on the cover that it was done by Yana-María Graver (who evidently did the drawings) with the collaboration of the executive board of APRIAS, which included Javier López Gómez, Adrián Pérez Castellón, Juan Carlos Alemán, Reyna Cruz H., Justina Urtecho (hard of hearing, now not active in the associa-

tion), Edda Salguera, Isidro Urtecho (deaf brother of Justina), and Sandra López (hearing sister of Javier and receptionist/secretary for the association). If Sheila Hougan worked on the project, she got no recognition. In my telephone interview with Yana-María in 1995, she implied that she and Sheila worked together on all of the projects having to do with sign language, but Sheila's name is not on the mimeographed copy that was given to me in 1997 by Noel Lam.

30. The acronym "SHIA" comes from the initials used to identify the Swedish Organization of Disabled Persons International Aid Association, which is an umbrella organization that administers projects abroad for a federation of thirteen different Swedish organizations representing persons with disabilities. One of the members of the federation is the Royal Swedish Deaf (SDR) Association. The grant proposals are sent to the member organizations, who approve or deny them, but the actual projects are administered by a SHIA representative who visits the country of the project regularly. In the 1980s and 1990s, SHIA had a resident administrator in Nicaragua. In 2002, SHIA had withdrawn, and a Danish organization was administering the funds sent by the SDR, which was still funding projects for the ANSNIC.

Ingvar Ekvall, a member of the board of the SDR, and like Andersson and Kjellberg, a militant advocate of sign language, first came to Nicaragua in 1993, but he did come multiple times during the rest of the decade. He also had a particularly strong influence on Javier, because Javier lived at Ingvar's house during his stay in Sweden. One of his trips was in 1995, because there is correspondence in the archives of PROGRESO in San José, Costa Rica, arranging a trip for Ekvall and Kerstin Kjellberg to visit Costa Rica on March 5, 1995, after they finished their visit in Nicaragua.

31. The linguistic transmission of at least some of this information must have been fascinating to watch. I watched a variation of what the 1990 situation was probably like when, in 1997, a Swedish representative came to the official presentation of the first printed dictionary on March 2, 1997, and was asked to address the crowd. He had a Swedish Sign Language/oral Swedish interpreter who also had excellent oral English skills and translated his sign into English. Then there was an oral English/oral Spanish translator who spoke to the oral Spanish/NSL interpreter. And every response went through the chain in reverse. Some variation of this method must have been used during, at least, parts of the 1990 visit. Gloria Minero was the Spanish/NSL translator (hearing mother of deaf daughter), or Morena Tórres, María Lourdes Palacios, or Jenifer Grigsby (deaf women with good Spanish lipreading skills) could have helped.

32. Josefa Gutiérrez, who is also considered a founding member, married a hearing man and had three children in the 1981–1983 period. She maintained

socialization ties with her deaf friends even during her marriage. She seems to have been atypical among her peers in this regard.

Appendix

1. Where I had multiple interviews with the same person, I list the date of the first interview with an asterisk. I met with Rúthy Durán, Silvia Ayón, Javier López Gómez, Irlanda Romero, Susana Rugama, Noel Lam, Ivette Aguilar, and others many, many times. Everyone I contacted during the six-week trips in 1994 or 1995, I contacted again multiple times in 1997 when I was in Nicaragua for ten months. I also conducted numerous interviews during the five two- to eight-week trips between 1999 and 2003.

2. Asociación Nacional de Sordos de Nicaragua (National Nicaraguan Association of the Deaf).

3. Asociación de Padres de Familia con Niños Discapacitados "Los Pipitos" (Association of Parents with Disabled Children, Los Pipitos).

4. Centro Ocupacional para Discapacitados (Occupational Center for the Disabled) now defunct.

5. Centro Nacional de Educación Especial (National Special Education Center, school founded in 1977, but renamed Escuela Melania Morales in 1987 in honor of a former teacher).

6. Instituto Nicaraguense de Seguridad Social y Bienestar (Nicaraguan Institute for Social Security and Welfare, governmental institution 1997–1990 whose work is now divided between the Ministry of the Family and the Social Security Institute).

7. Instituto Nicaraguense de Adaptación Technologica (Nicaraguan Technical Training Institute).

8. Initials used in Nicaragua for the Swedish International Development Agency.

References

Aguirre Heredia, O. 1995. Los Gestos Como Forma de Comunicacion. M.A. thesis, School of Journalism, Central American University, Managua, Nicaragua.

Anderson, B. 1991. *Imagined Communities: Reflections on the Origin and Spread of Nationalism.* London: Verso.

Archivo Nacional, Caja No. 112, Años 1950–1964, Educación Pública: Acuerdo y Correspondencia. Proyecto Del Presupuesto De La Secretaria De Educación Pública Para El Año Fiscal 1949–1950.

Archivo Nacional, Caja No. 112, Años 1950–1964, Educación Pública: Acuerdo y Correspondencia. Relación De Asignaciones Personales Personal Permanente—Ministerio De Educación Pública, 26 De Julio De 1963.

Asociación Nacional de Sordos de Nicaragua (ANSNIC) 1997. *Diccionario del Idioma da Señas de Nicaragua.* Managua, Nicaragua: Copy Fast, S.A.

Best, H. 1943. *Deafness and the Deaf in the United States, Considered Primarily in Relation to Those Sometimes More or Less Erroneously Known as "Deaf-Mutes."* New York: Macmillan.

Birnholz, J., and B. Benacerraf. 1983. The Development of Human Fetal Hearing. *Science* 222:516–18.

Corea Fonseca, E. 2000. *Historia de la Medicina en Nicaragua.* Privately published book distributed to doctors in Nicaragua.

DeCasper, A., and W. Fifer. 1980. Of Human Bonding: Newborns Prefer Their Mothers' Voices. *Science* 208:1174–76.

DeCasper, A., and M. Spence. 1991. Auditorily Mediated Behavior during the Perinatal Period: A Cognitive View. In *Newborn Attention: Biological Constraints and the Influence of Experience,* ed. M. Weiss and P. Zelazo, 142–76. Norwood, N.J.: Ablex.

El Nuevo Diario, September 16, 2004. "Sordo-muditos nicas asombran al mundo." Available on the Internet at: http://www.elnuevodiario.com.ni/cgi-bin/print.pl?id=nacional-20040917-12.

Fischer, R. and Lane, H., eds. 1993. *Looking Back: A Reader on the History of Deaf Communities and Their Sign Languages.* Hamburg: Signum.

Gallaudet, T. A. 1856. Letter to the President of the New England Gallaudet Association. *American Annals of the Deaf and Dumb* 9:186–87.

Groce, N. 1985. *Everyone Here Spoke Sign Language: Hereditary Deafness on Martha's Vineyard.* Cambridge, Mass.: Harvard University Press.

Grooteman, B. 1990. *Informe Sobre El Centro Ocupacional para Discapacitados (C.O.D.) Periodo 1981–1990.* Unpublished report to Werkgroep C.O.D. Villa Libertad/Holanda.

Guerrero, E. et al. 1993. *La Empleada Domestica en Nicaragua: Solo Lava, Cocina y Limpia!.* Managua, Nicaragua: Centro de Estudios y Analisis Socio Laborales (CEAL), Area de la Mujer.

Goffman, E. 1963. *Stigma: Notes on the Management of Spoiled Identity.* Englewood Cliffs, N.J.: Prentice Hall.

Hougen, S. 1993. Deaf Education in Nicaragua. *Nicaragua Through Our Eyes: The Bulletin of the US Solidarity Community Benjamin Linder,* 7(6): 7; 12.

Infante Cespedes, M. 1995. *Sordera: Mitos Y Realidades.* San José, Costa Rica: Editorial Technologica de Costa Rica.

Instituto Nicaraguense de Estadisticas y Censos. 1982. *Anuario Estadistico de Nicaragua, 1981.* Managua, Nicaragua: Author.

———. 1984. *Anuario Estadistico de Nicaragua, 1983.* Managua, Nicaragua: Author.

———. 1985. *Boletin de Estadisticas Sociales, Segundo Semestre 1984.* Managua, Nicaragua: Author.

———. 1986. *Anuario Estadistico de Nicaragua 1986.* Managua, Nicaragua: Author.

———. 1989. *Nicaragua en Cifras: Años 1983–1987.* Managua, Nicaragua: Author.

———. 1992. *Compendio Estadistico 1987–1991.* Managua, Nicaragua: Author.

———. 1995. *Censos Nacionales 1995: Cifras Oficiales Finales, Republica de Nicaragua.* Managua, Nicaragua: Author.

Johnson, D., and R. Whitehead. 1989. Effect of Maternal Rubella on Hearing and Vision: A Twenty Year Post-Epidemic Study. *American Annals of the Deaf* 137:232–42.

Kegl, J. 1994. The Nicaraguan Sign Language Project: An Overview. *Signpost* 7(1): 40–46.

Kegl, J., and J. McWhorter. 1996. Perspectives on an Emerging Language. In *Proceedings of the Stanford Child Language Research Forum.* New York: Cambridge University Press.

Kegl, J., A. Senghas, and M. Coppola. 1999. Creation through Contact: Sign Language Emergence and Sign Language Change in Nicaragua. In *Language Creation and Language Change,* ed. M. DeGraff. Cambridge, Mass.: MIT Press.

Kosko, B. 1993. *Fuzzy Thinking: The New Science of Fuzzy Logic.* New York: Hyperion.

La Gaceta. 1946. Crear Escuela de Enseñanza Especial. February 6.

———. 1946. Nombrar Director de la Escuela de Enseñanza Especial al Dr. Emilio Lacayo. February 6.

———. 1946. Alquilar lugar para la Escuela de Enseñanza Especial. February 22.

———. 1946. Nombrar a Dora Santiesteban profesora de la Escuela Especial de Retrasados Mentales. February 22.

———. 1947. Reglamento de la Escuela de Enseñanza Especial para niños anormales. June 19.

———. 1983. Cancelase. May 23.

———. 1989a. Personería Jurídica, Decreto A.N. June 15.

———. 1989b. Apruebanse Estatutos "APRIAS." November 7.

———. 1995. Ley de Prevención, Rehabilitación y Equiparación de Oportunidades para las Personas con Discapacidad, Ley No. 202. September 27.

———. 1997. Decreto No. 50–97. De Reglamento a la Ley 202 de Prevención, Rehabilitación y Equiparación de Oportunidades para la Persona con Discapacidad. August 25.

Lane, H., ed. 1984a. *The Deaf Experience: Classics in Language and Education.* Cambridge, Mass.: Harvard University Press.

———. 1984b. *When the Mind Hears: A History of the Deaf.* London: Penguin.

Mairena Martinez, M. 1997. Singular Proceso a Punta de Señas. *El Nuevo Diario,* August 27.

Mántica Abaunza, C. 2002. *Album de Los Mántica de Nicaragua.* Managua, Nicaragua: Ediciones de PAVSA.

Marenco Tercero, E. 1997. Nicas envian 60 mil remesas mensuales. *El Observador Económico* 63:24–25.

———. 2003. Los Niños Me Dan Mucha Energía. (article about Natalia Popova and her work) *La Prensa,* June 8.

Meier, R. 1991. Language Acquisition by Deaf Children. *American Scientist* 79:60–70.

Ministerio de Educación. 1984. Cinco Años de Educación en la Revolución. Managua, Nicaragua: Author.

———. 1990. Boletin Informativo 1990. Managua, Nicaragua: Author.

———. 1990. Informe de Matricula 1990. Managua, Nicaragua: Author.

———. 1992. Boletin Estadistico 1991. Managua, Nicaragua: Author.

———. 1993. Informe de Matricula 1992. Managua, Nicaragua: Author.

———. 1993. Boletin Informativo. Managua, Nicaragua: Author.

———. 1994. Boletin Informativo. Managua, Nicaragua: Author.

———. 1995a. Informe de Matricula. Managua, Nicaragua: Author.

———. 1995b. Introducción a la Educación Especial: Necesidades en Educación Especial. Typescript, pp. 1–10.

———. 1997a. Boletin Informativo Educación Especial 1989–1996. Managua, Nicaragua: Author.

———. 1997b. Cobertura de Atención, Servicios Educativos Especiales 1990–1997. Managua, Nicaragua: Author.

———. 1997c. Matricula Final 1997. Managua, Nicaragua: Author.

Miron, G. 1996. *Special Needs Education in Nicaragua.* Stockholm: Institute of International Education.

Monahan, L. 1996. Signing, Oralism and the Development of the New Zealand Deaf Community: An Ethnography and History of Language Ideologies. Ph.D. diss., University of California, Los Angeles.

Morford, J. 1996. Insights to Language from the Study of Gesture: A Review of Research on the Gestural Communication of Non-Signing Deaf People. *Language & Communication* 16:165–78.

Renzi, R., and L. Alaniz. 1997. Condiciones de Vida de los Hogares Urbanos de León, Granada y Managua. *El Observador Economico* 61:37–54.

Romero, E. 2003. Agentes encubiertos vigilan a sospechoso. *La Prensa,* August 21.

Schein, J. 1989. *At Home among Strangers.* Washington D.C.: Gallaudet University Press.

Schow, R., and M. Nerbonne. 1996. Introduction to *Audiologic Rehabilitation,* 3d ed. Boston: Allyn & Bacon.

Senghas, A. 1995. Children's Contribution to the Birth of Nicaraguan Sign Language. Ph.D. diss., Massachusetts Institute of Technology, Cambridge.

Senghas, A., and M. Coppola. 2001. Children Creating Language: How Nicaraguan Sign Language Acquired a Spatial Grammar. *Psychological Science* 12(4): 323–28.

Senghas, R. 1997. An "Unspeakable, Unwriteable" Language: Deaf Identity, Language and Personhood among the First Cohort of Nicaraguan Signers. Ph.D. diss., University of Rochester, New York.

Stach, B. 1998. *Clinical Audiology: An Introduction.* San Diego: Singular.

Stokoe, W. 1960. Sign Language Structure: An Outline of the Visual Communication Systems of the American Deaf. Studies in Linguistics, Occasional Papers No. 8. Buffalo, N.Y.: University of Buffalo.

Valentine, M. 1949. *Educación del sordomudo en el hogar.* Tegucigalpa: Talleres Tipograficos Nacionales.

Index

Page numbers in italics denote figures, photographs, and tables.